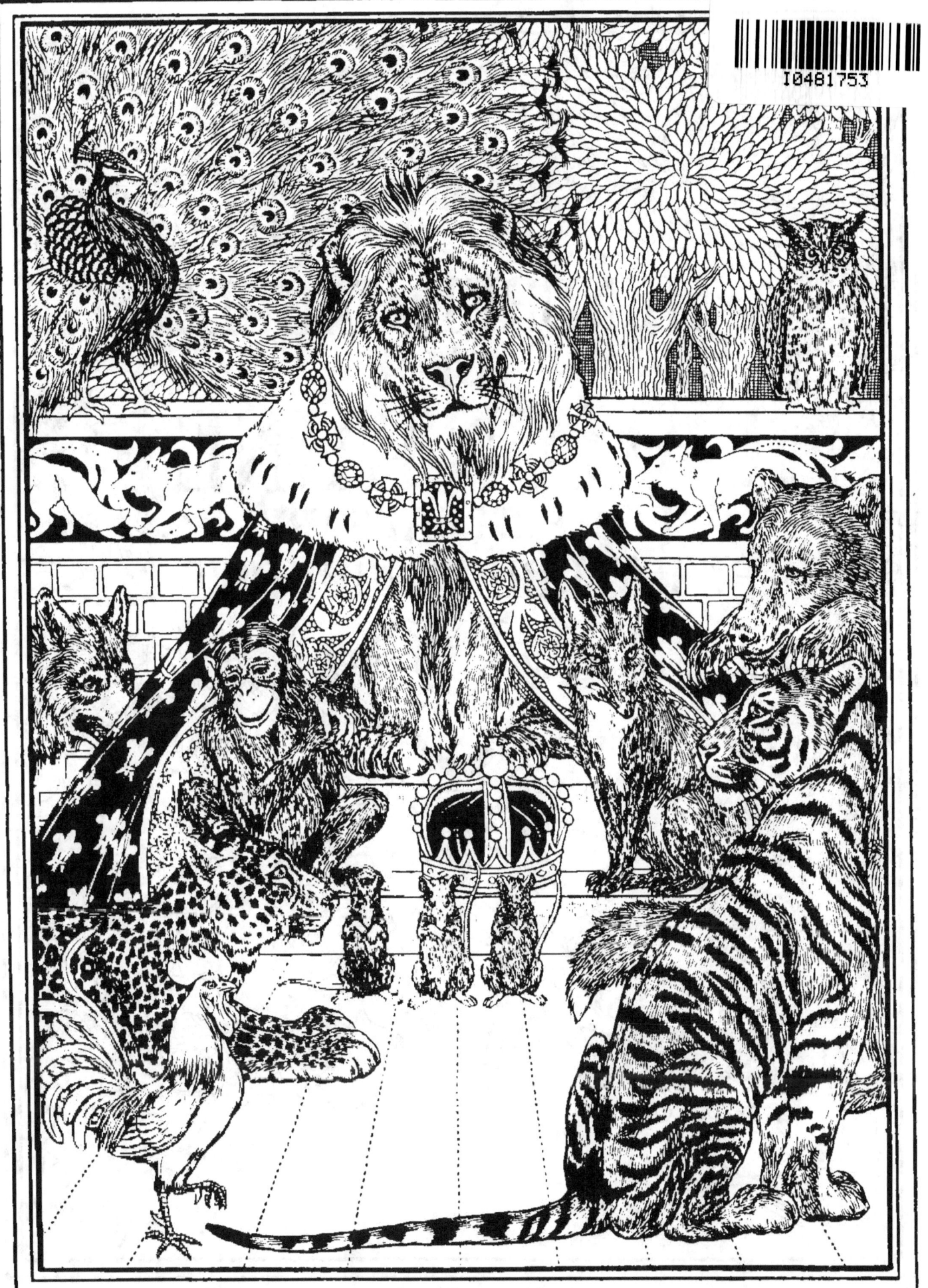

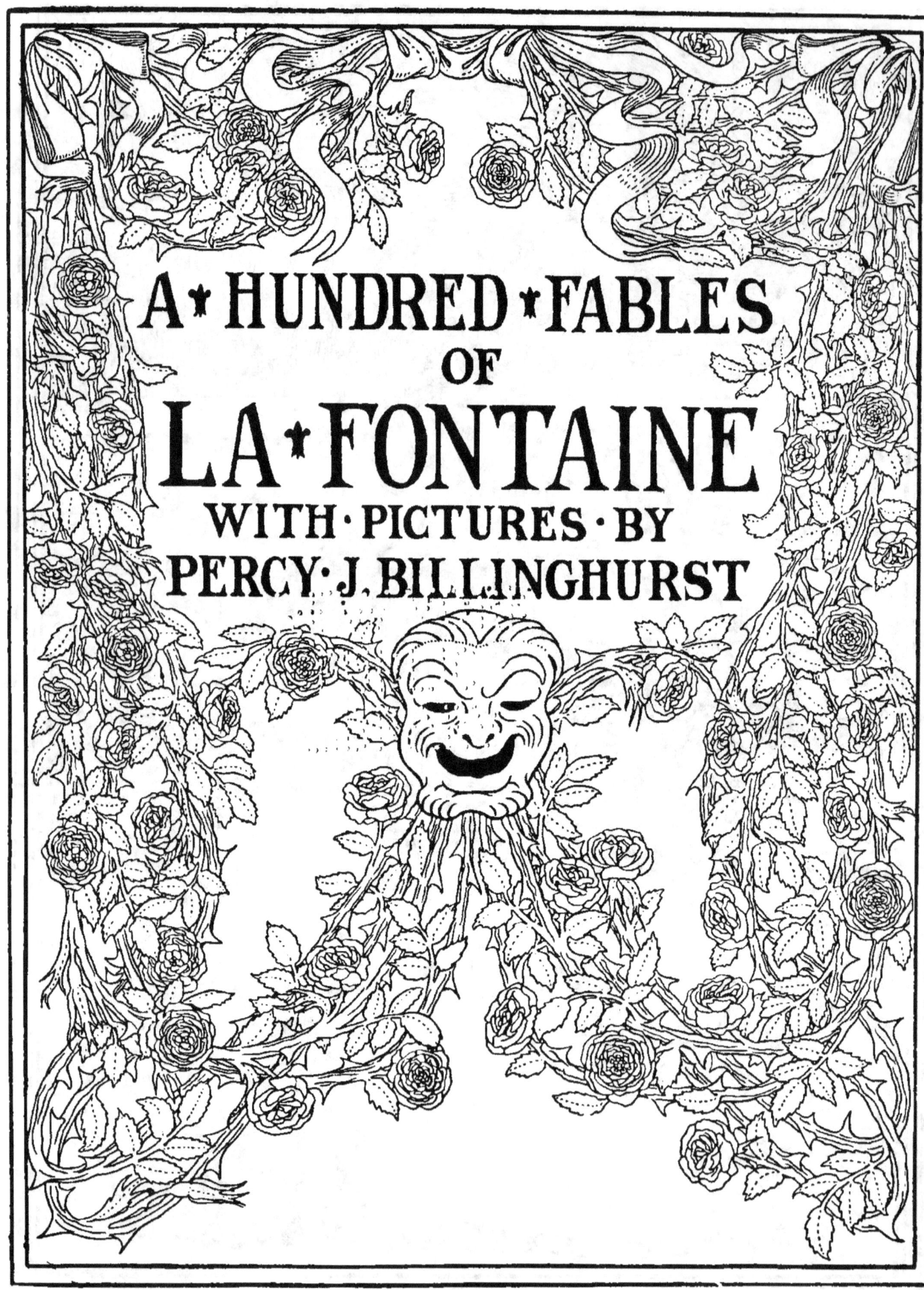

A ∗ HUNDRED ∗ FABLES
OF
LA ∗ FONTAINE
WITH ∗ PICTURES ∗ BY
PERCY ∗ J. BILLINGHURST

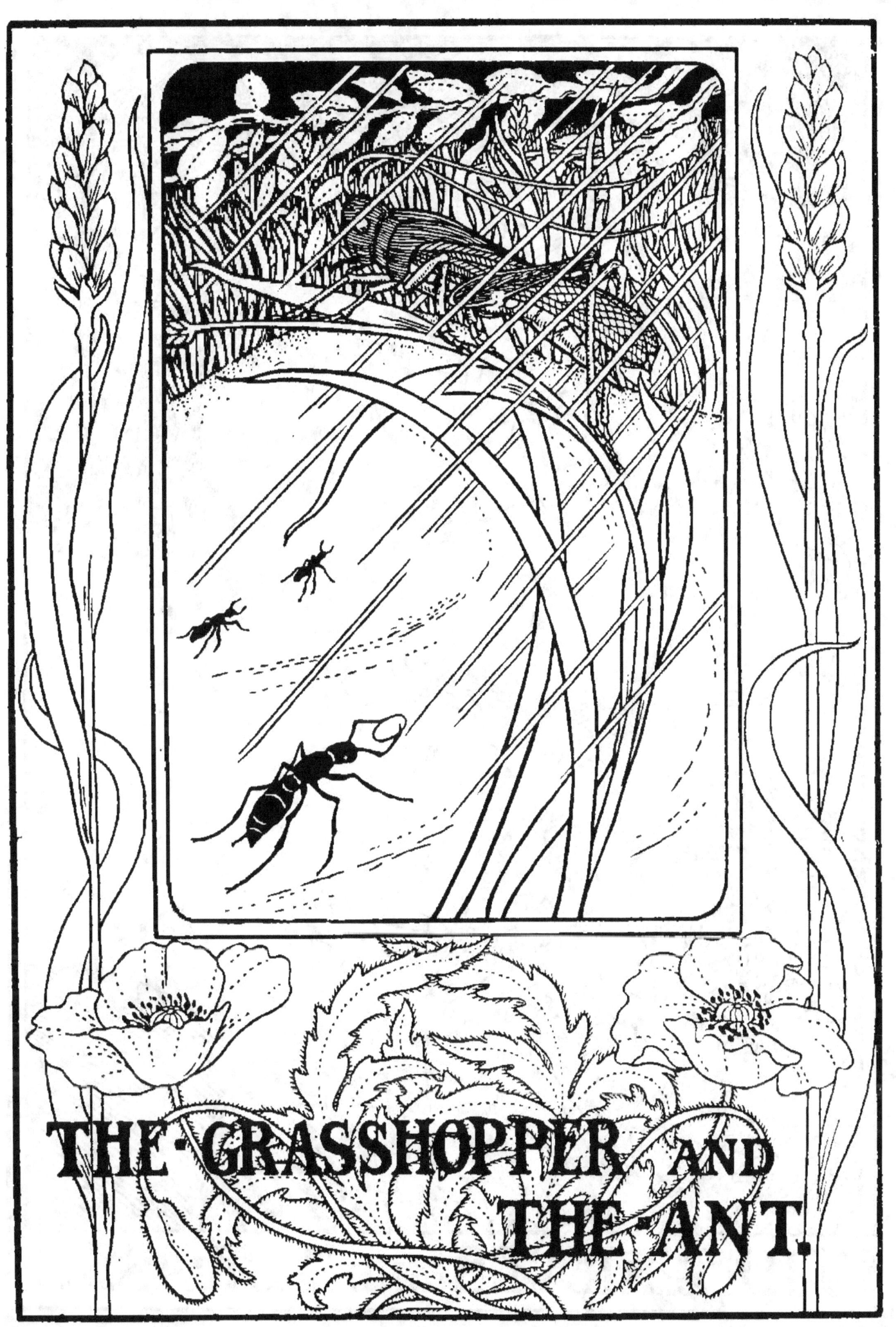

THE·GRASSHOPPER AND
THE·ANT.

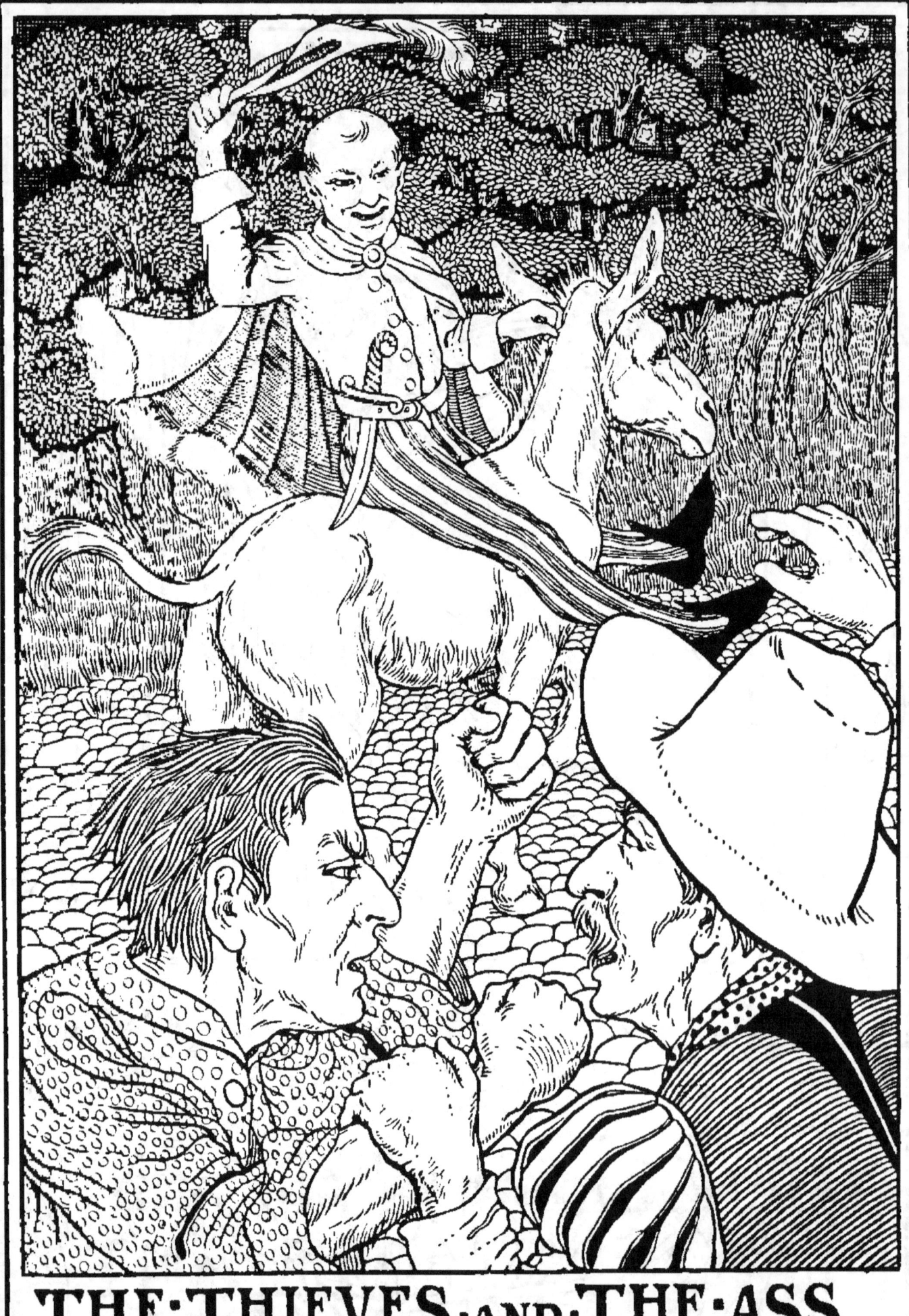

THE·THIEVES·AND·THE·ASS.

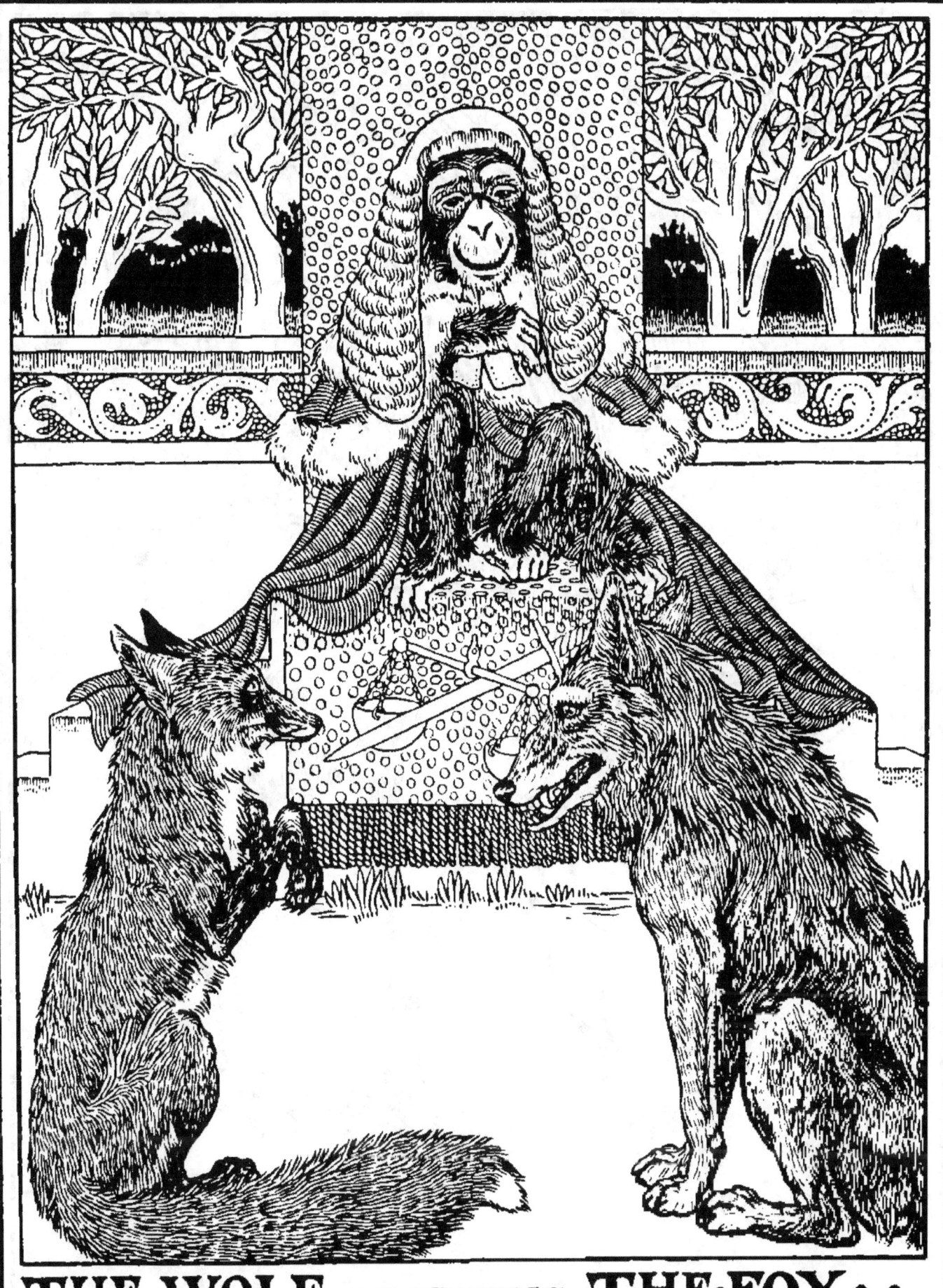

THE·WOLF·ACCUSING·THE·FOX··
·BEFORE·THE·MONKEY···

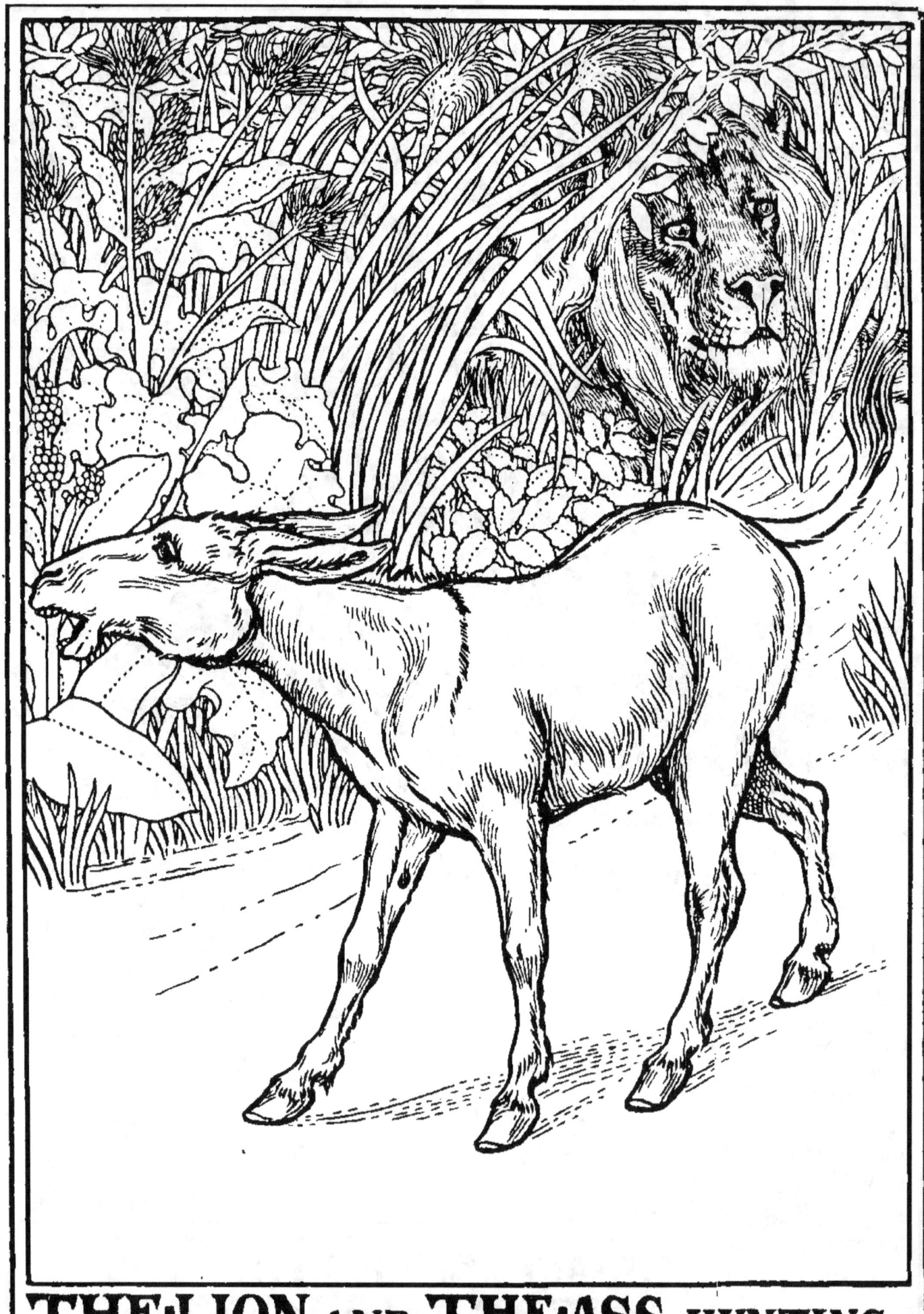

THE·LION·AND·THE·ASS·HUNTING.

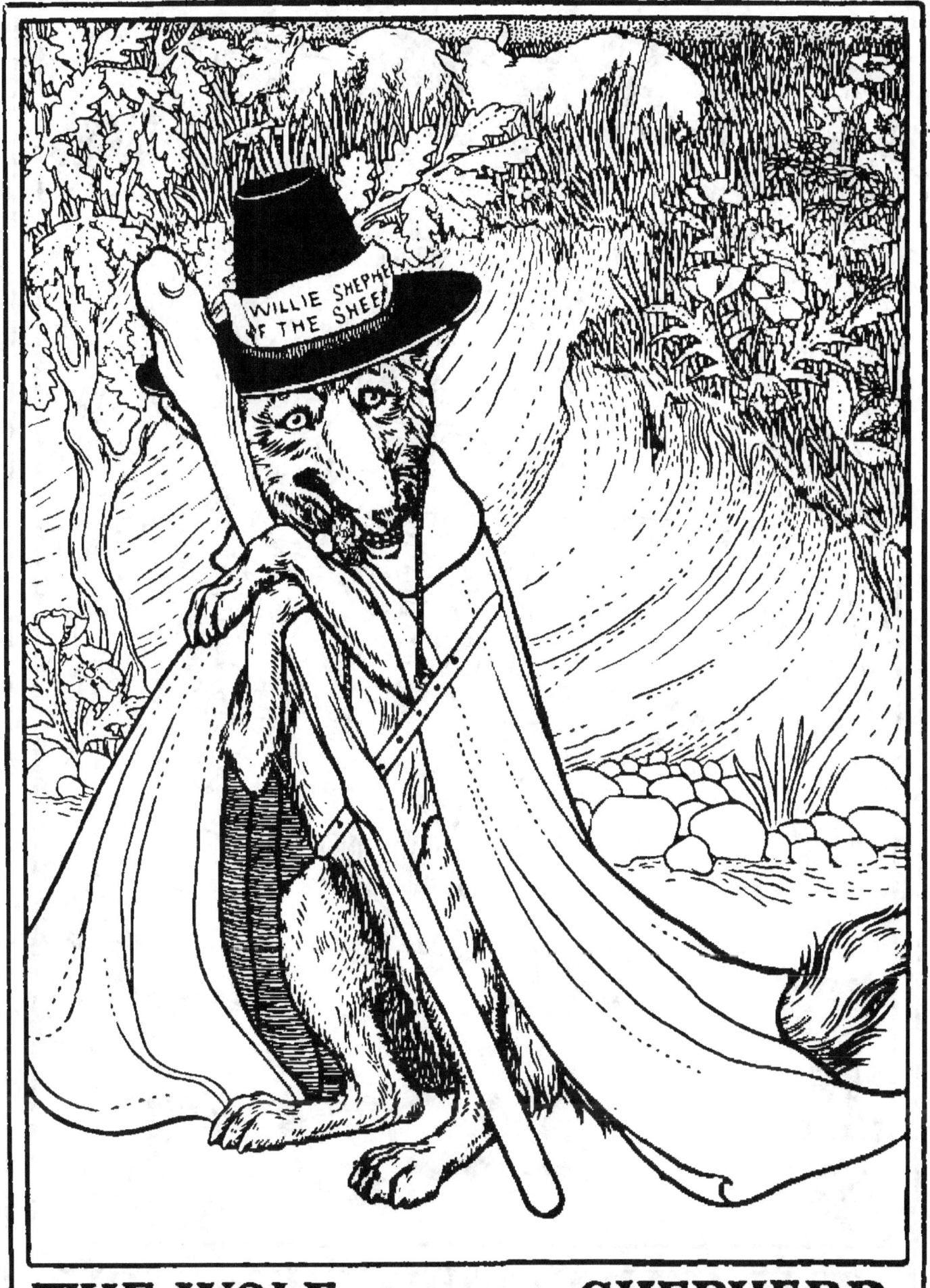

THE·WOLF·TURNED·SHEPHERD.

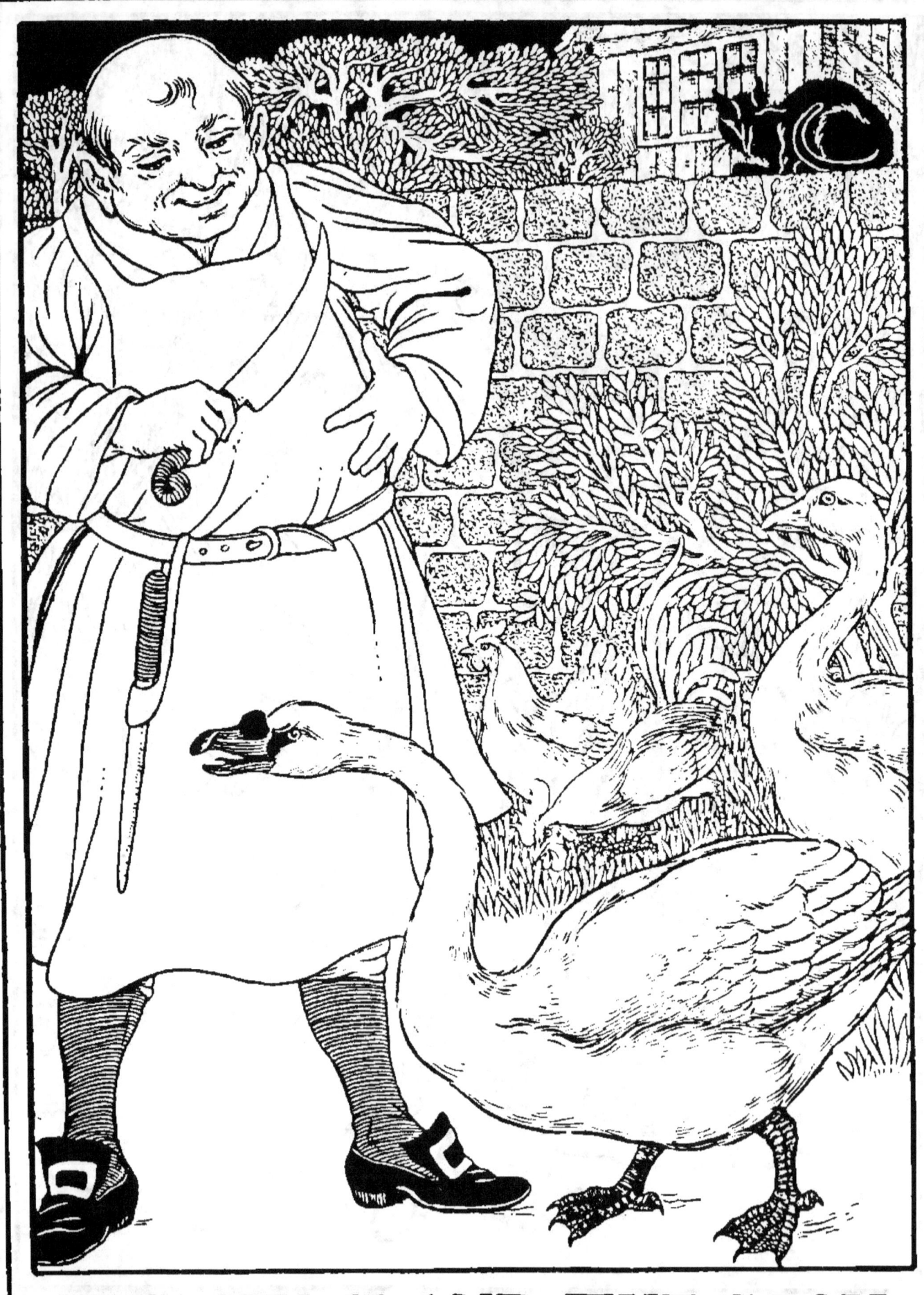

THE·SWAN·AND·THE·COOK.

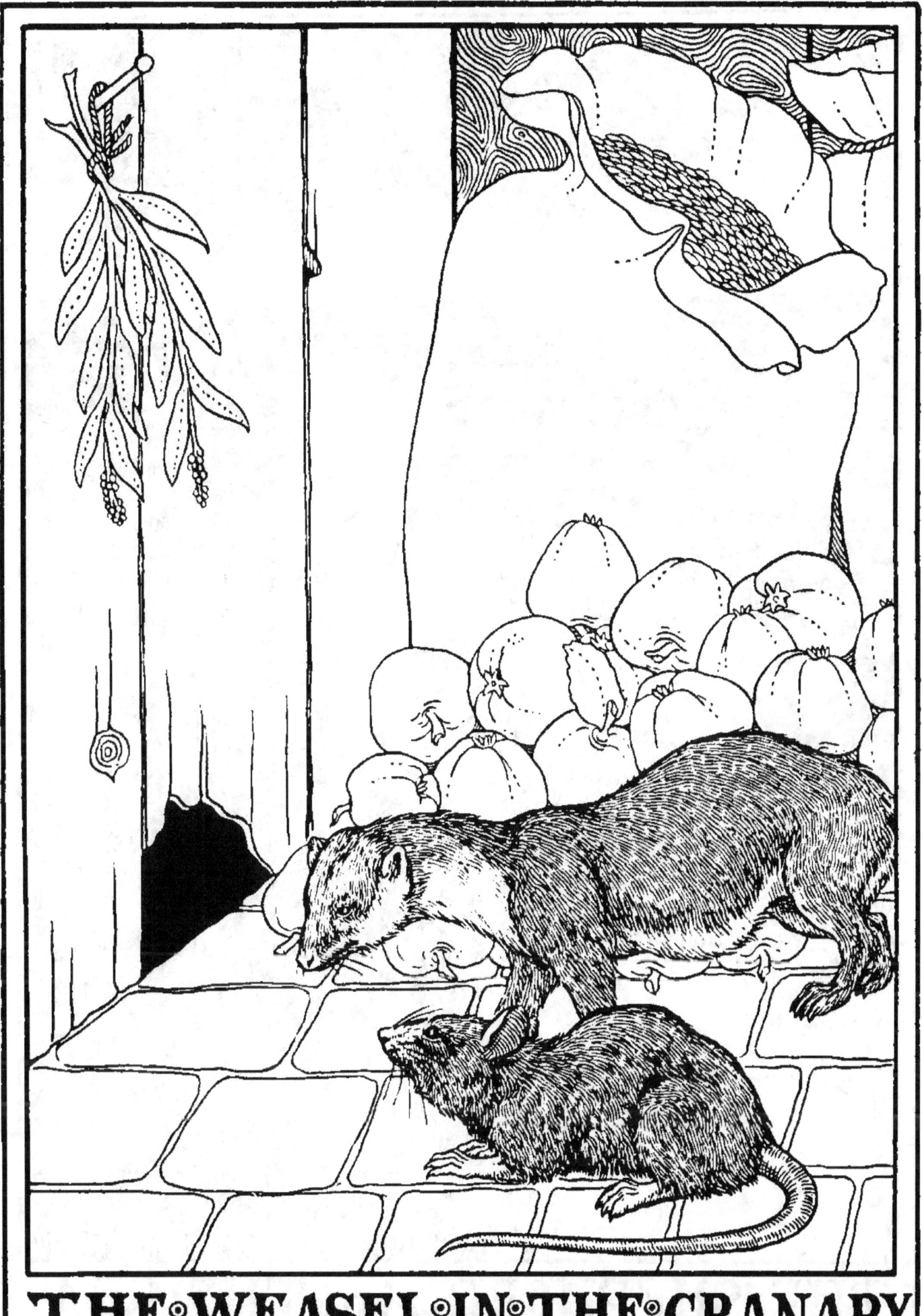

THE·WEASEL·IN·THE·GRANARY

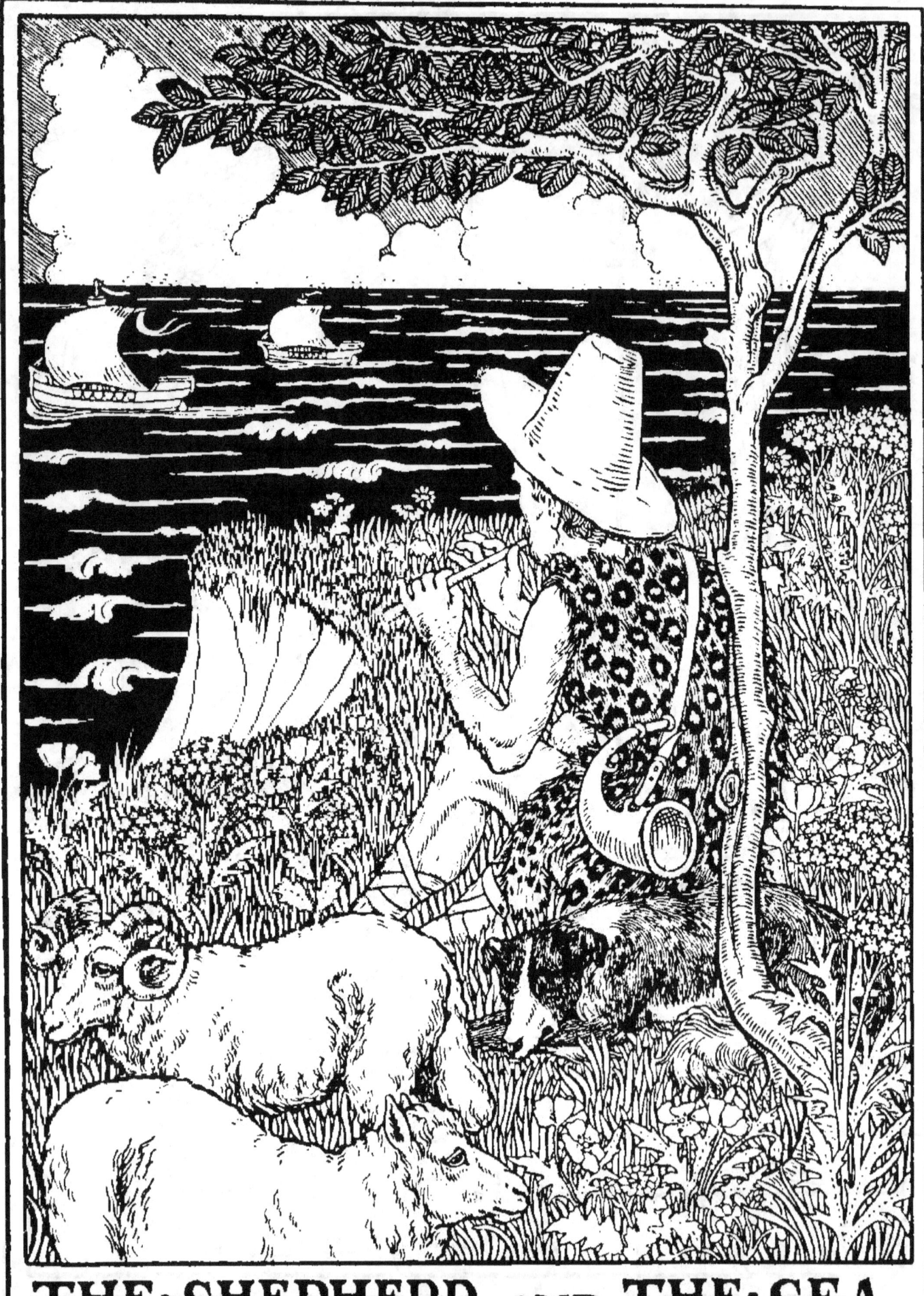

THE·SHEPHERD·AND·THE·SEA.

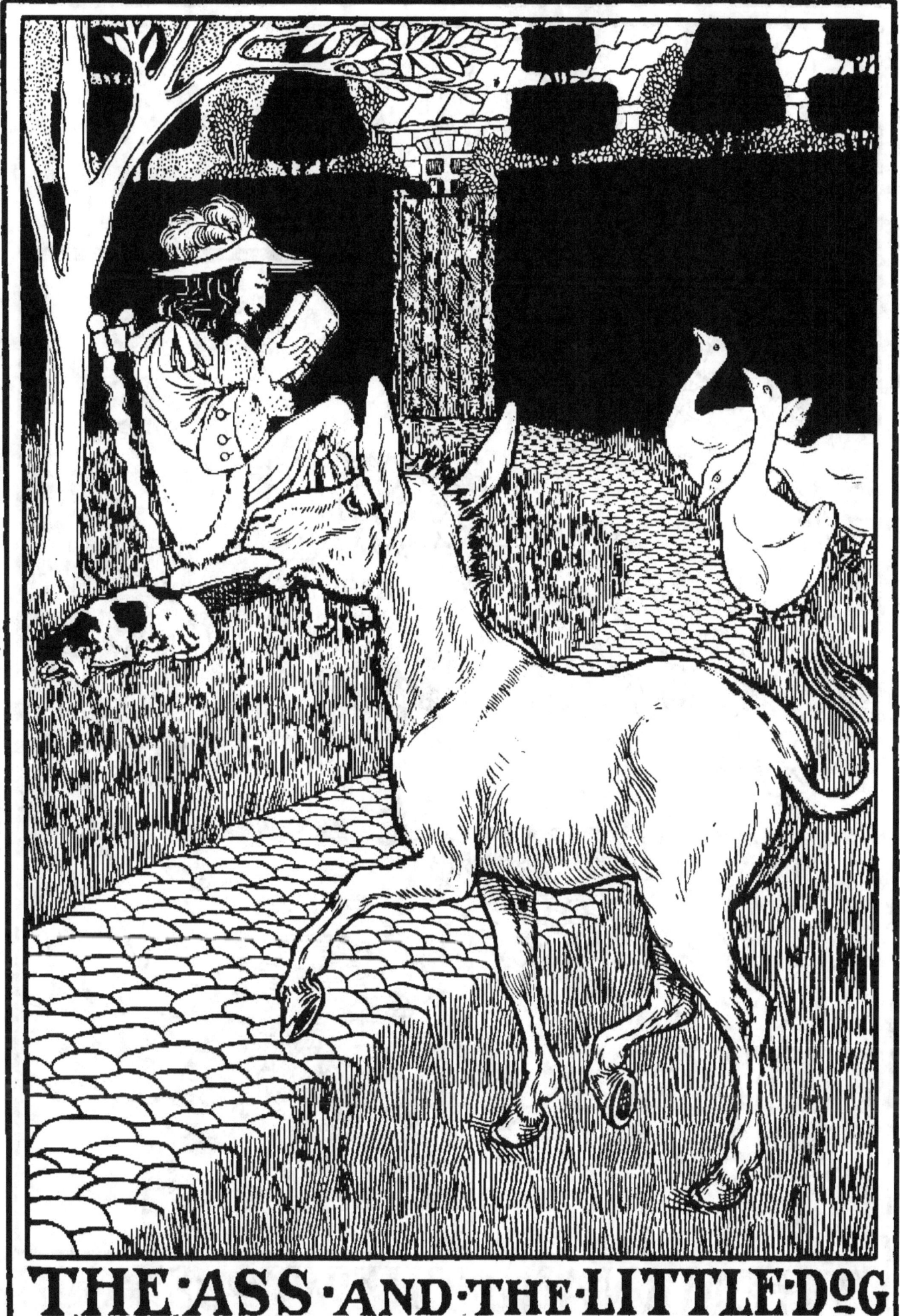

THE·ASS·AND·THE·LITTLE·DOG

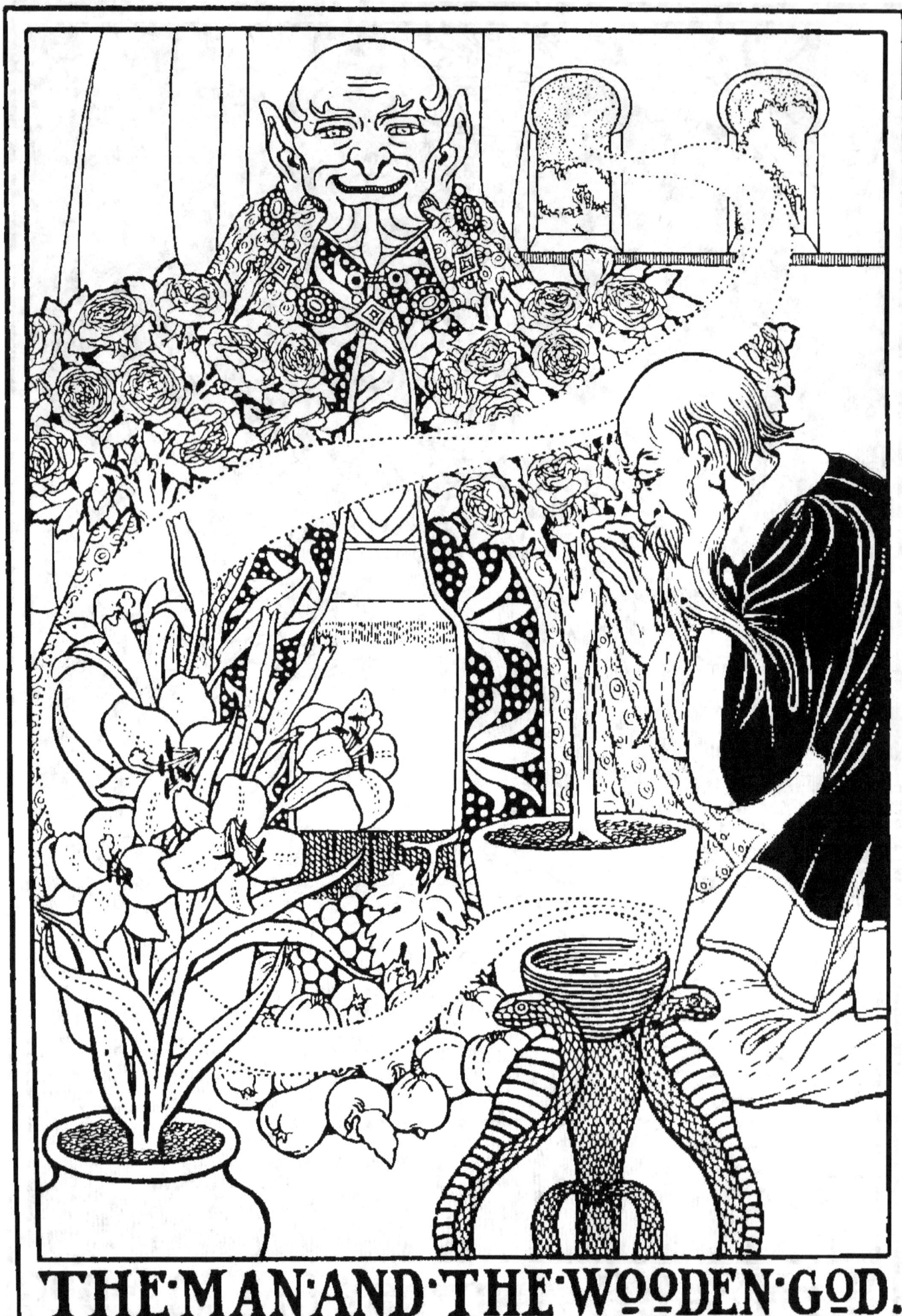

THE·MAN·AND·THE·WOODEN·GOD.

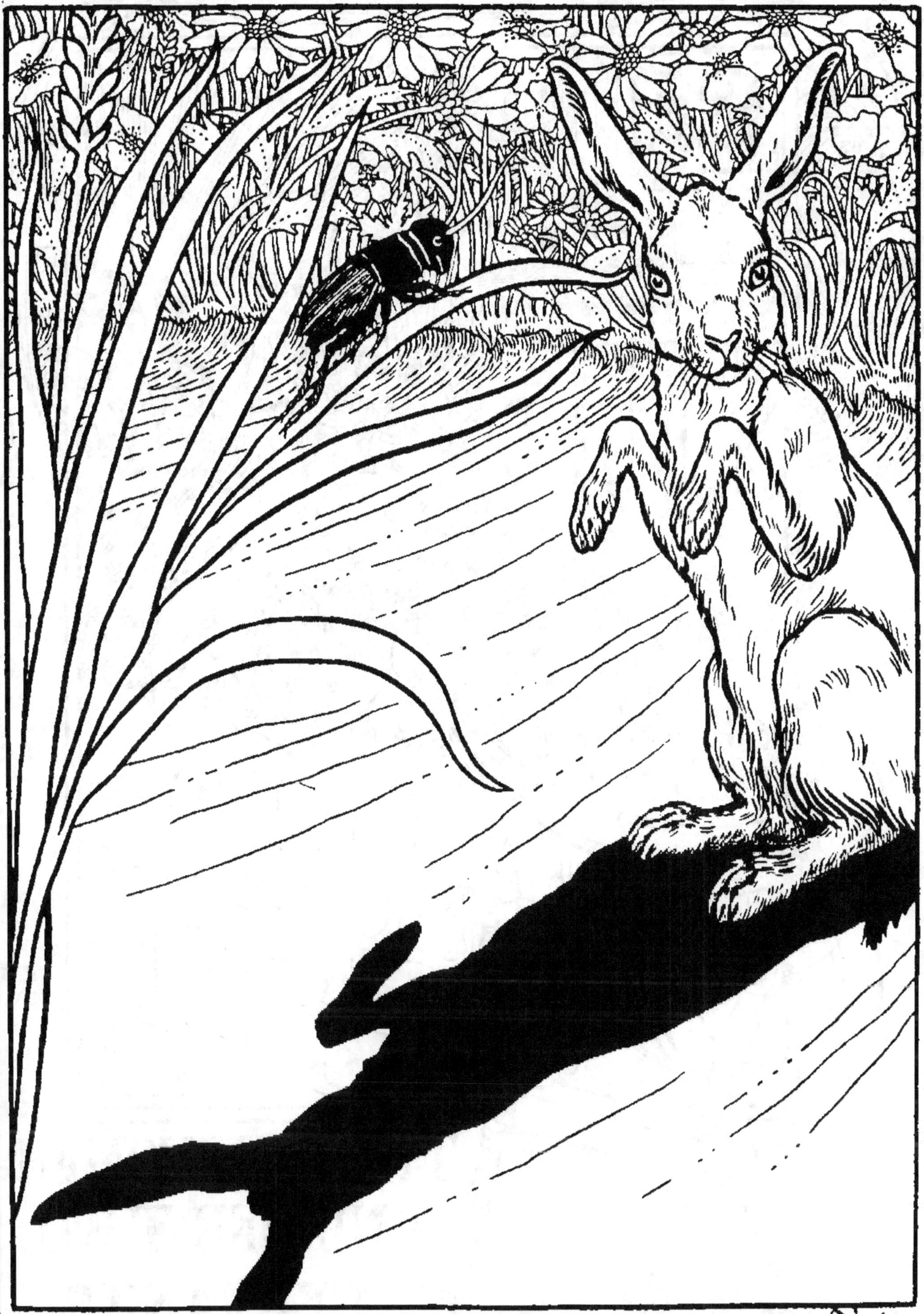

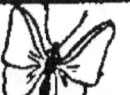

THE·EARS·OF·THE·HARE.

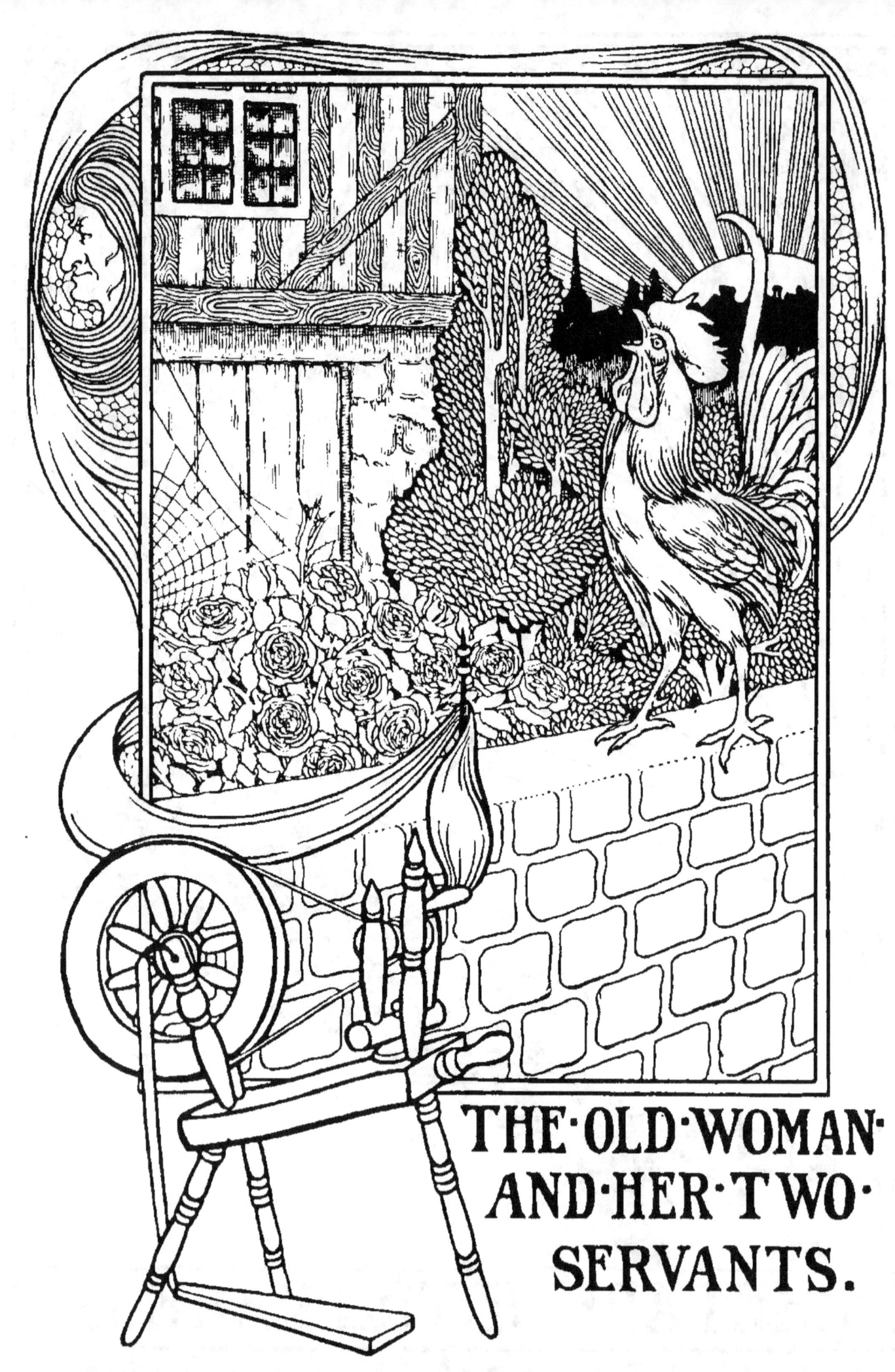

THE·OLD·WOMAN·
AND·HER·TWO·
SERVANTS.

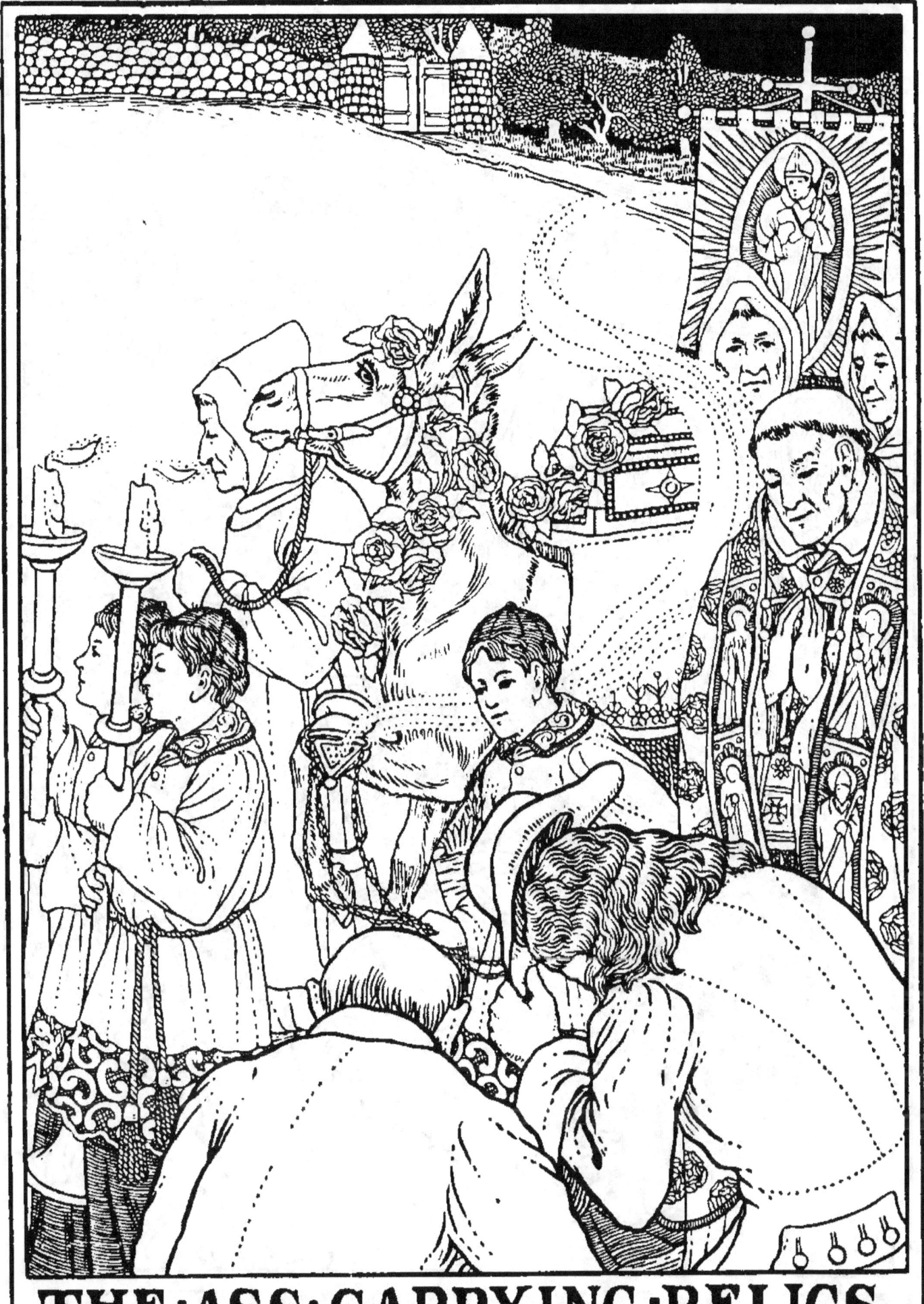

THE·ASS·CARRYING·RELICS.

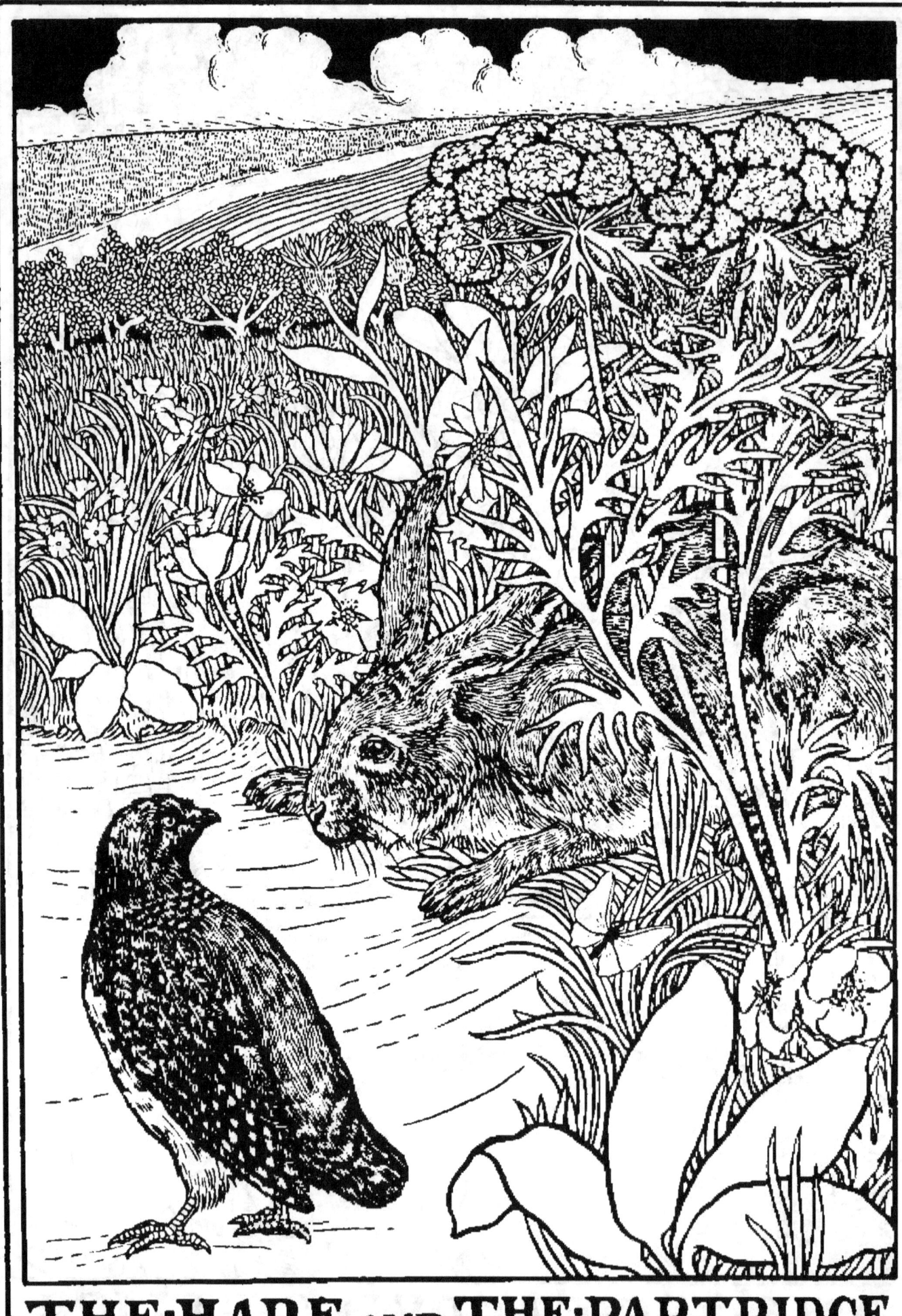

THE·HARE·AND·THE·PARTRIDGE.

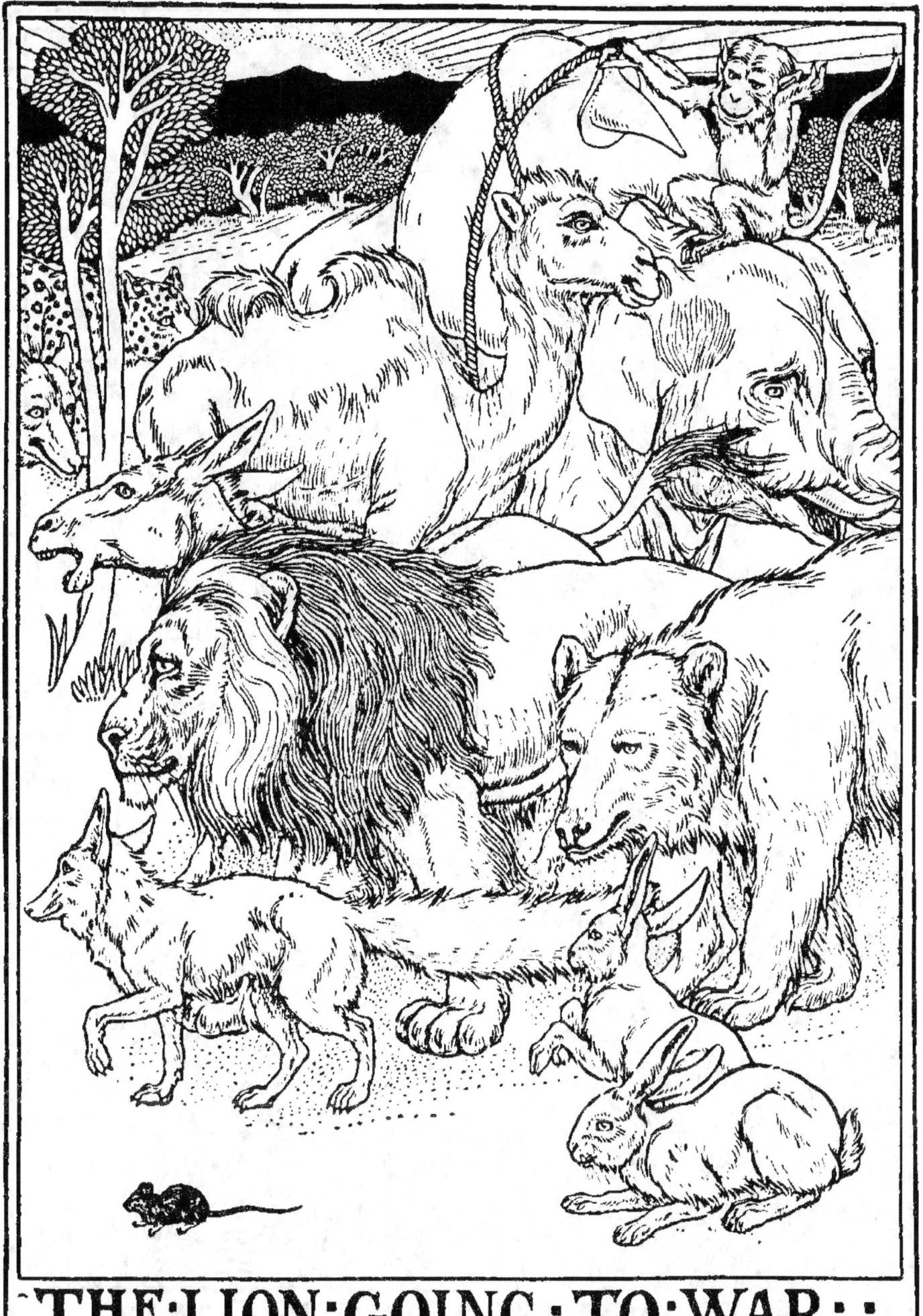

THE·LION·GOING·TO·WAR··

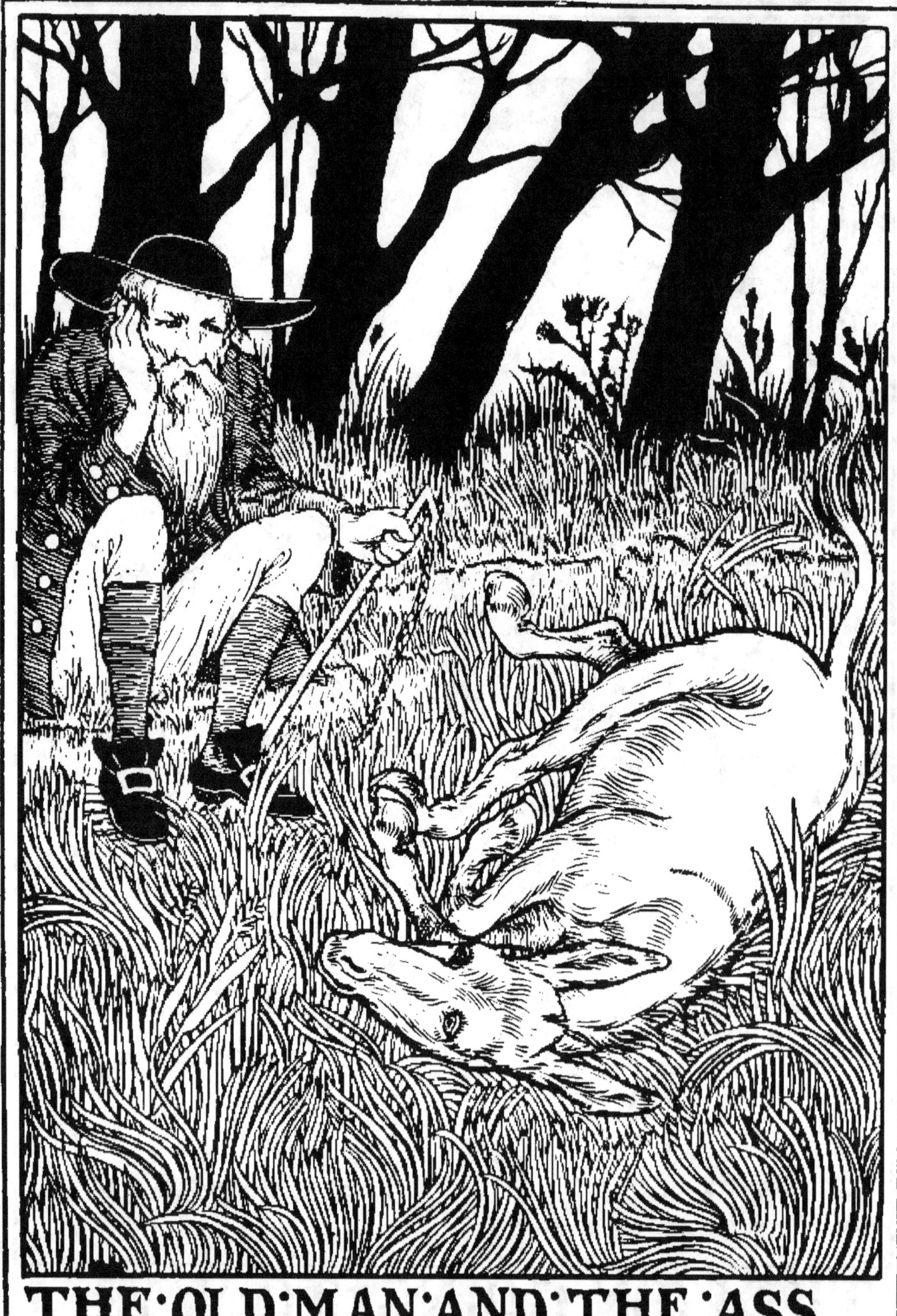

THE·OLD·MAN·AND·THE·ASS.

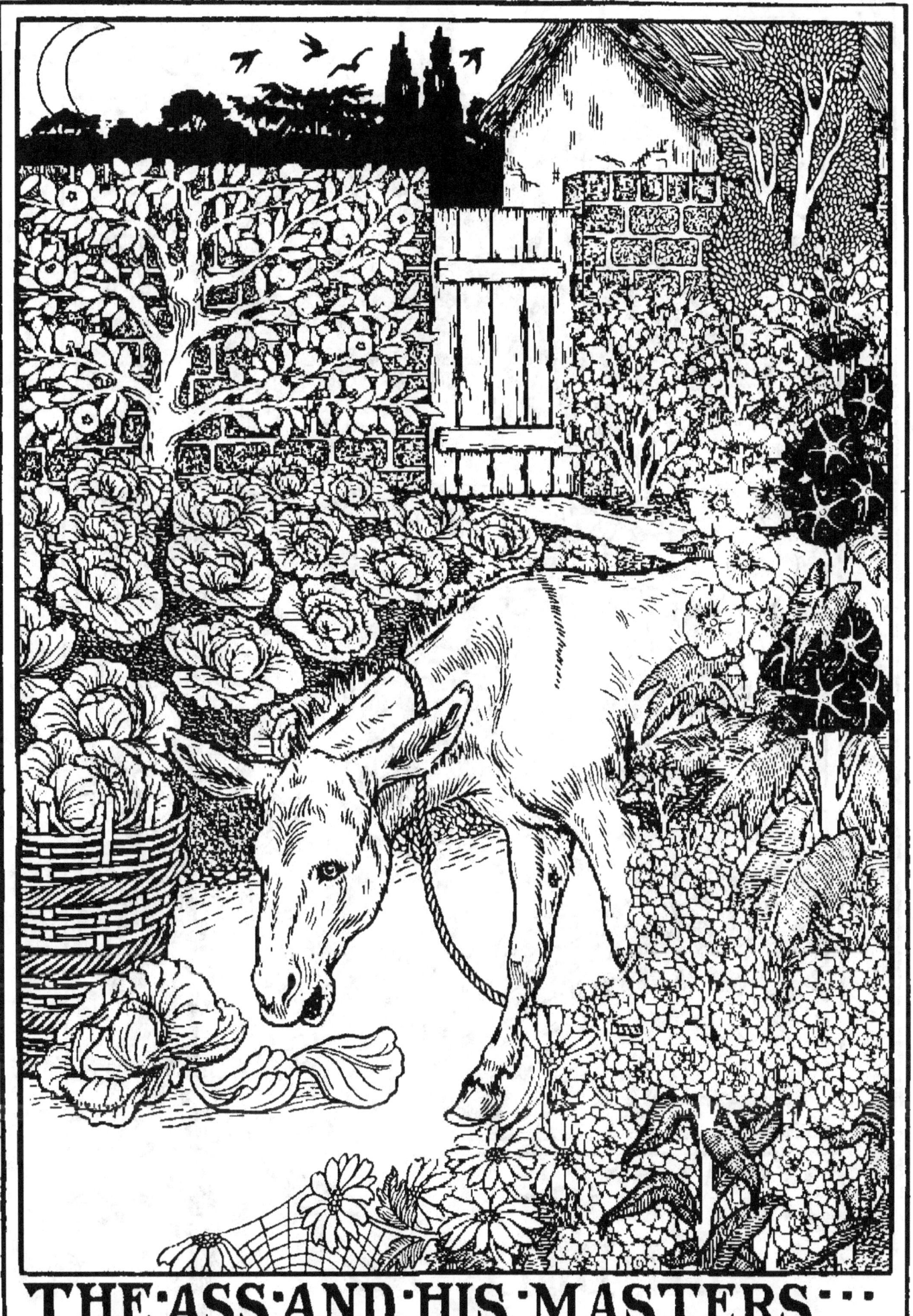

THE·ASS·AND·HIS·MASTERS···

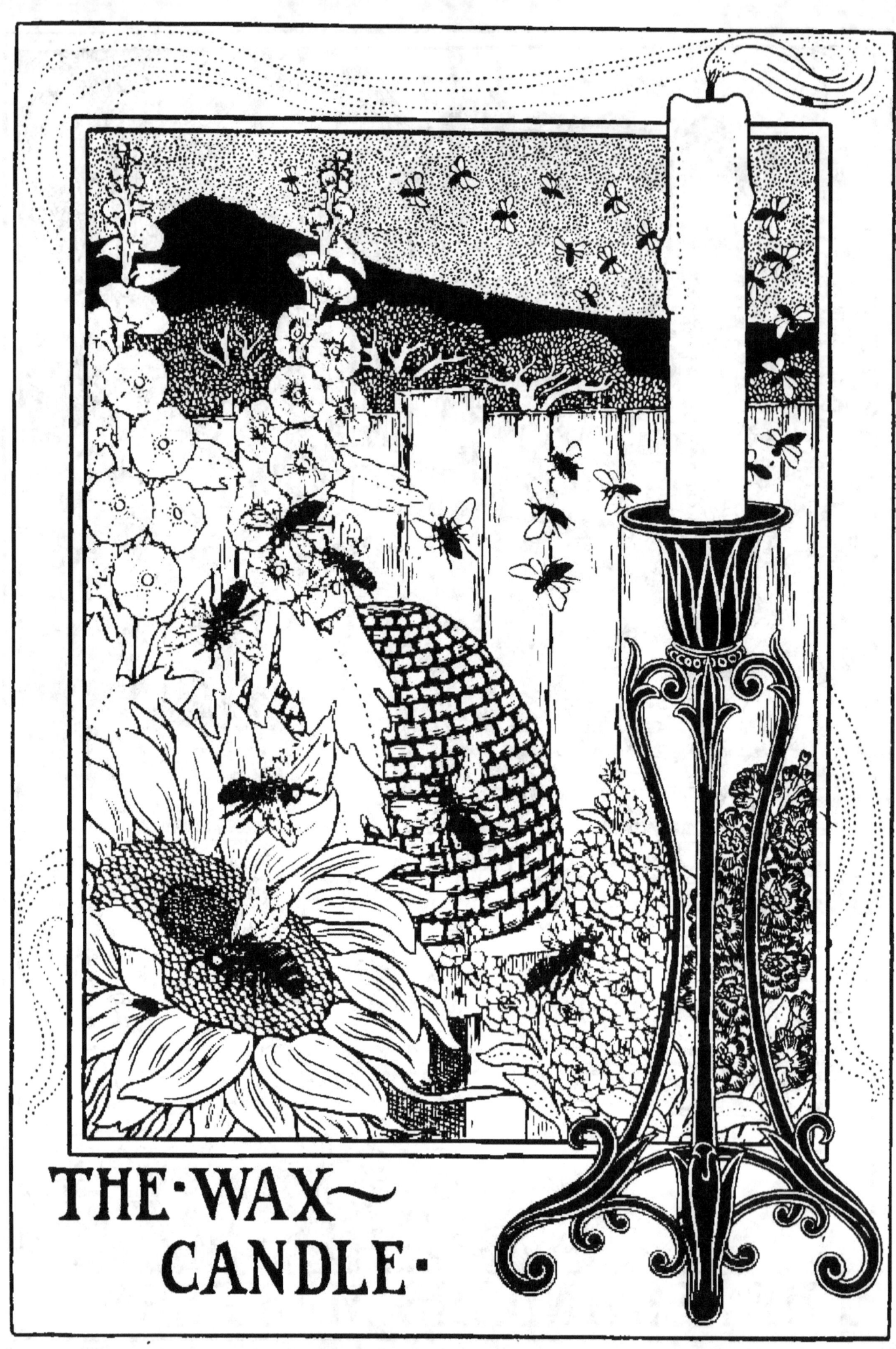

THE·WAX~
CANDLE·

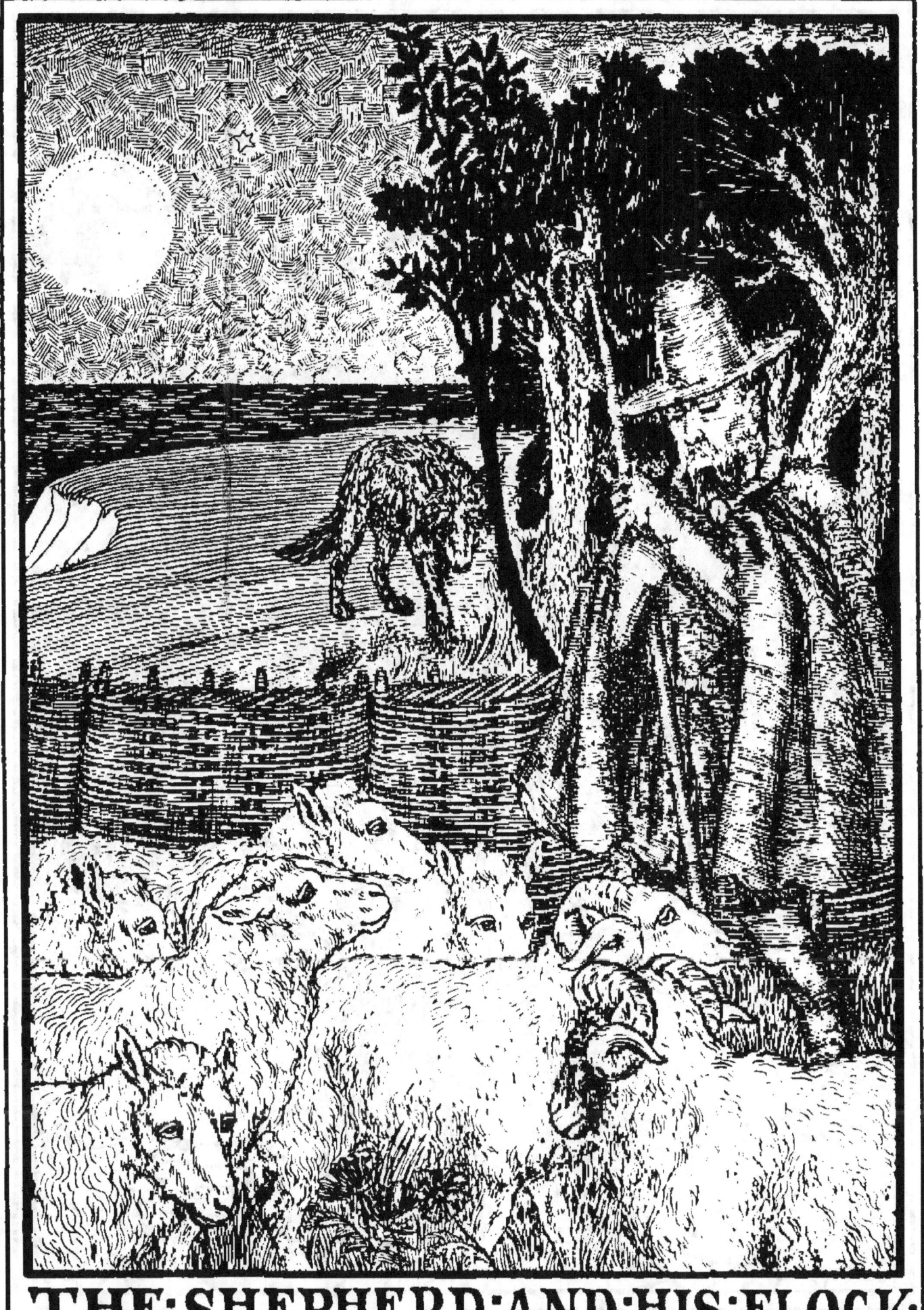

THE·SHEPHERD·AND·HIS·FLOCK·

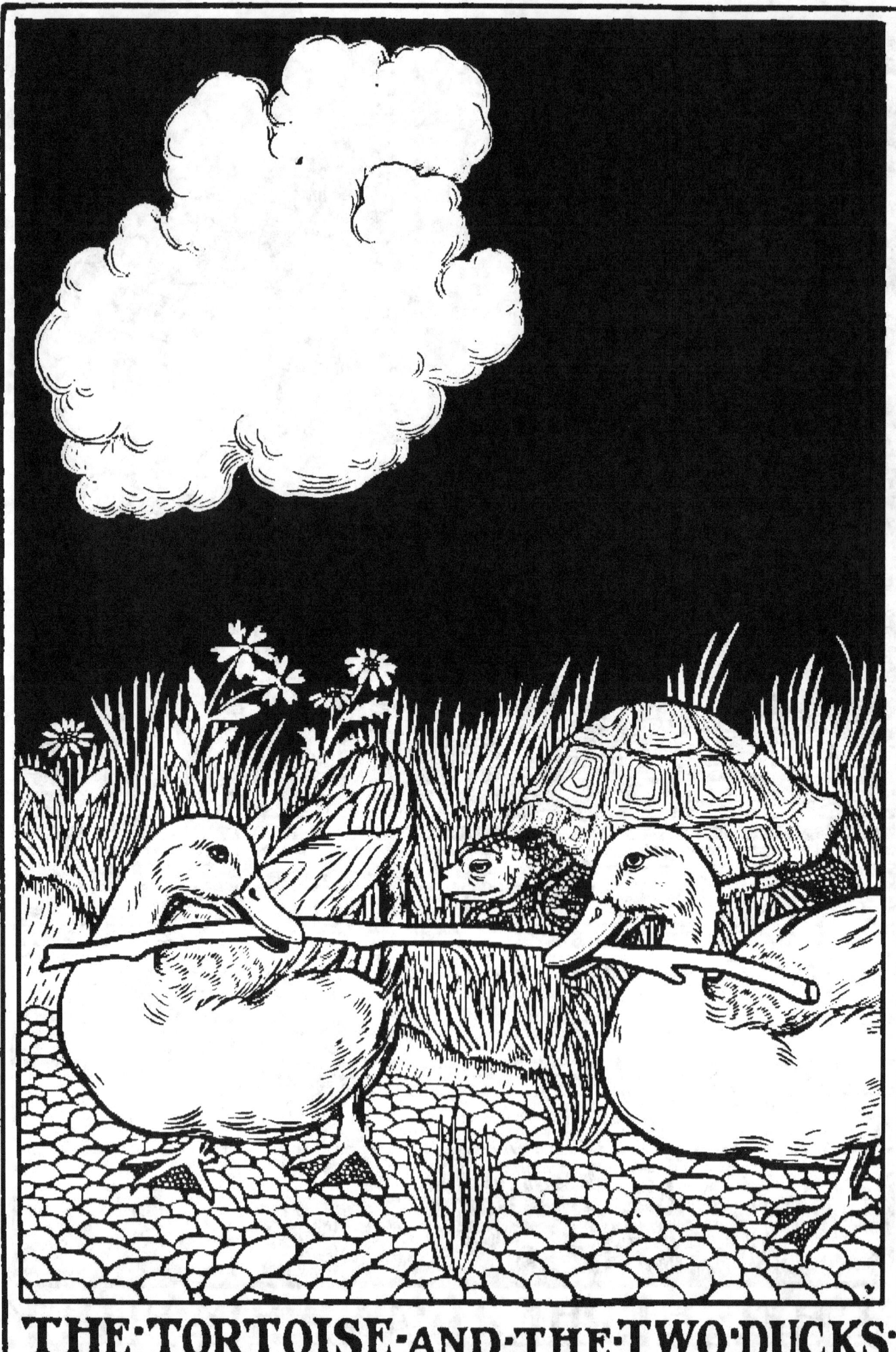

THE·TORTOISE·AND·THE·TWO·DUCKS·

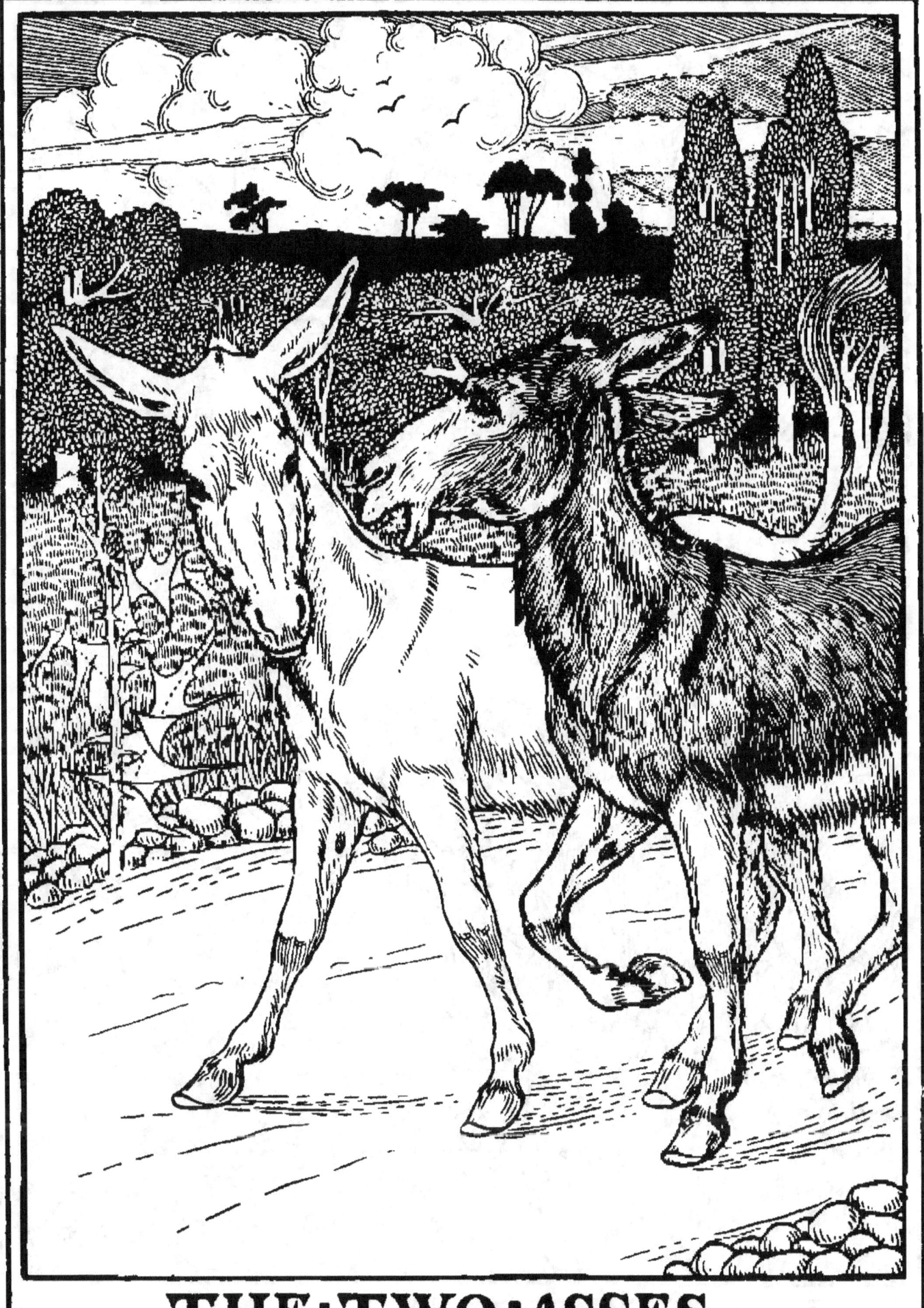

THE·TWO·ASSES.

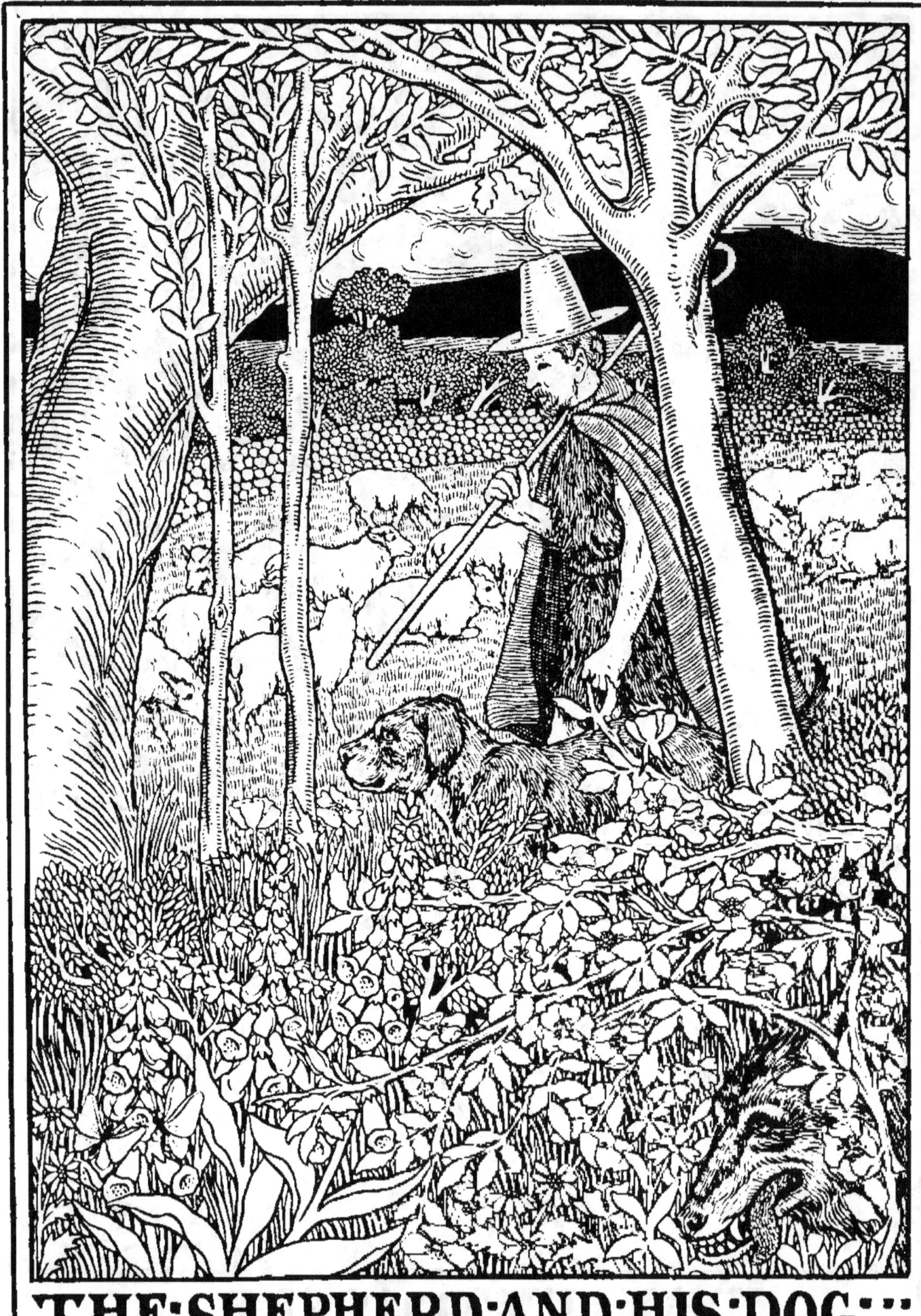

THE·SHEPHERD·AND·HIS·DOG···

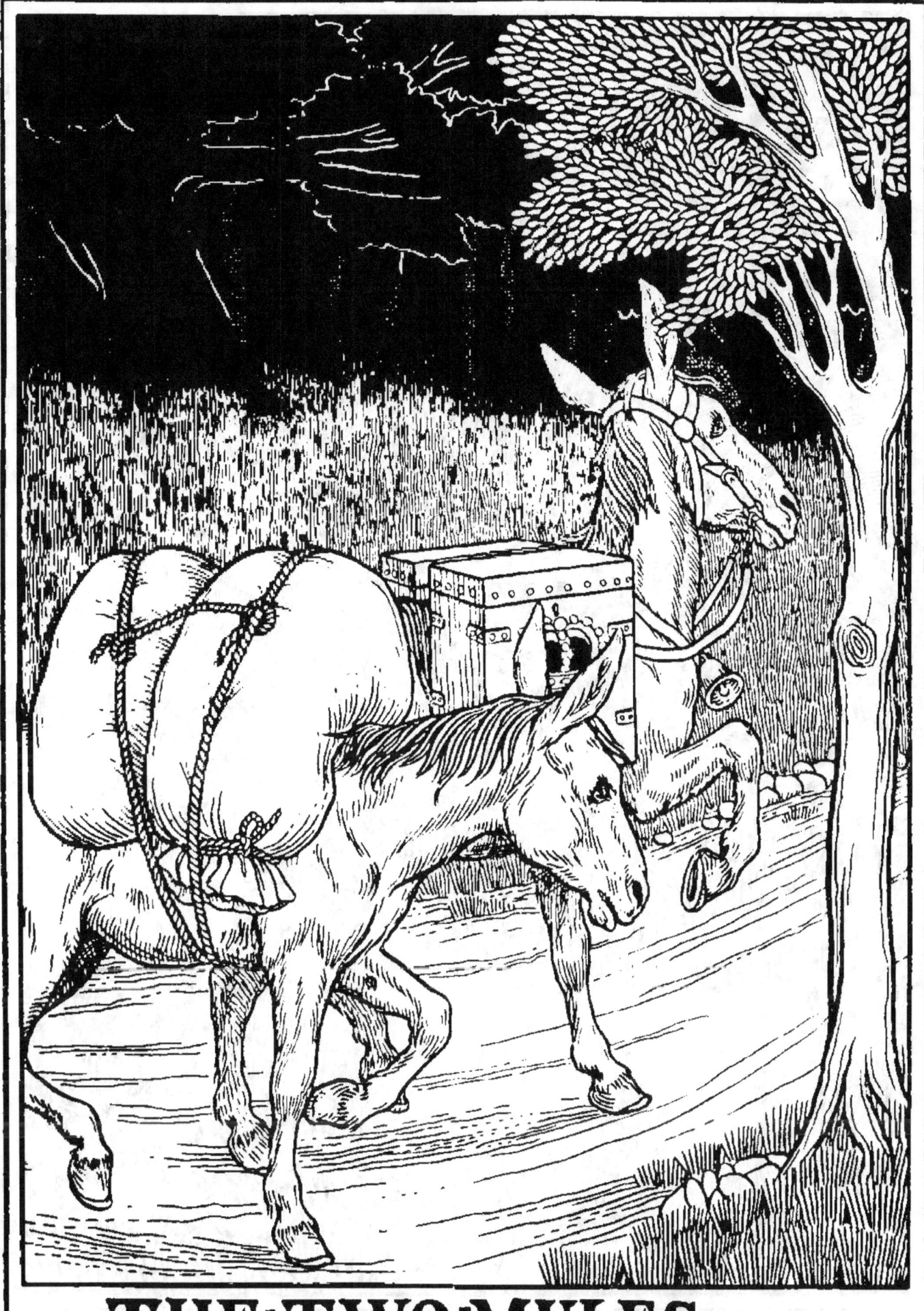

THE·TWO·MULES.

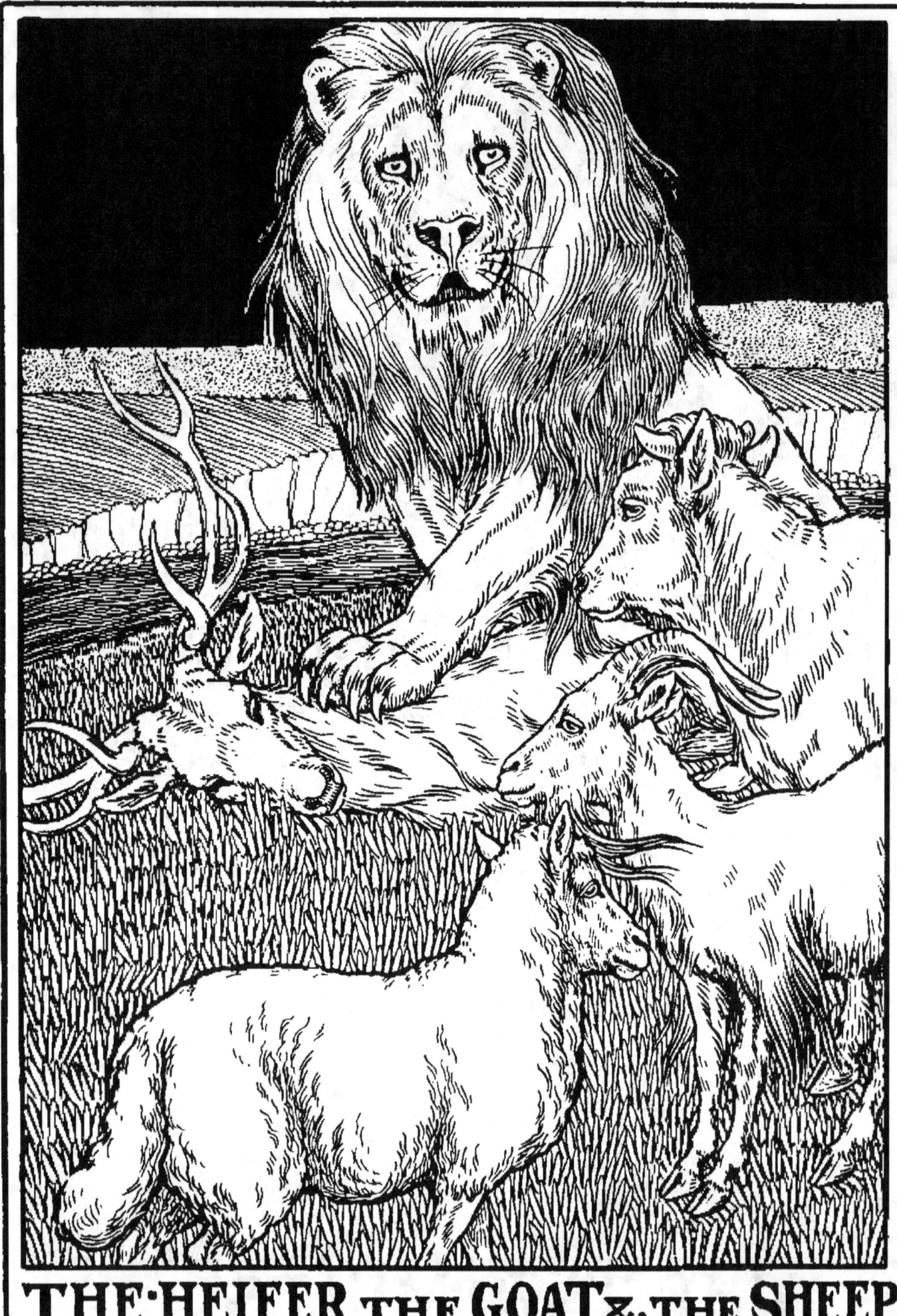

THE·HEIFER, THE GOAT, & THE SHEEP.

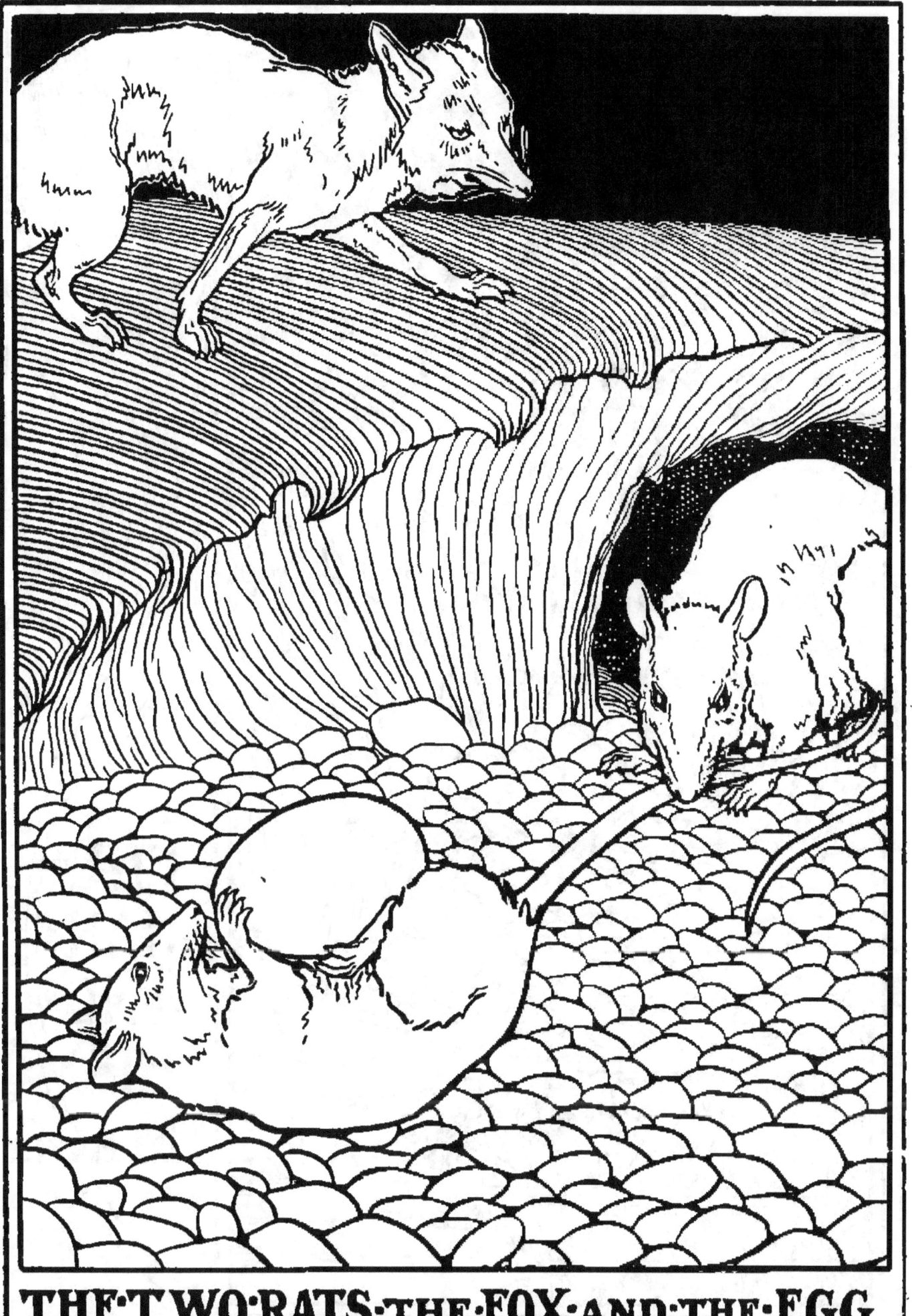

THE·TWO·RATS·THE·FOX·AND·THE·EGG.

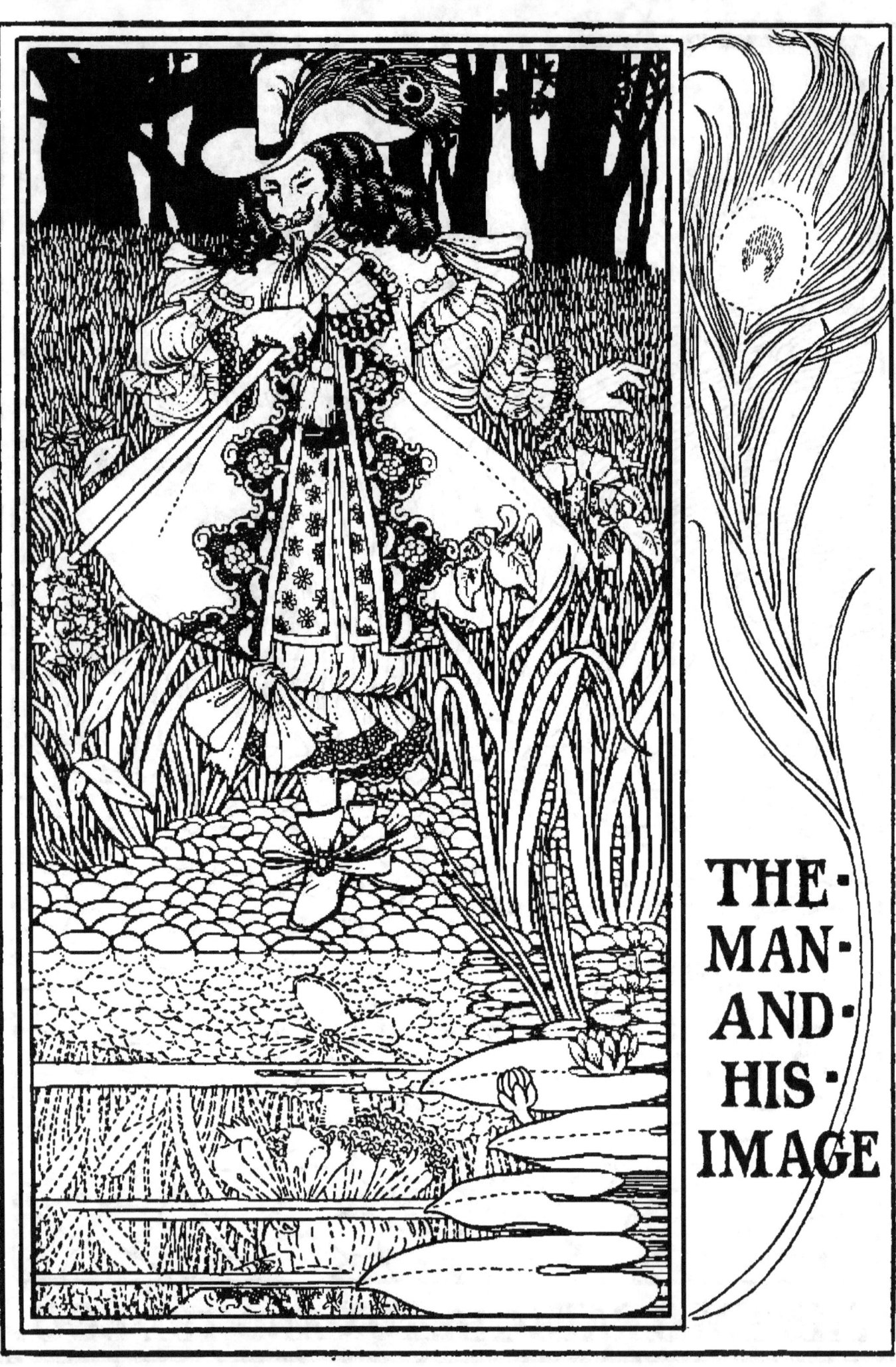

THE·
MAN·
AND·
HIS·
IMAGE

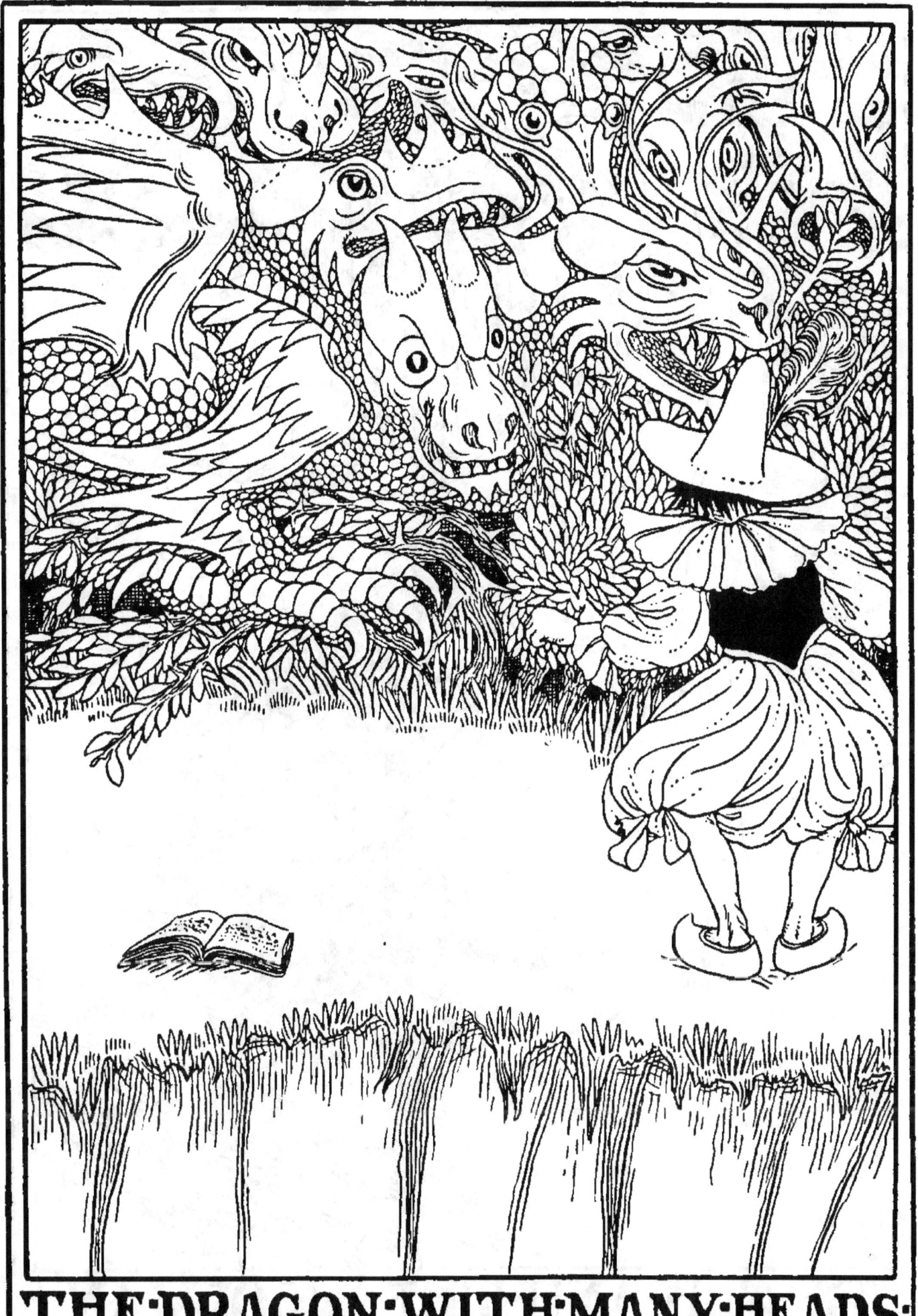

THE·DRAGON·WITH·MANY·HEADS·

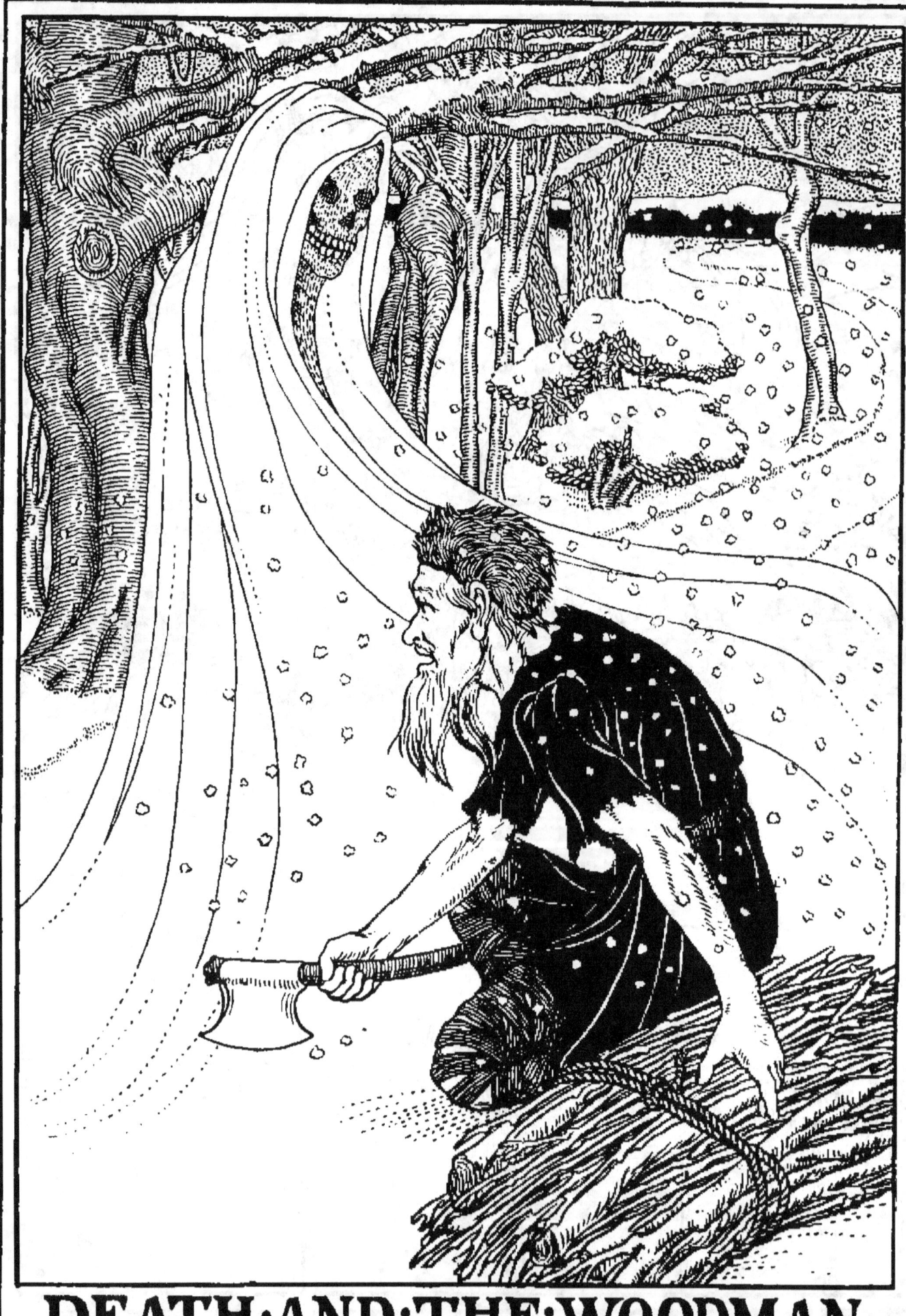

DEATH·AND·THE·WOODMAN.

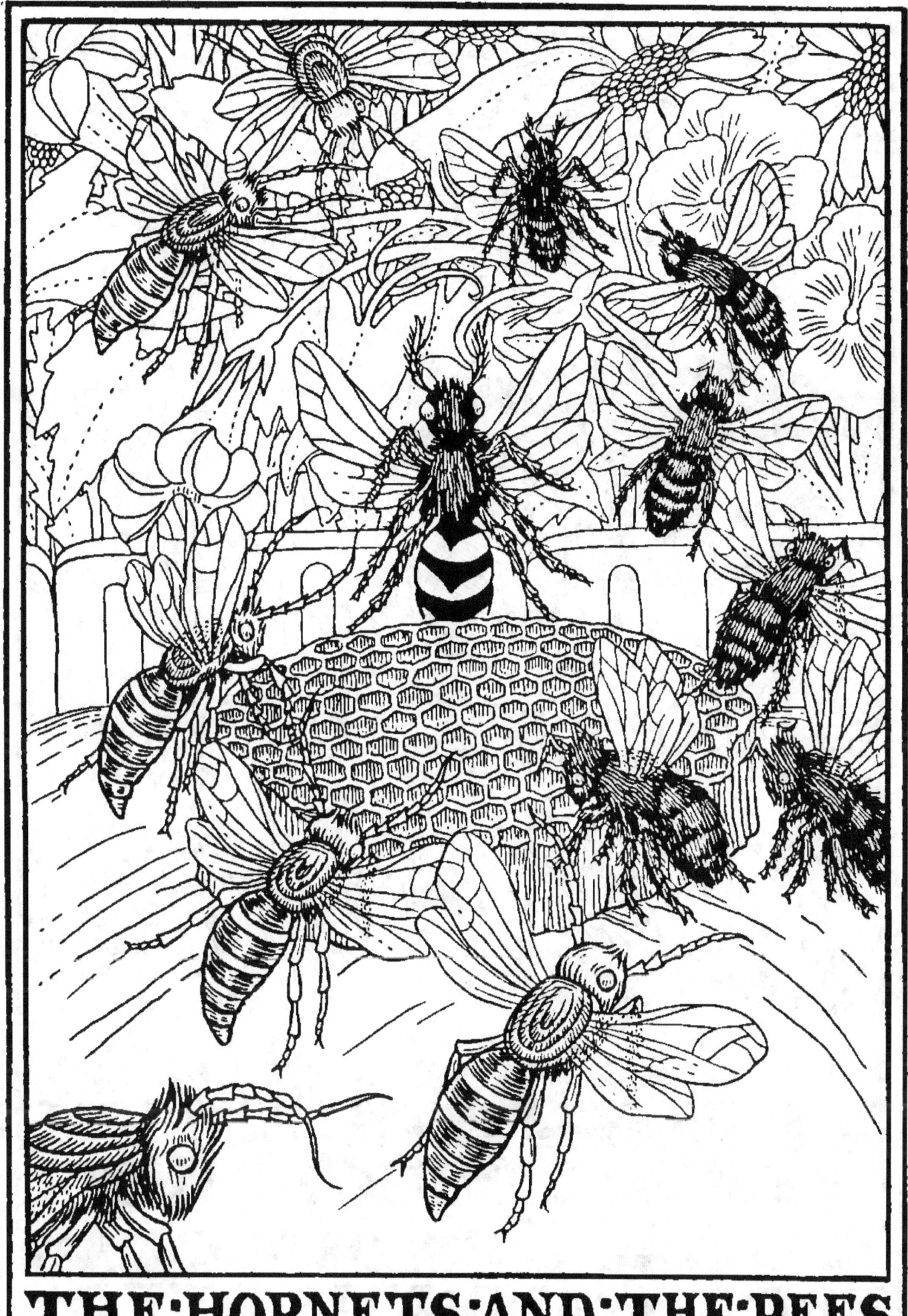

THE·HORNETS·AND·THE·BEES

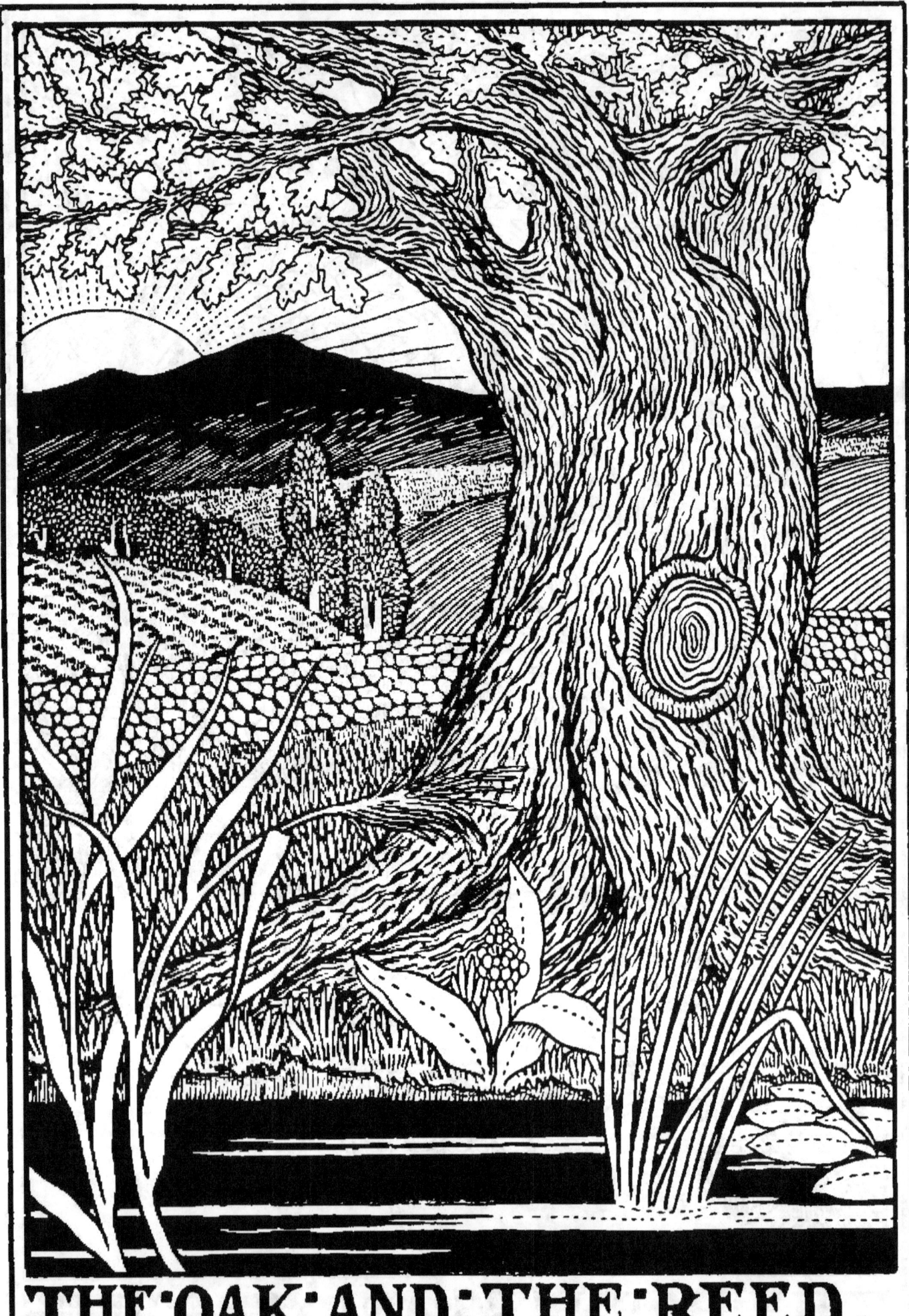

THE·OAK·AND·THE·REED.

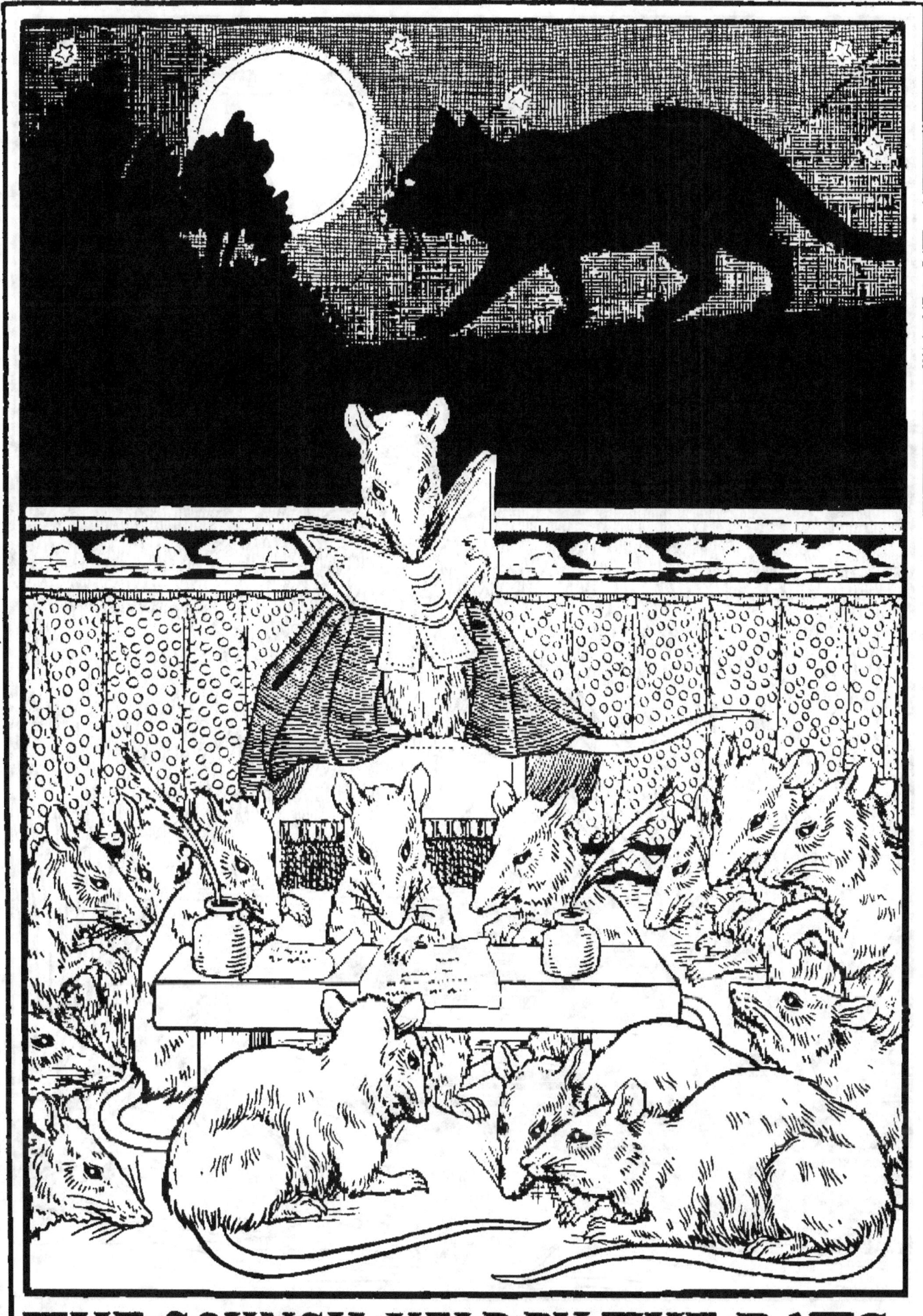

THE·COUNCIL·HELD·BY·THE·RATS.

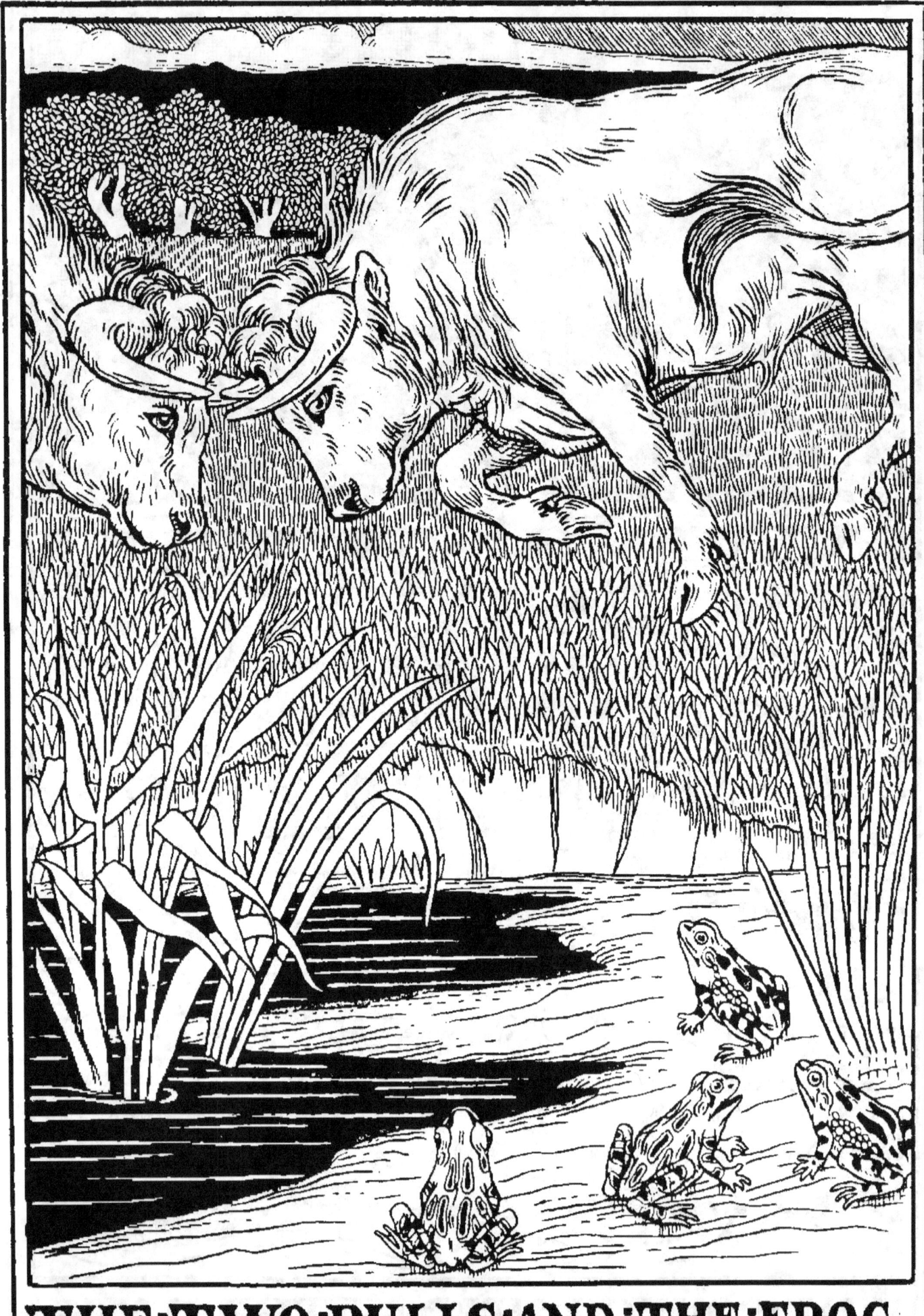

THE·TWO·BULLS·AND·THE·FROG.

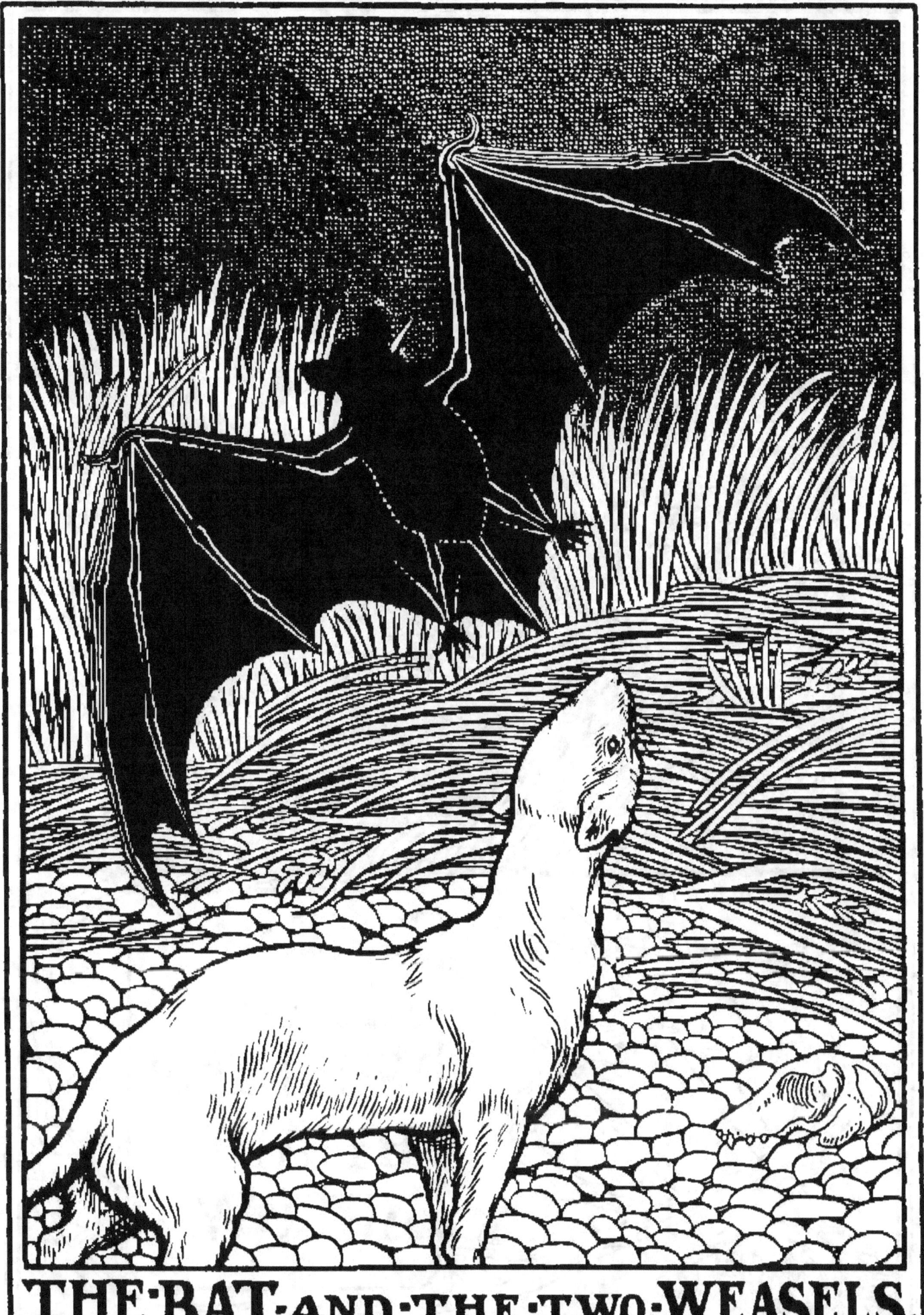

THE·BAT·AND·THE·TWO·WEASELS.

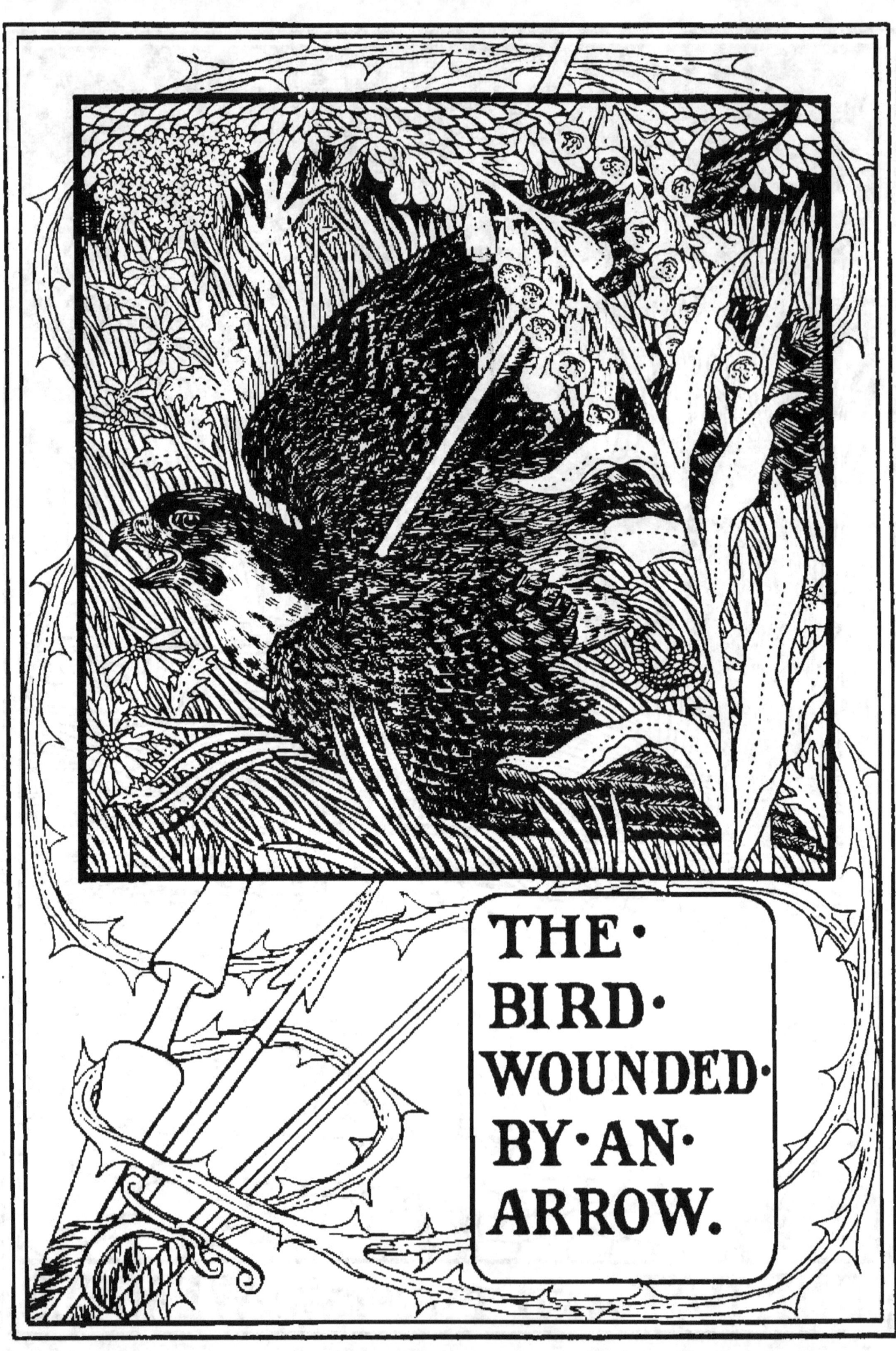

THE·
BIRD·
WOUNDED·
BY·AN·
ARROW.

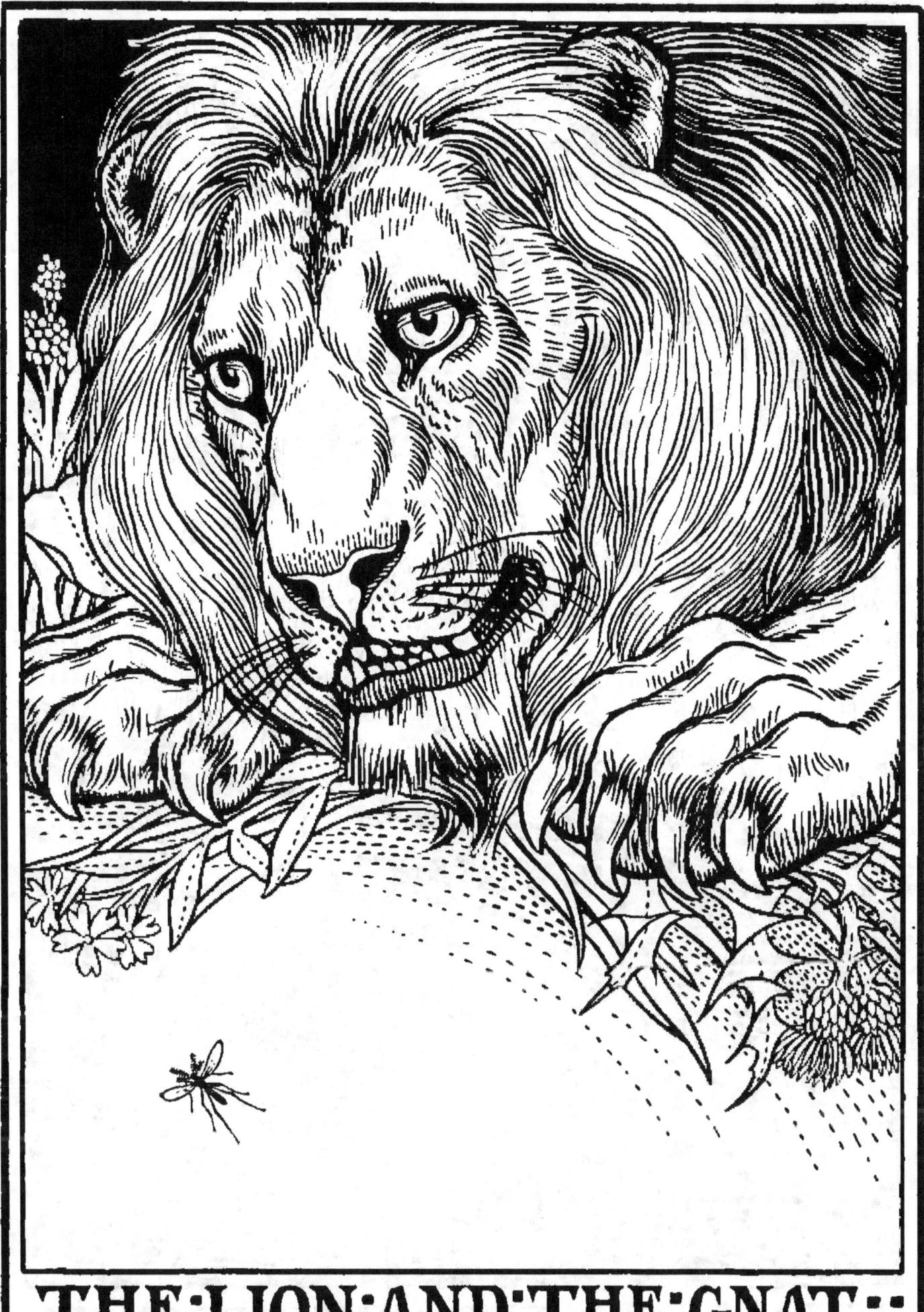

THE·LION·AND·THE·GNAT··

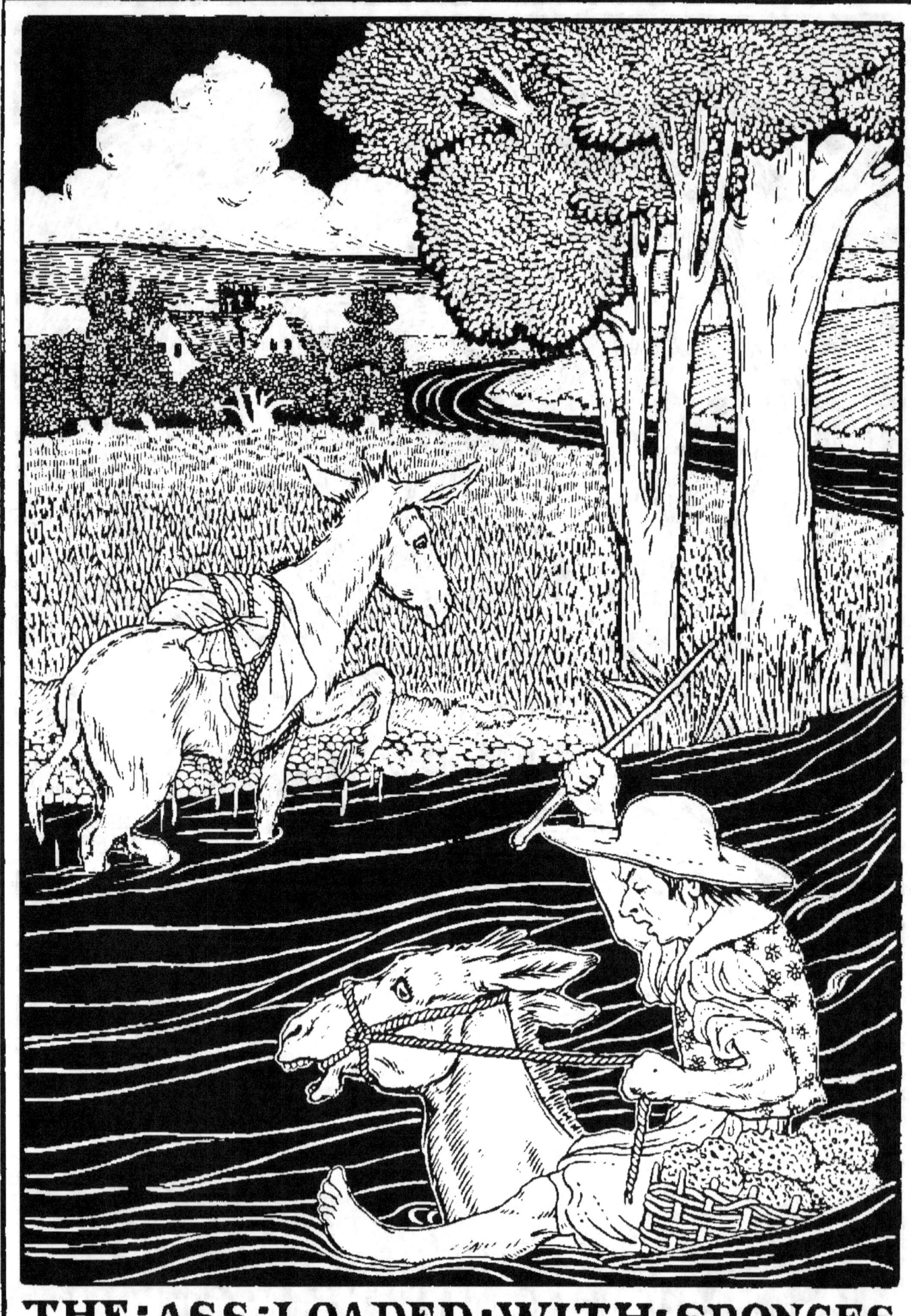

THE·ASS·LOADED·WITH·SPONGES.

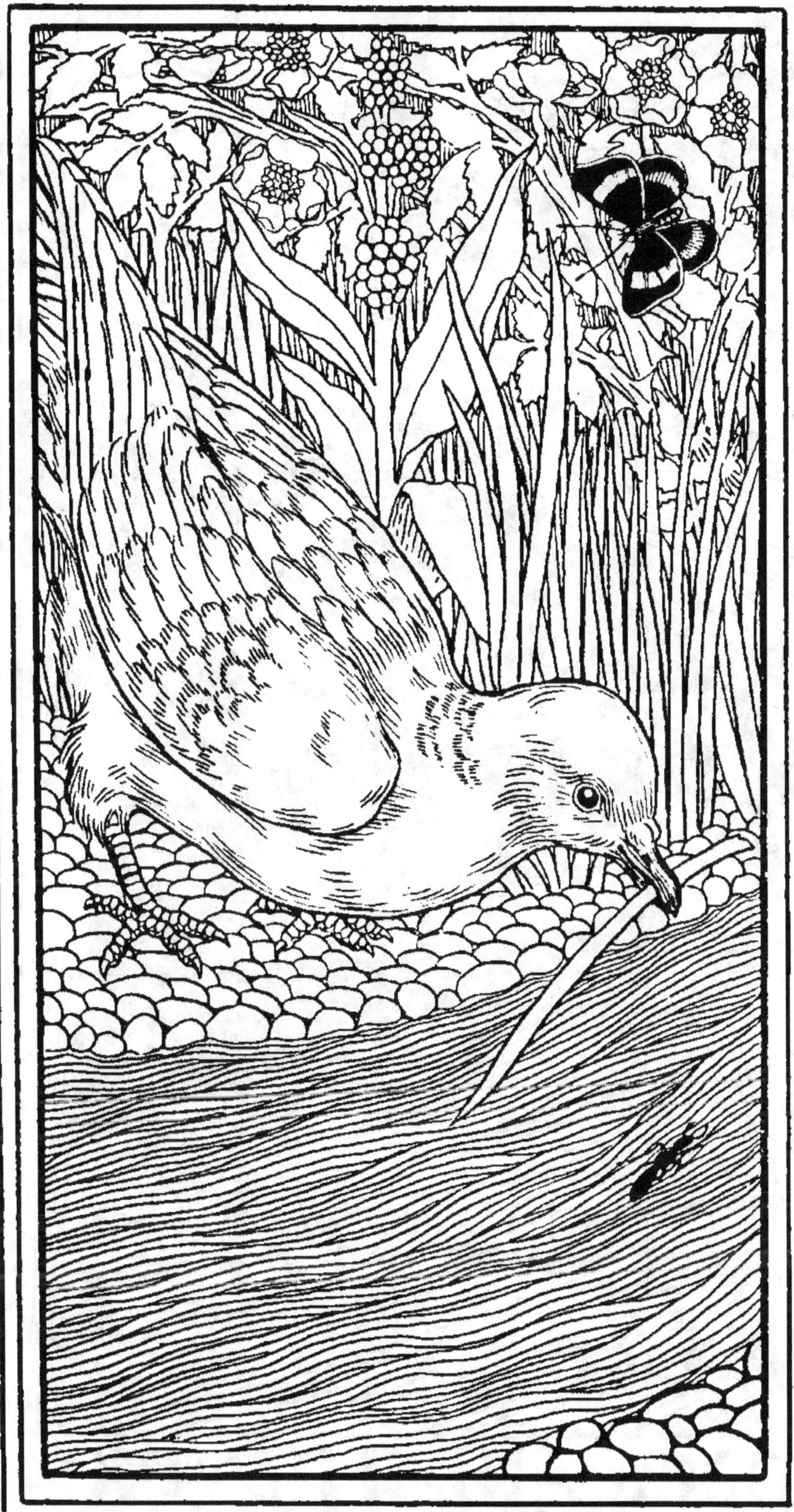

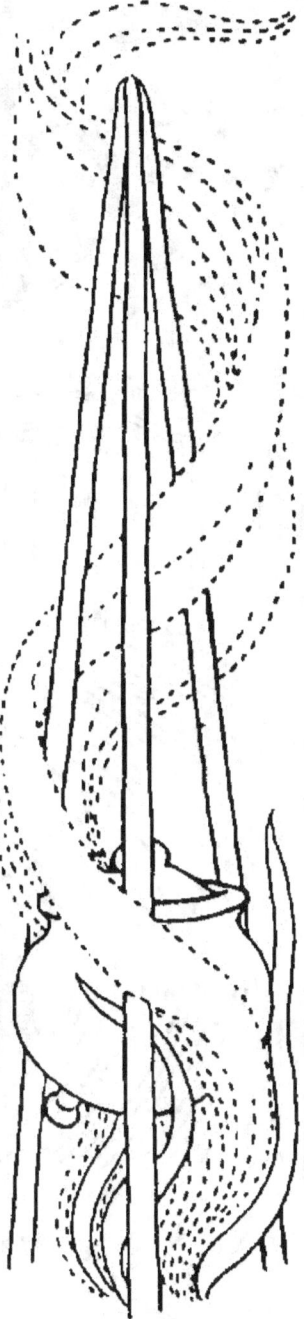

THE·
DOVE·
AND·
THE·
ANT.

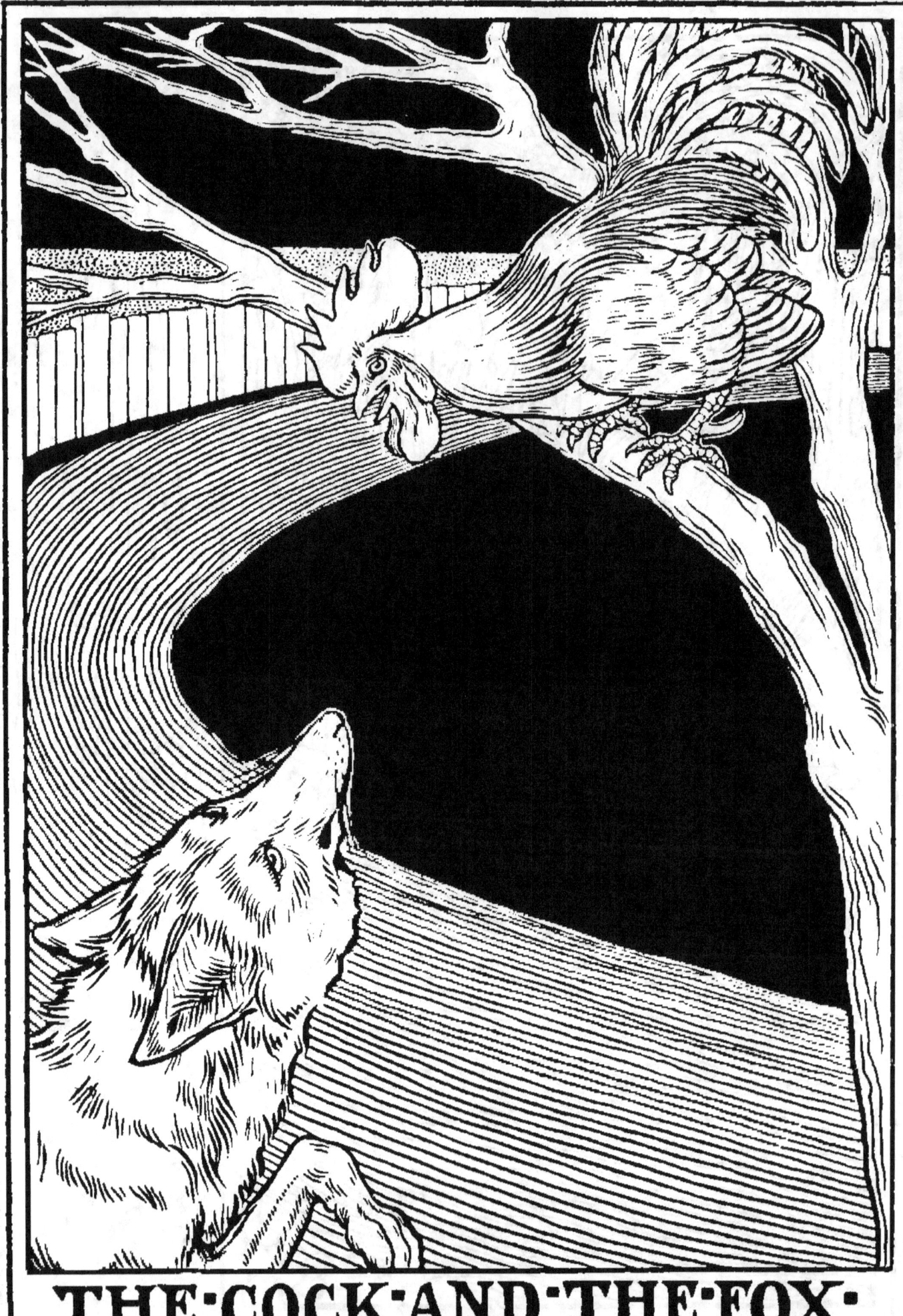

THE·COCK·AND·THE·FOX·

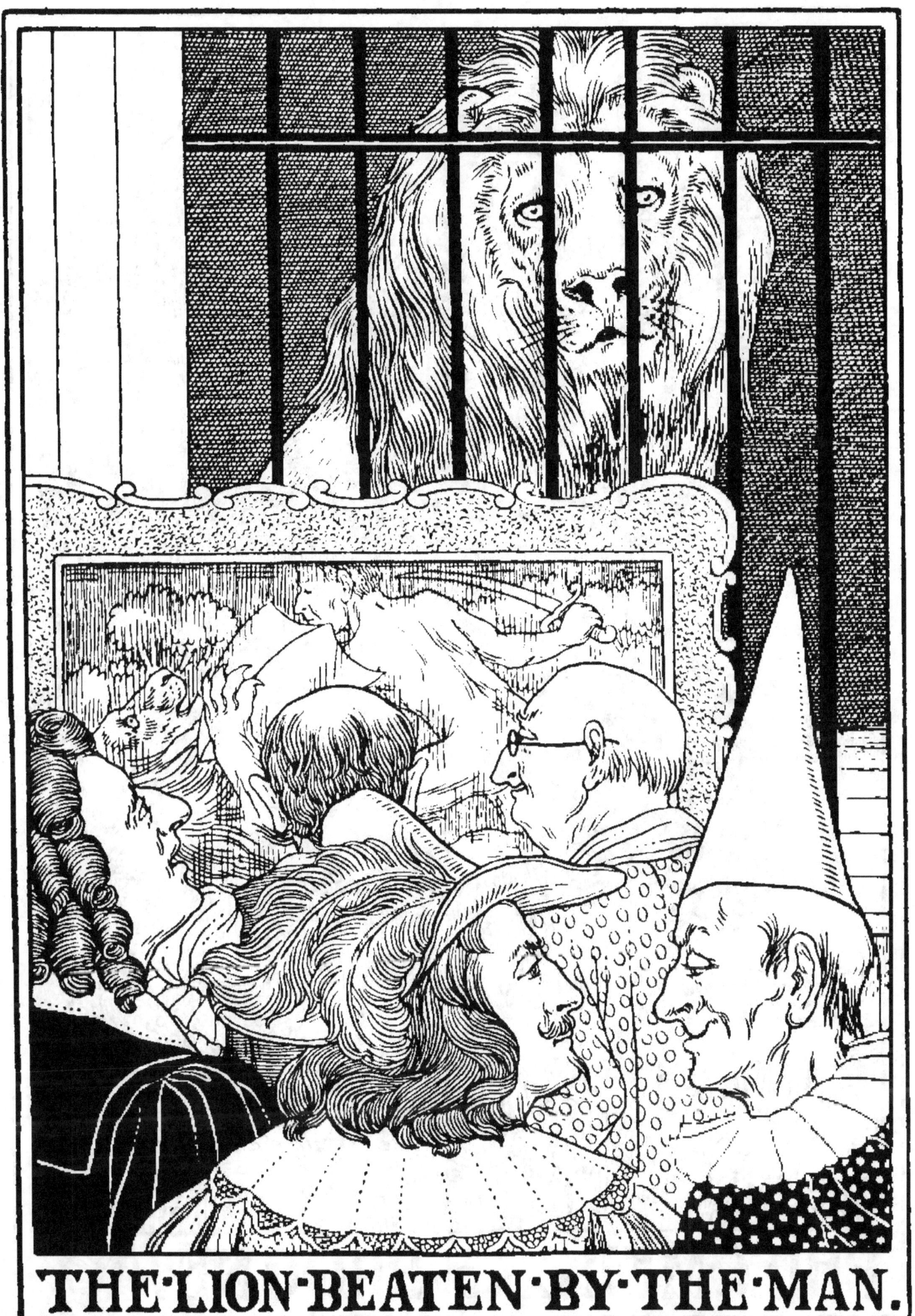

THE·LION·BEATEN·BY·THE·MAN.

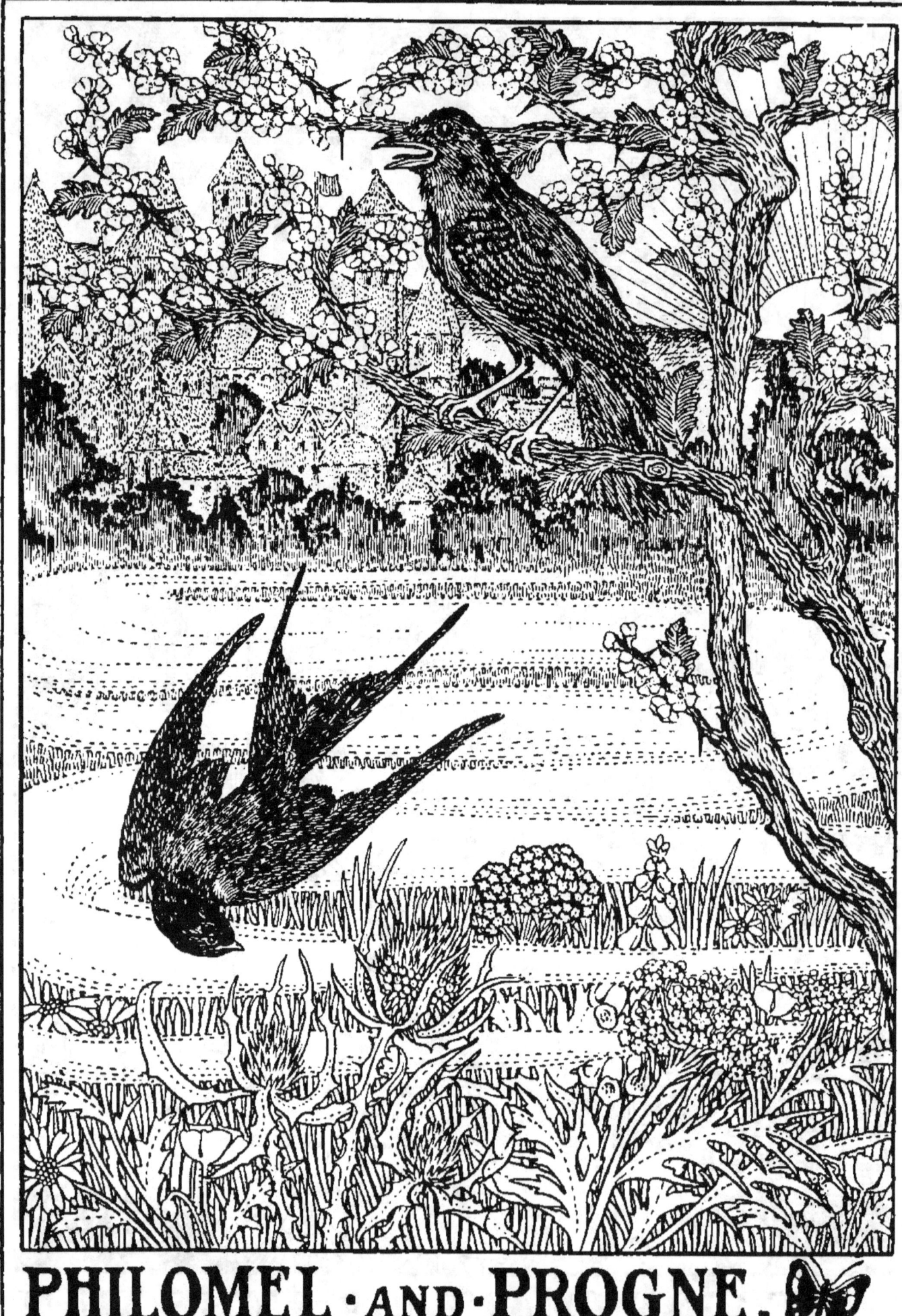

PHILOMEL · AND · PROGNE.

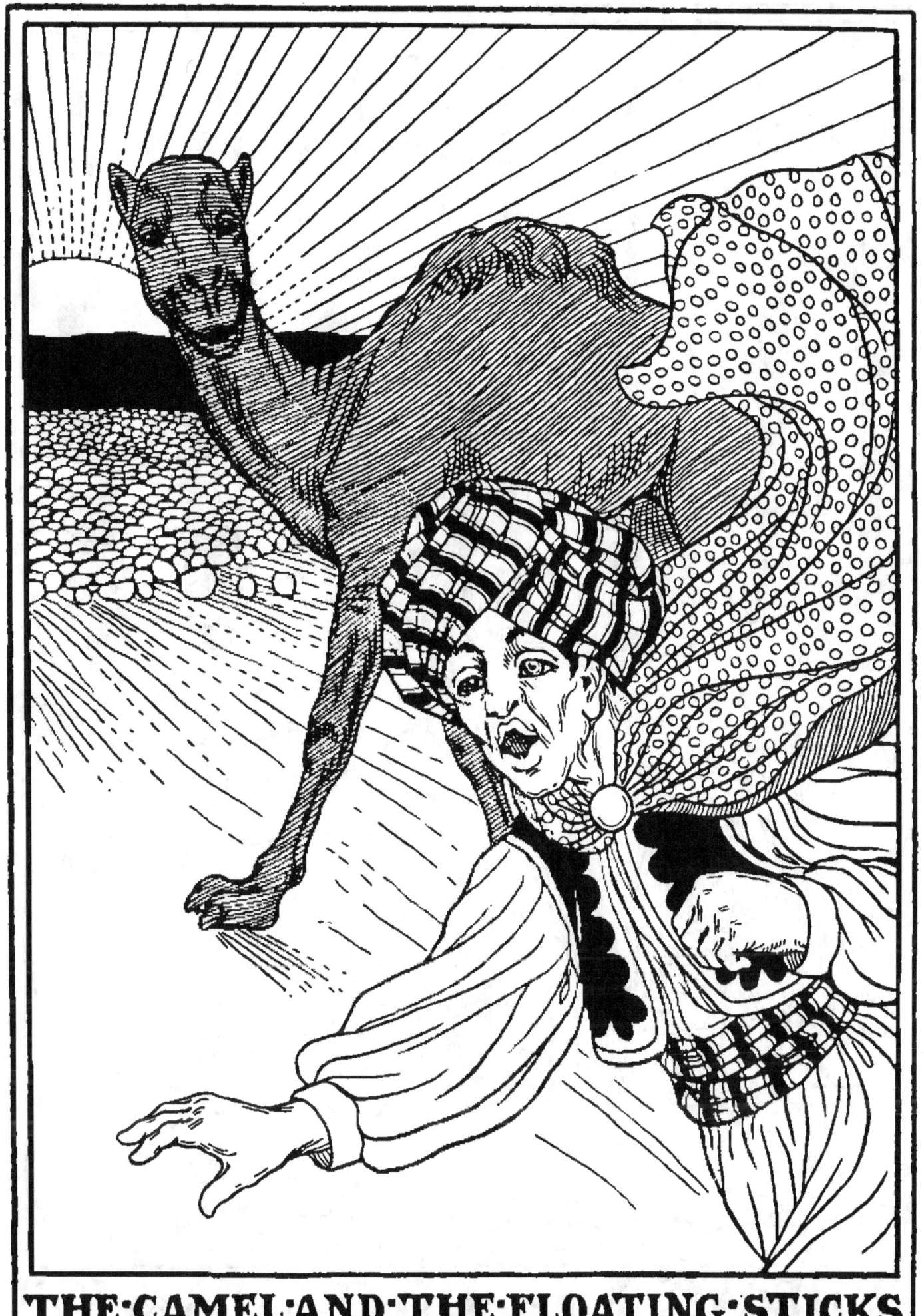

THE·CAMEL·AND·THE·FLOATING·STICKS

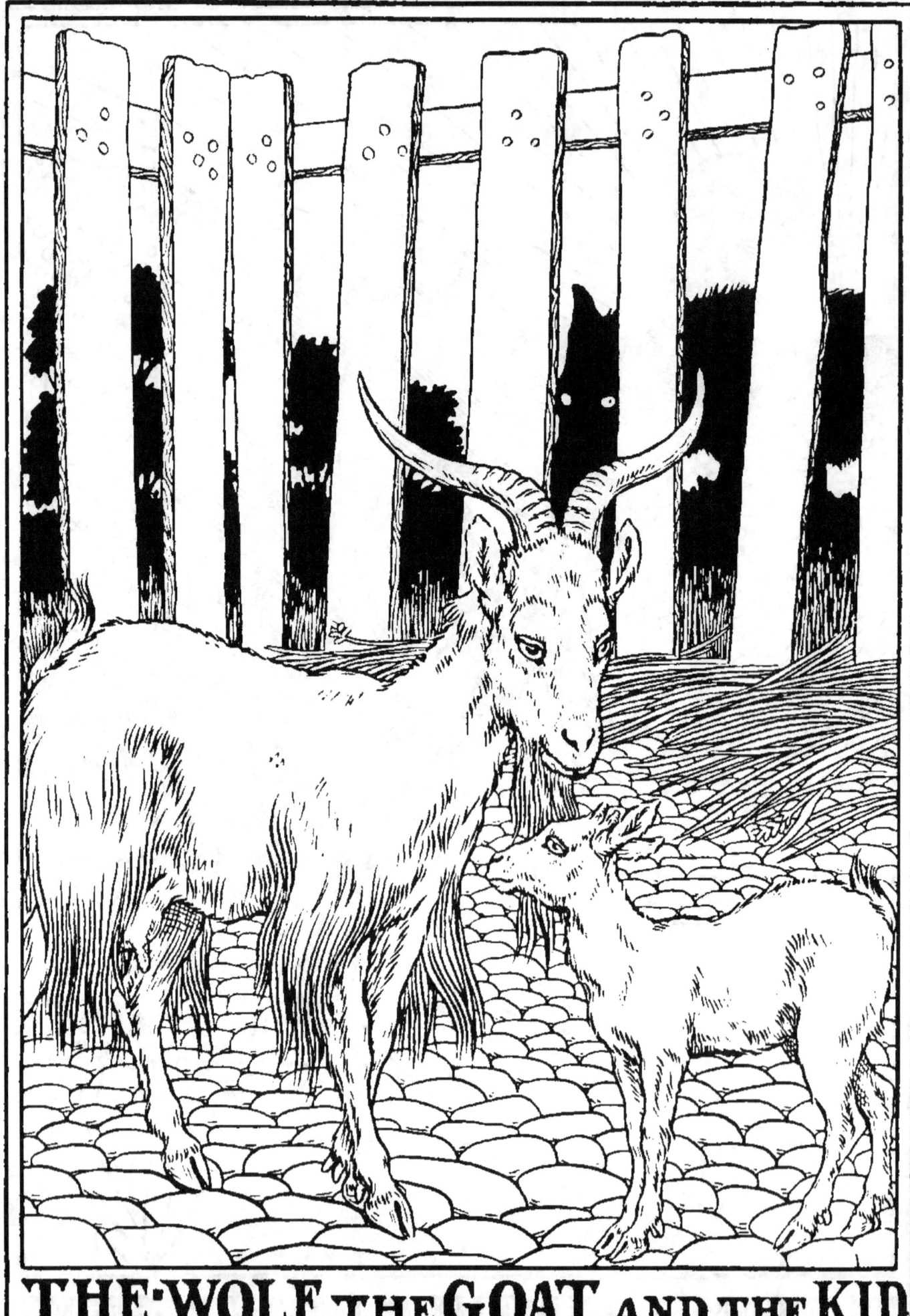

THE·WOLF, THE GOAT, AND THE KID

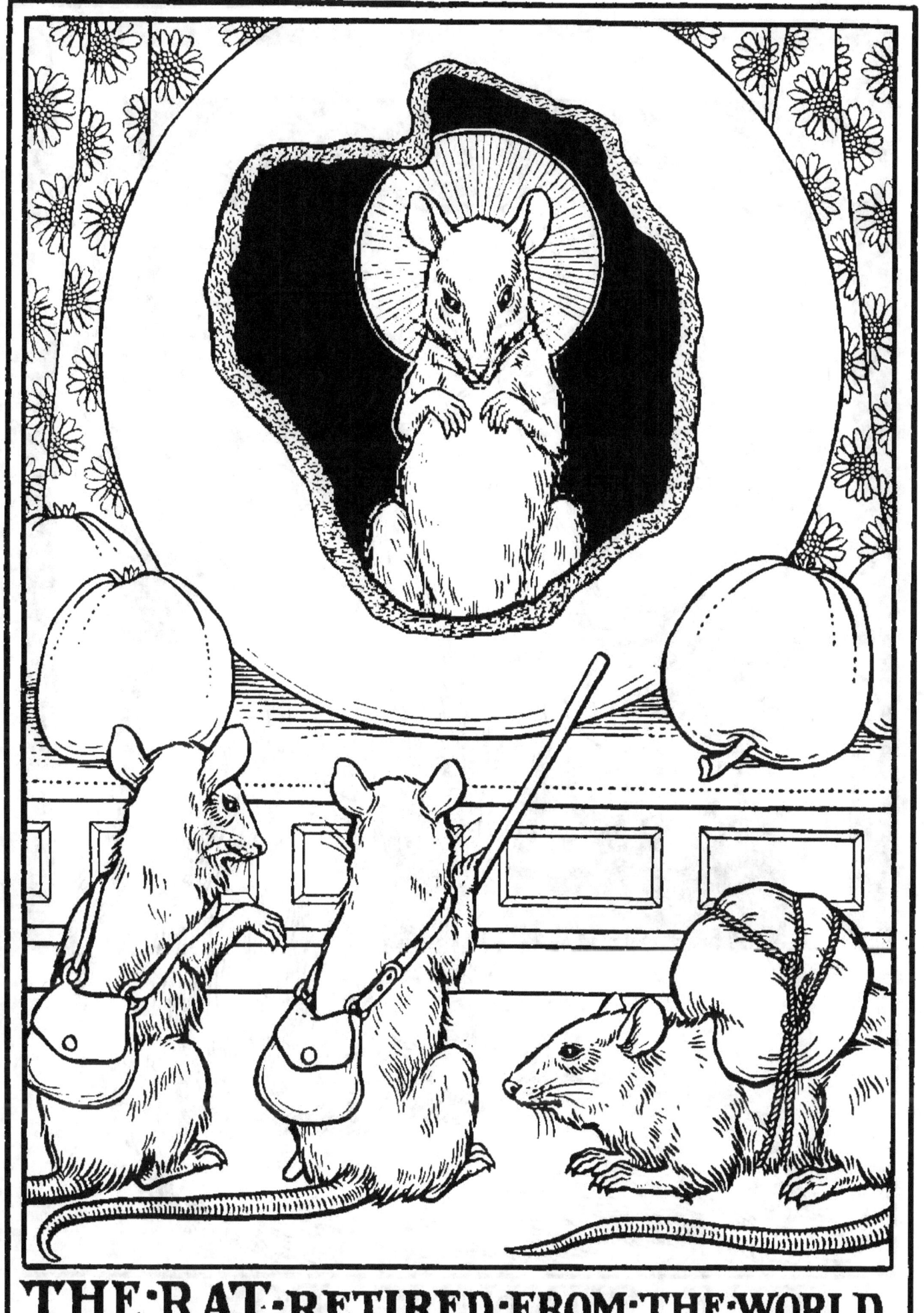

THE·RAT·RETIRED·FROM·THE·WORLD.

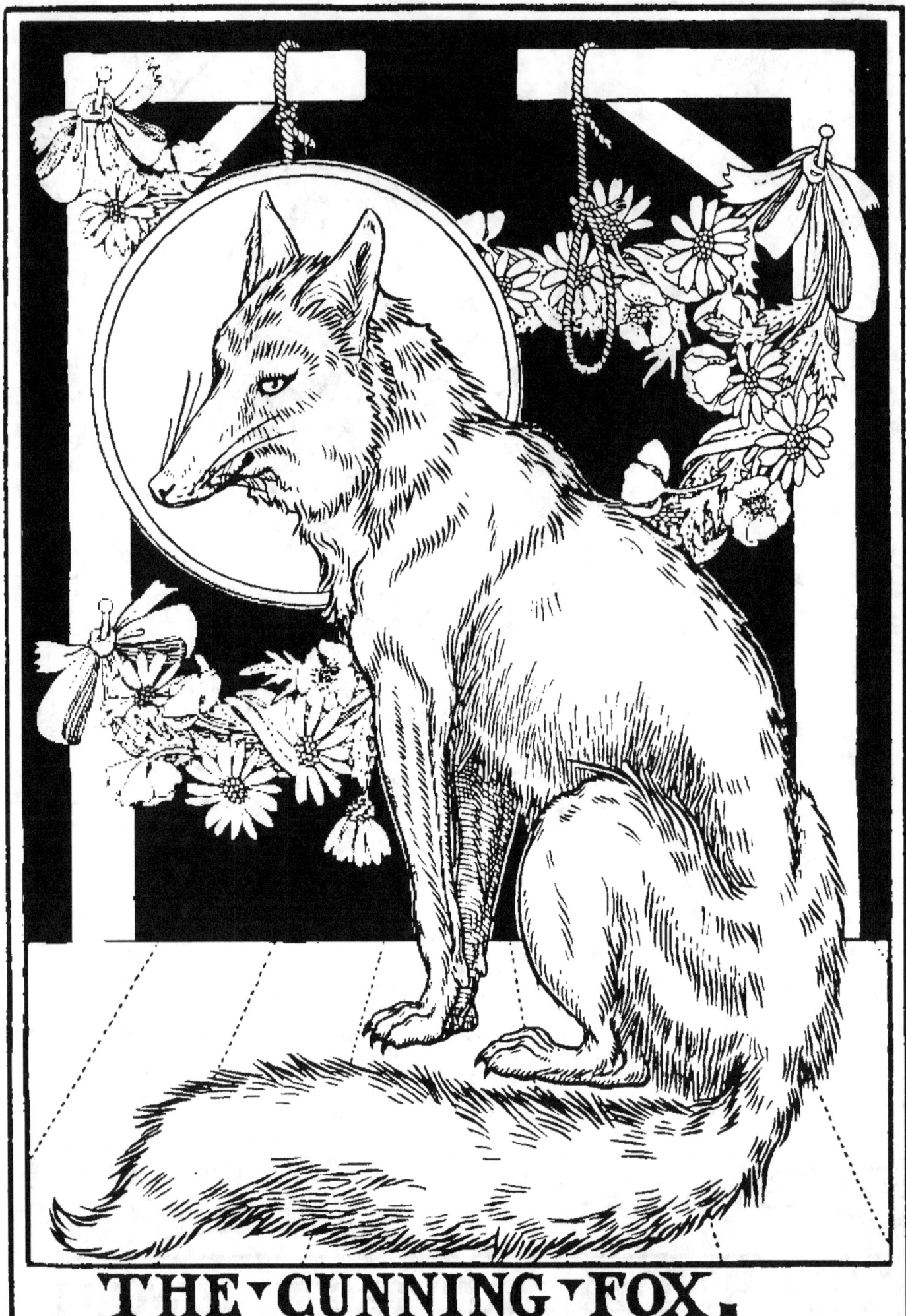

THE·CUNNING·FOX.

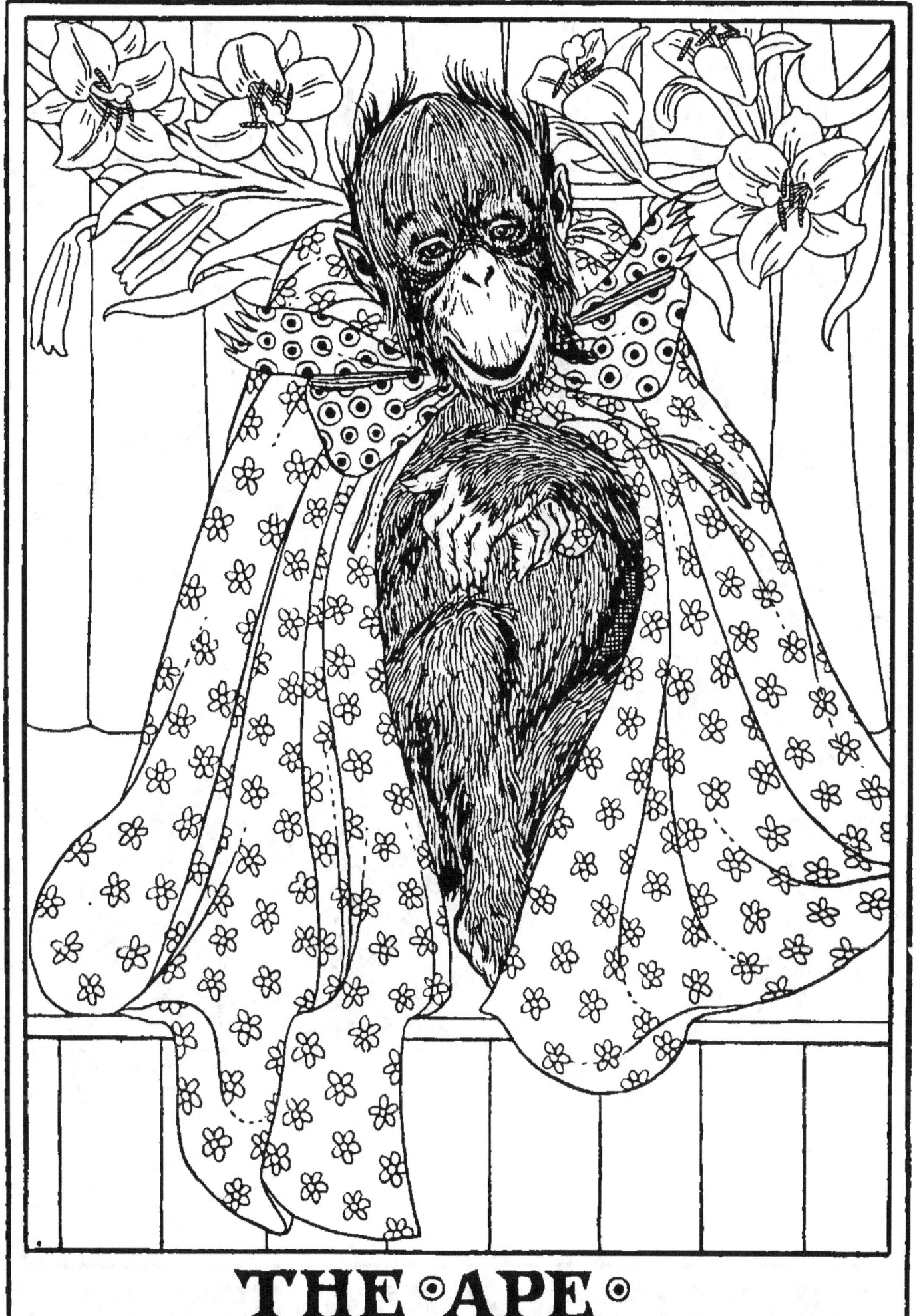

THE •APE• ◦

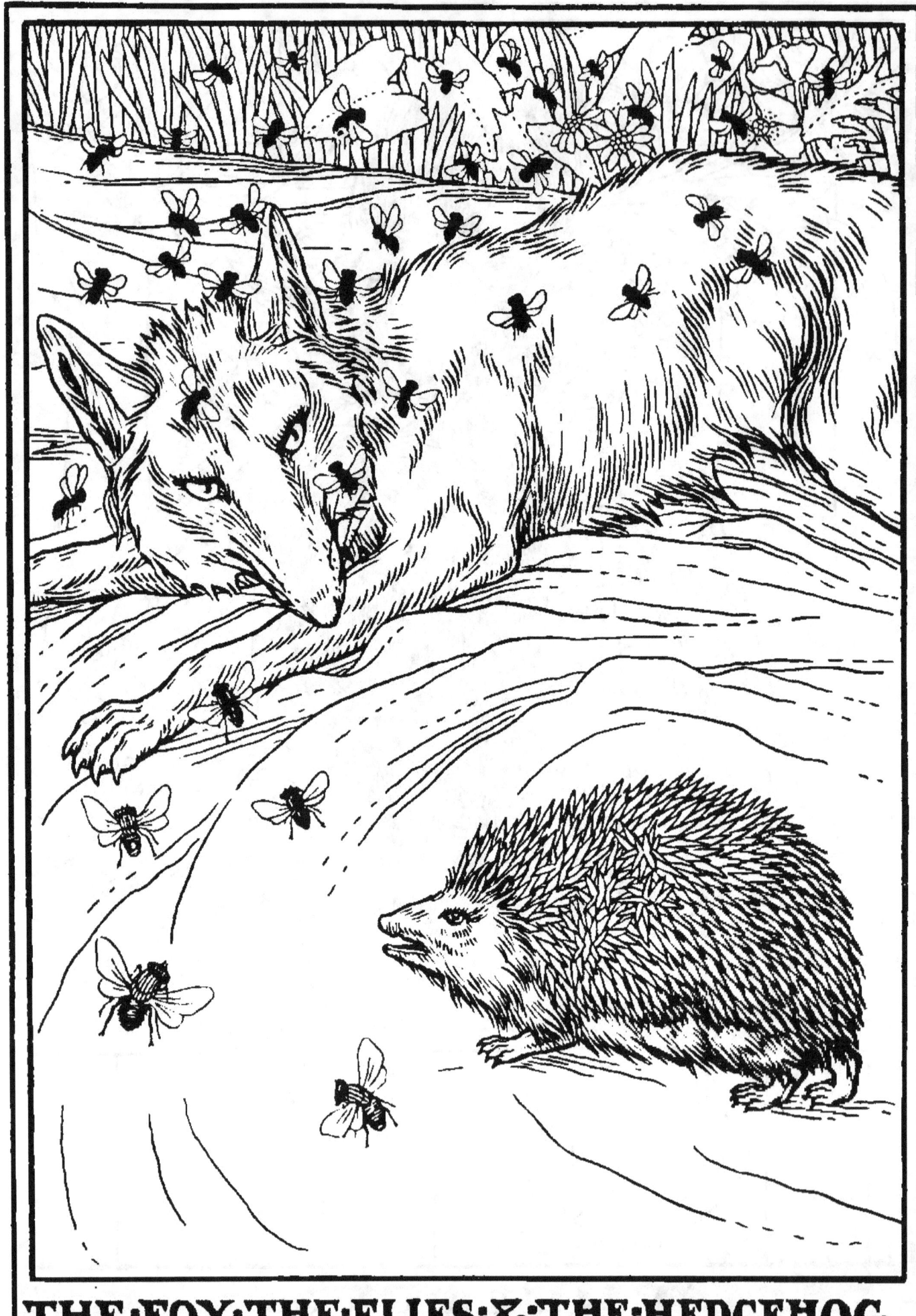

THE·FOX·THE·FLIES·&·THE·HEDGEHOG.

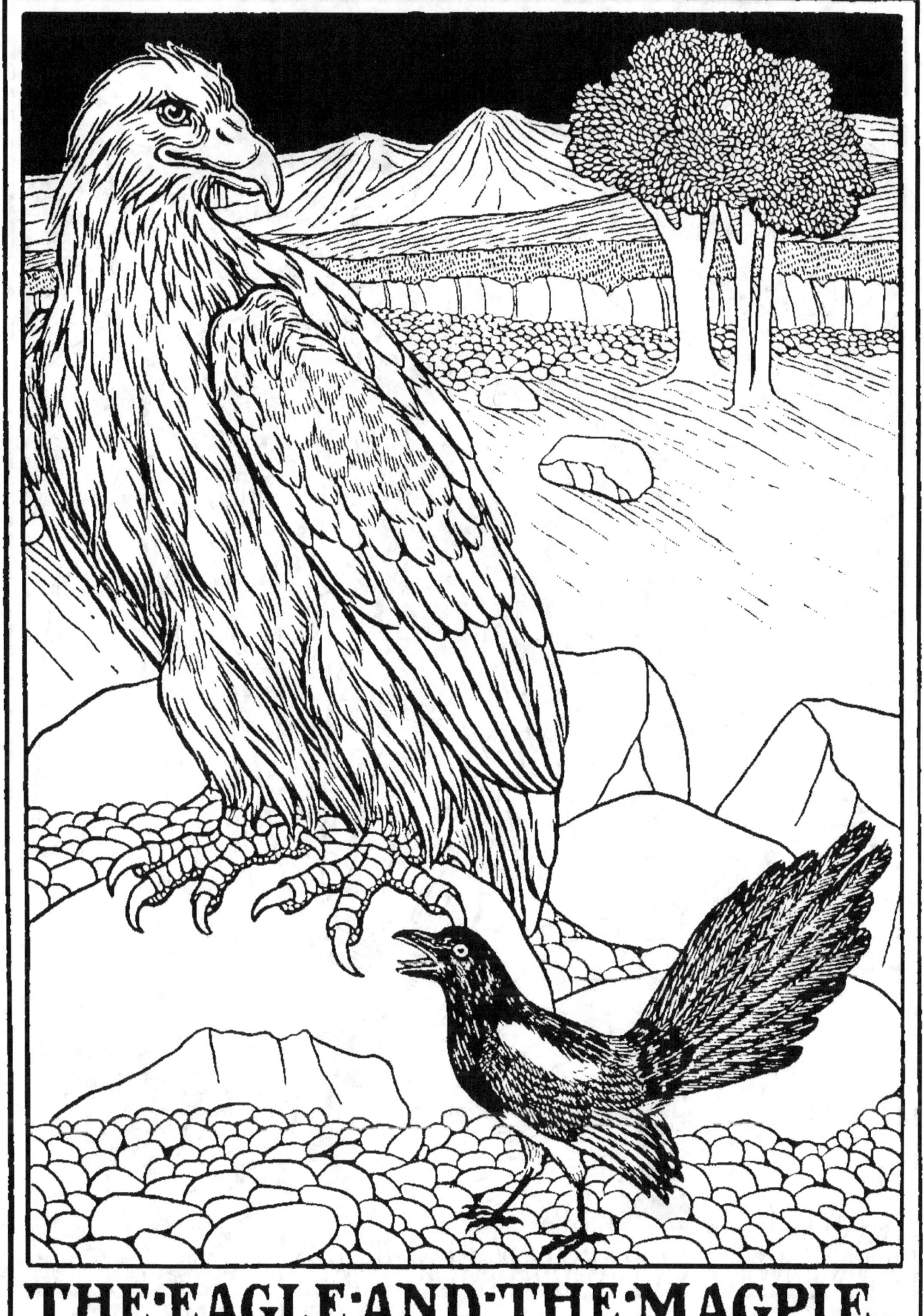

THE·EAGLE·AND·THE·MAGPIE.

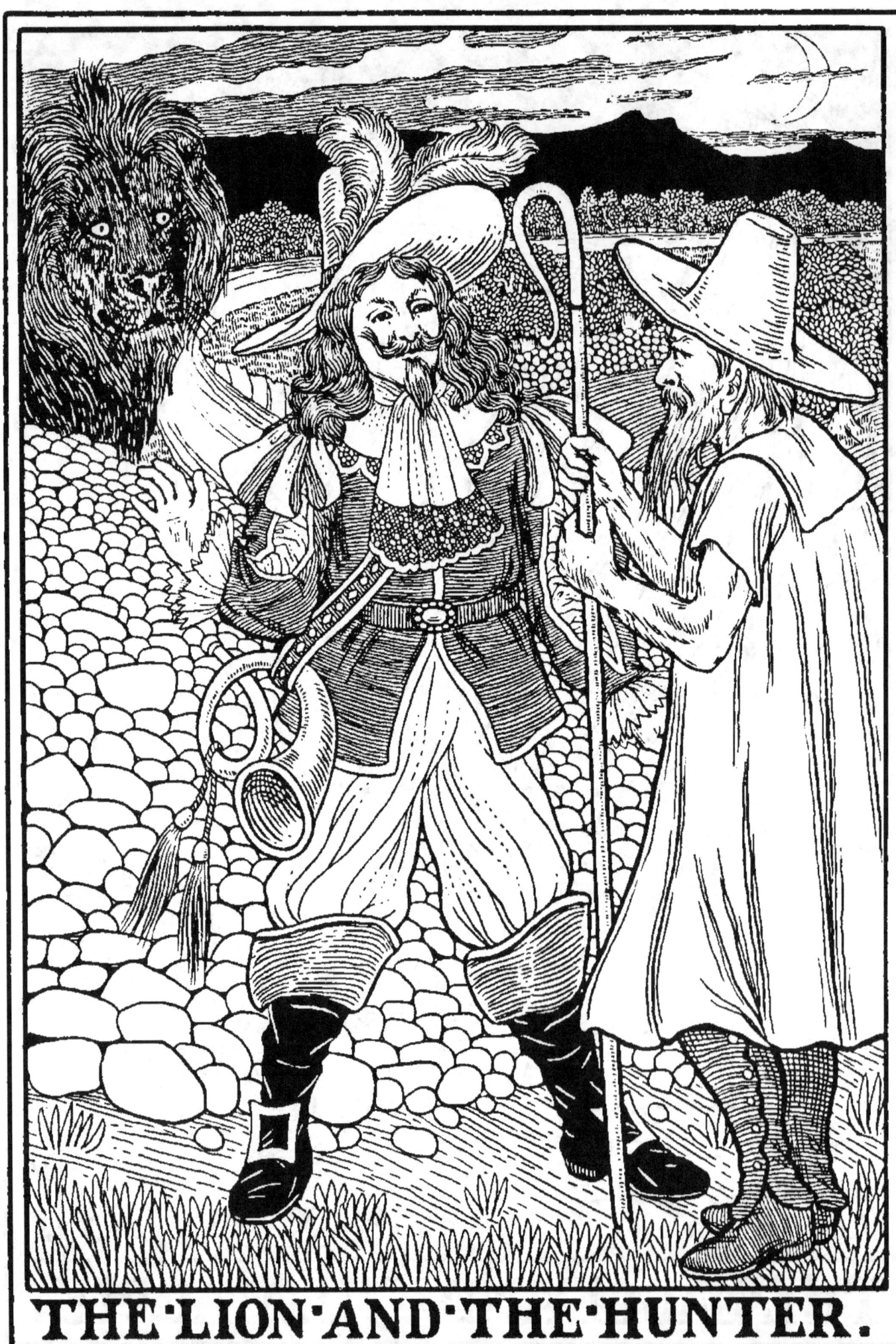

THE·LION·AND·THE·HUNTER.

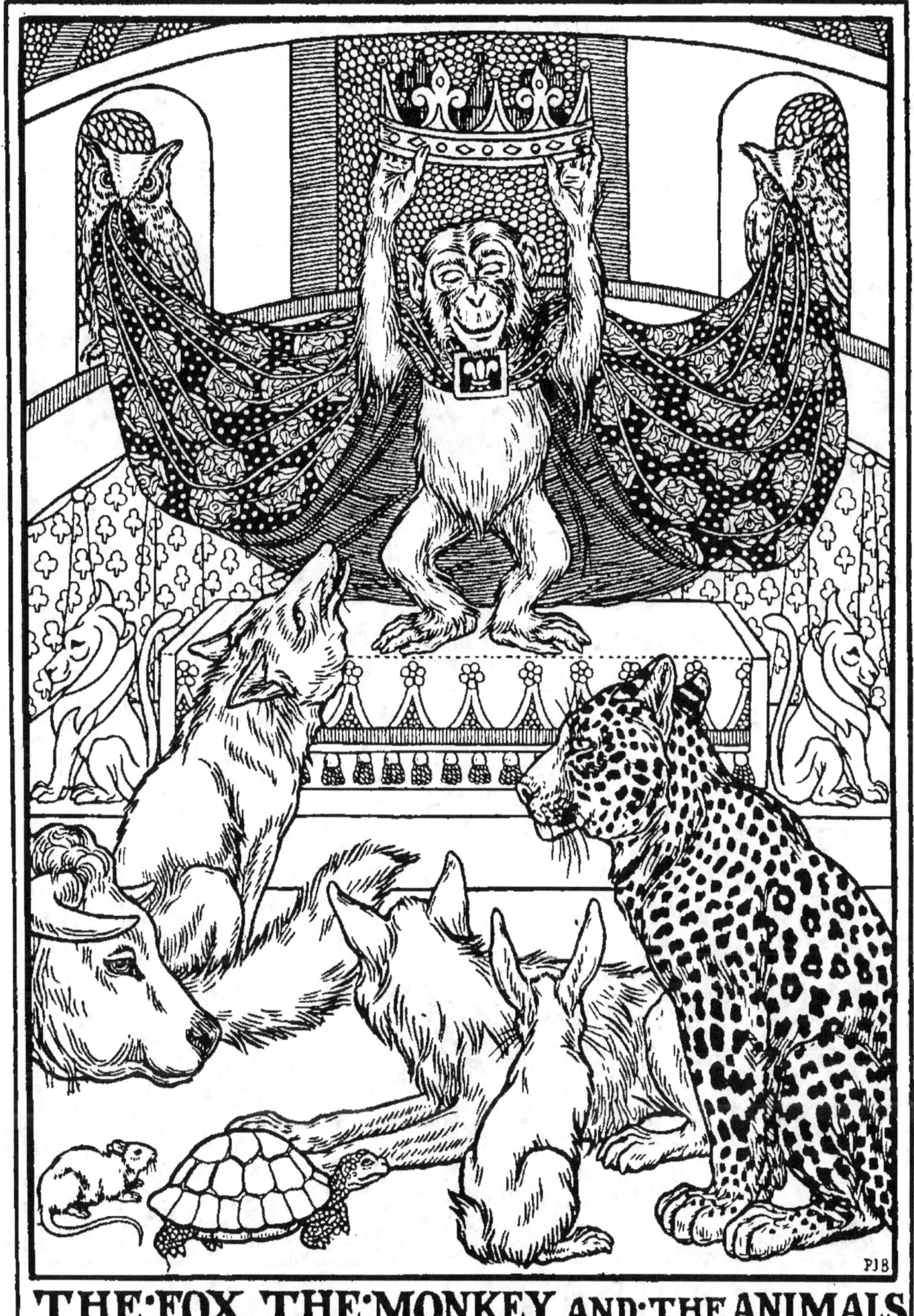

THE·FOX, THE·MONKEY, AND·THE·ANIMALS

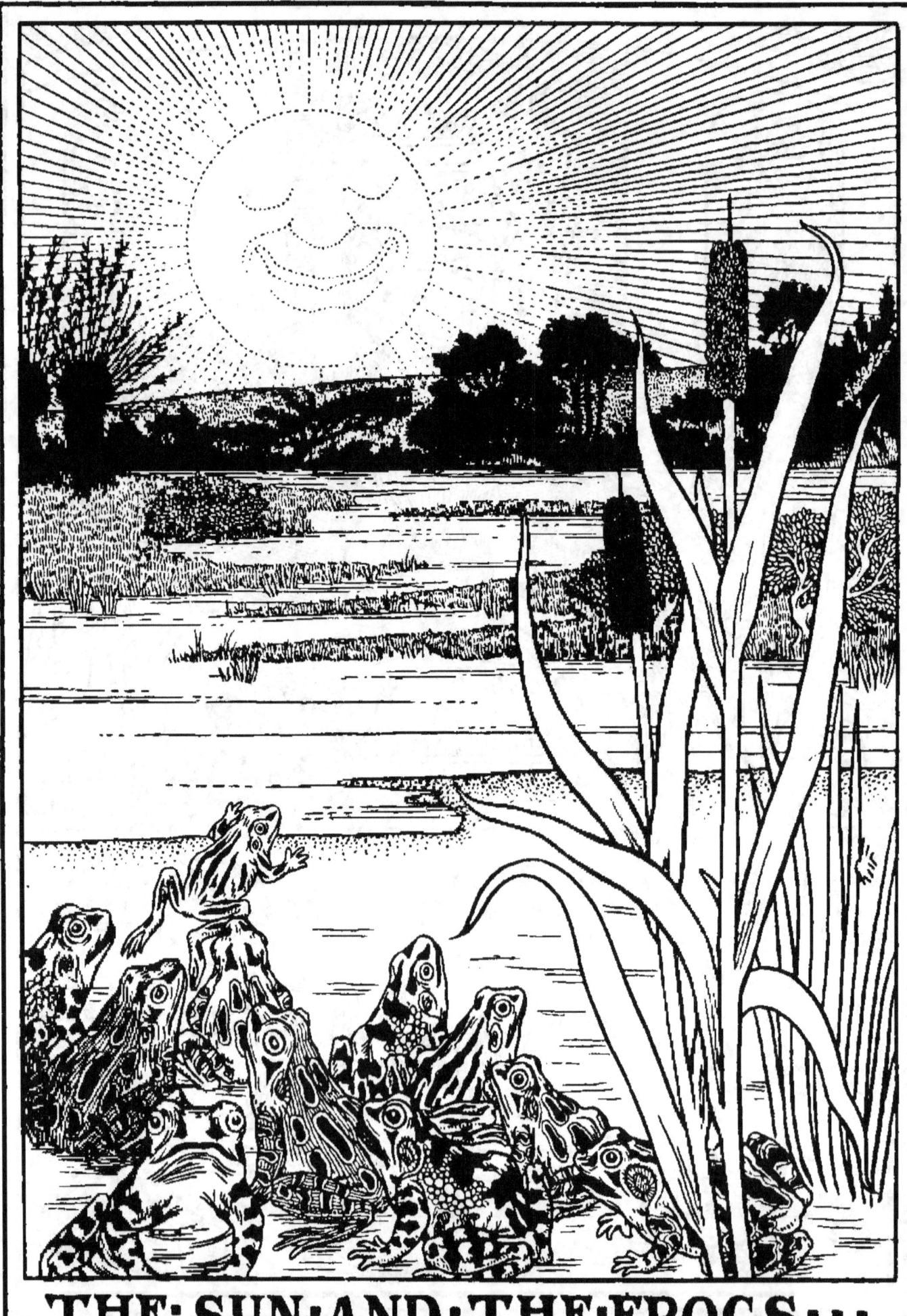

THE·SUN·AND·THE·FROGS···

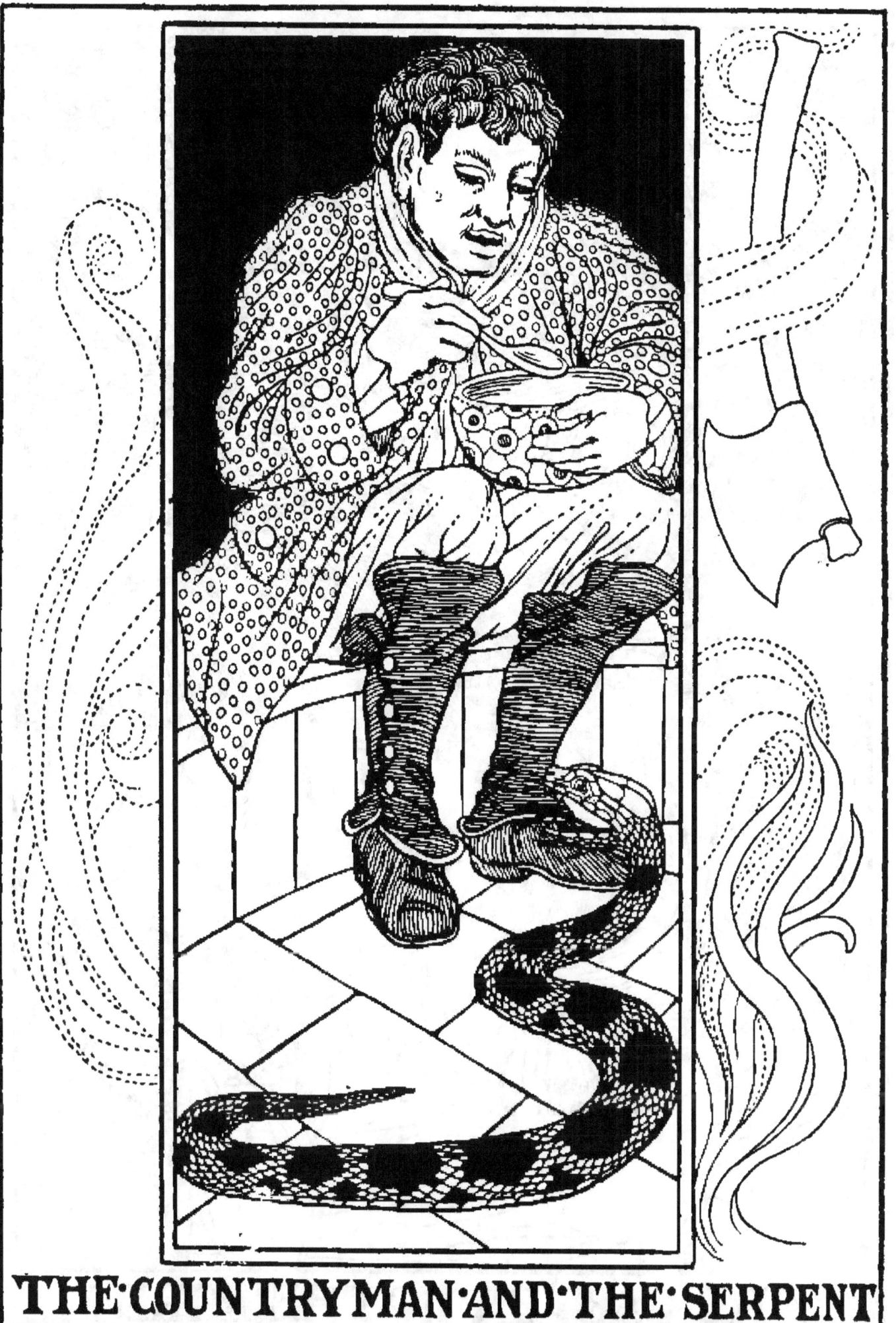

THE·COUNTRYMAN·AND·THE·SERPENT

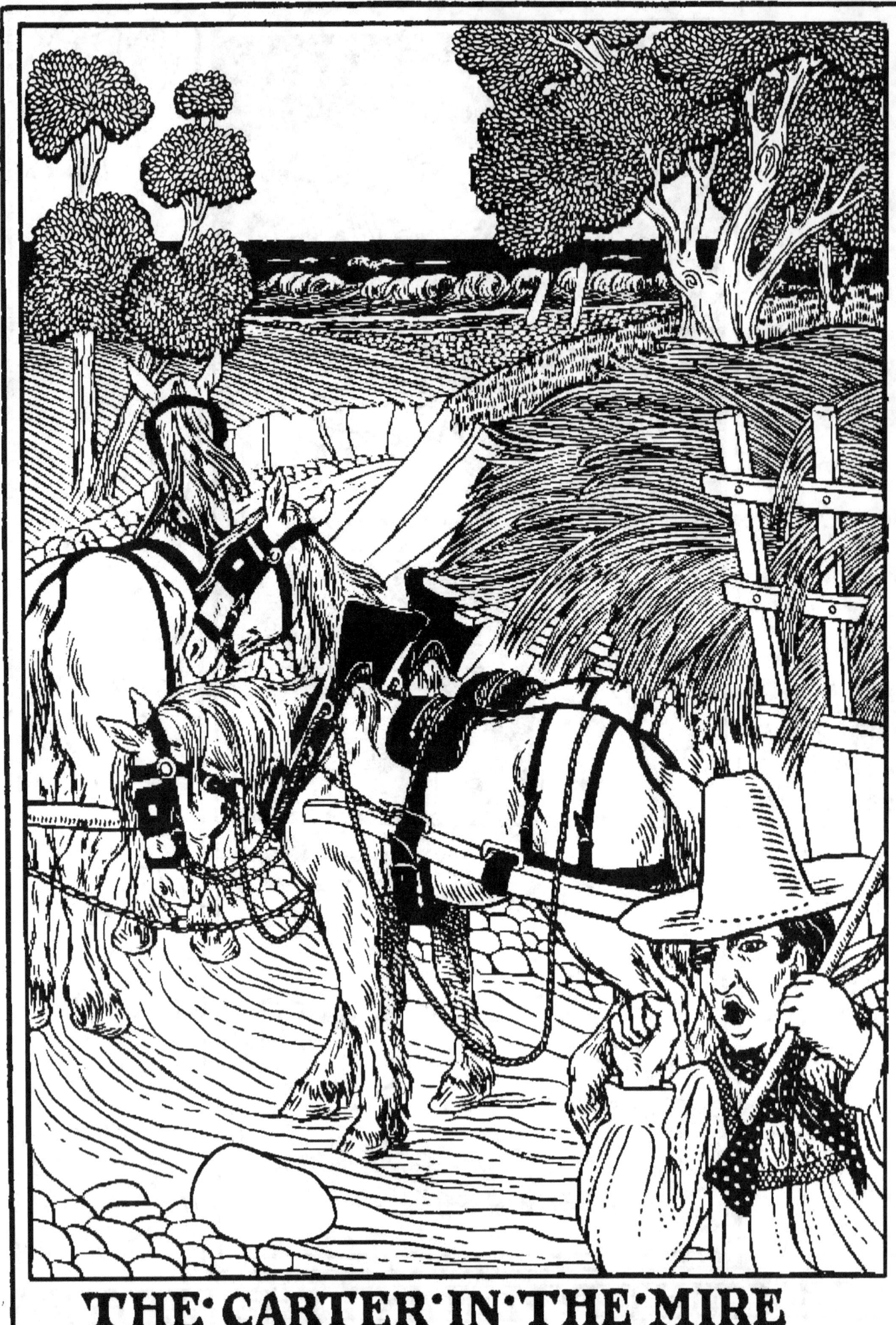

THE·CARTER·IN·THE·MIRE

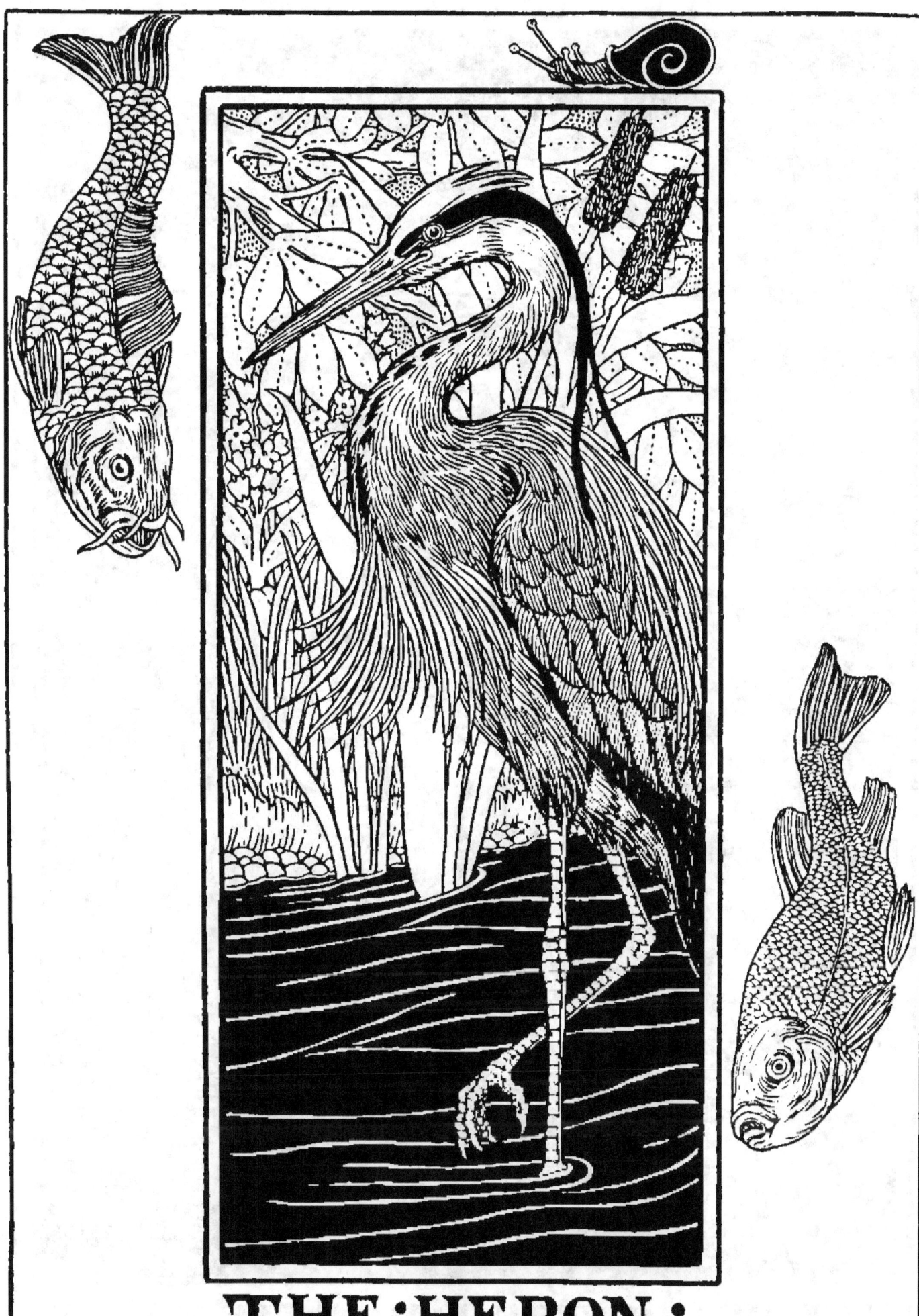

THE · HERON ·

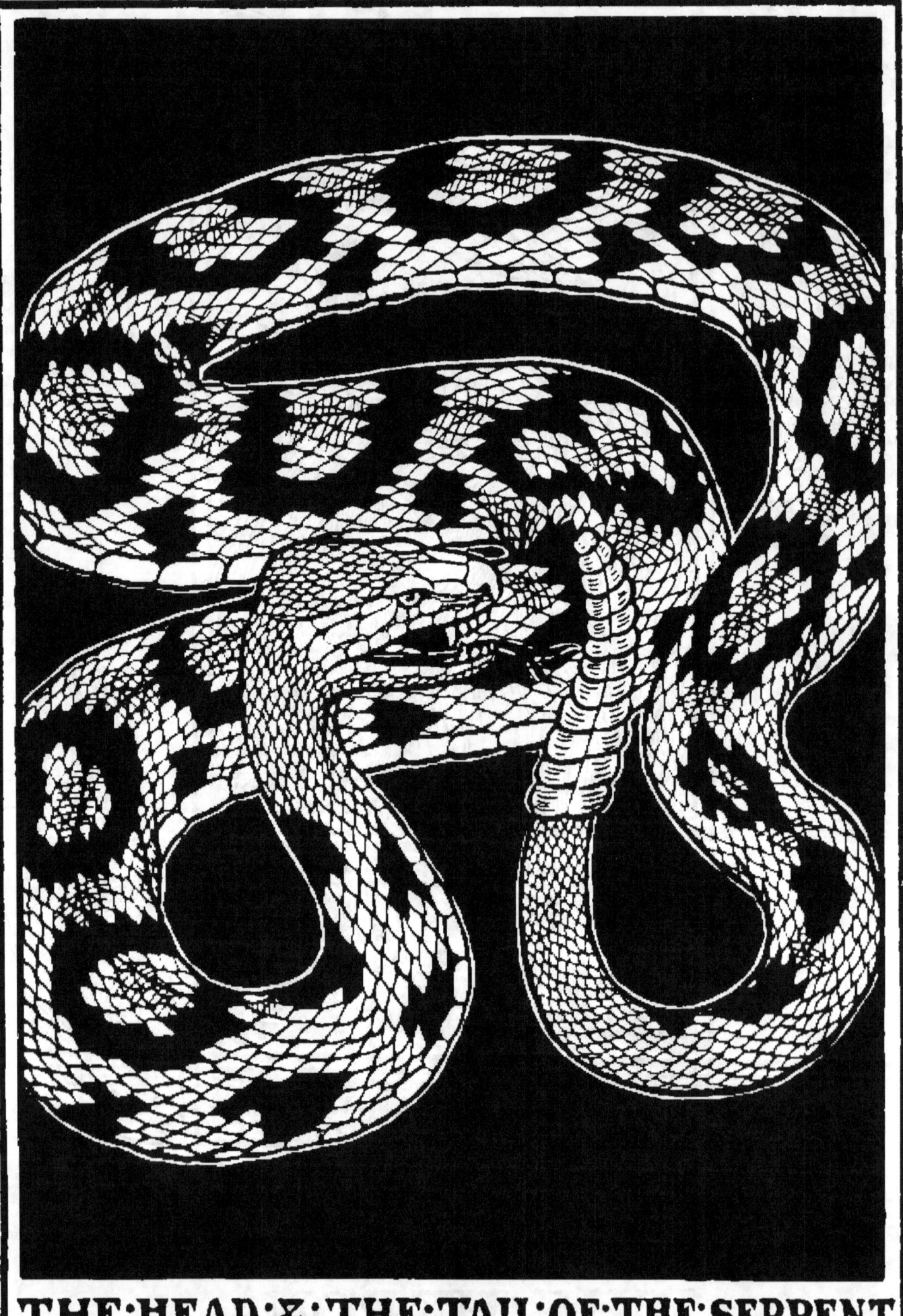

THE·HEAD·&·THE·TAIL·OF·THE·SERPENT

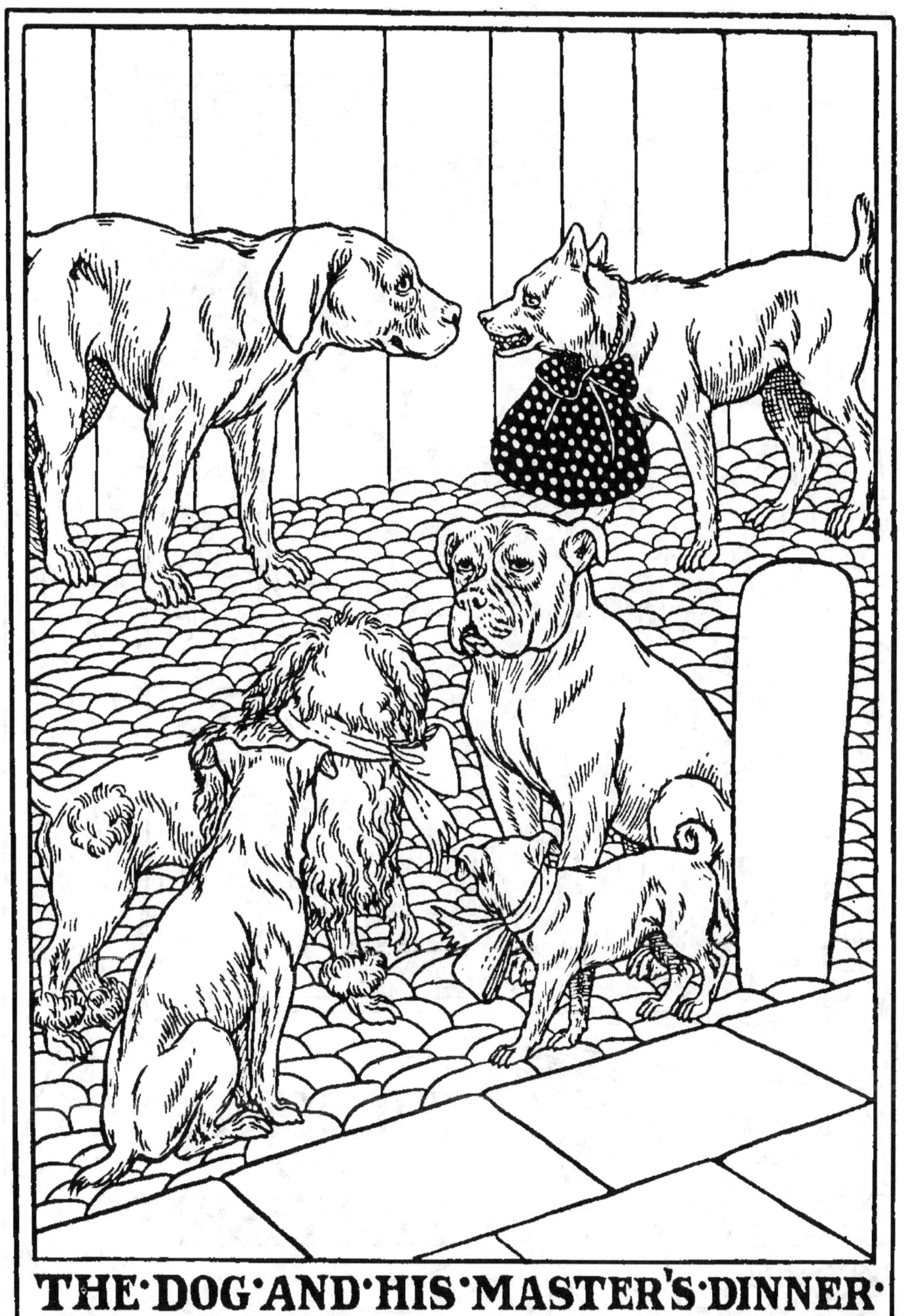

THE·DOG·AND·HIS·MASTER'S·DINNER·

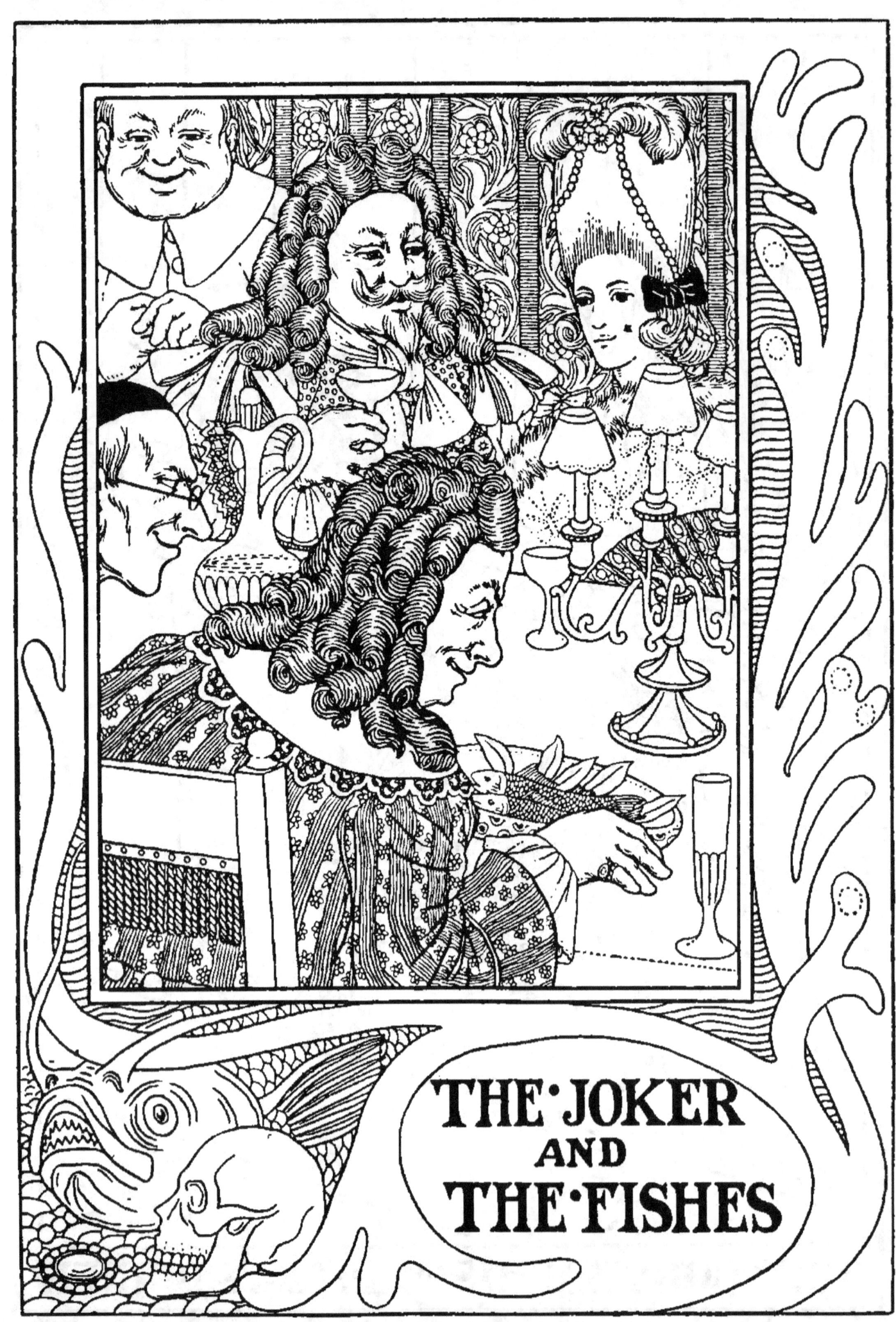

THE·JOKER
AND
THE·FISHES

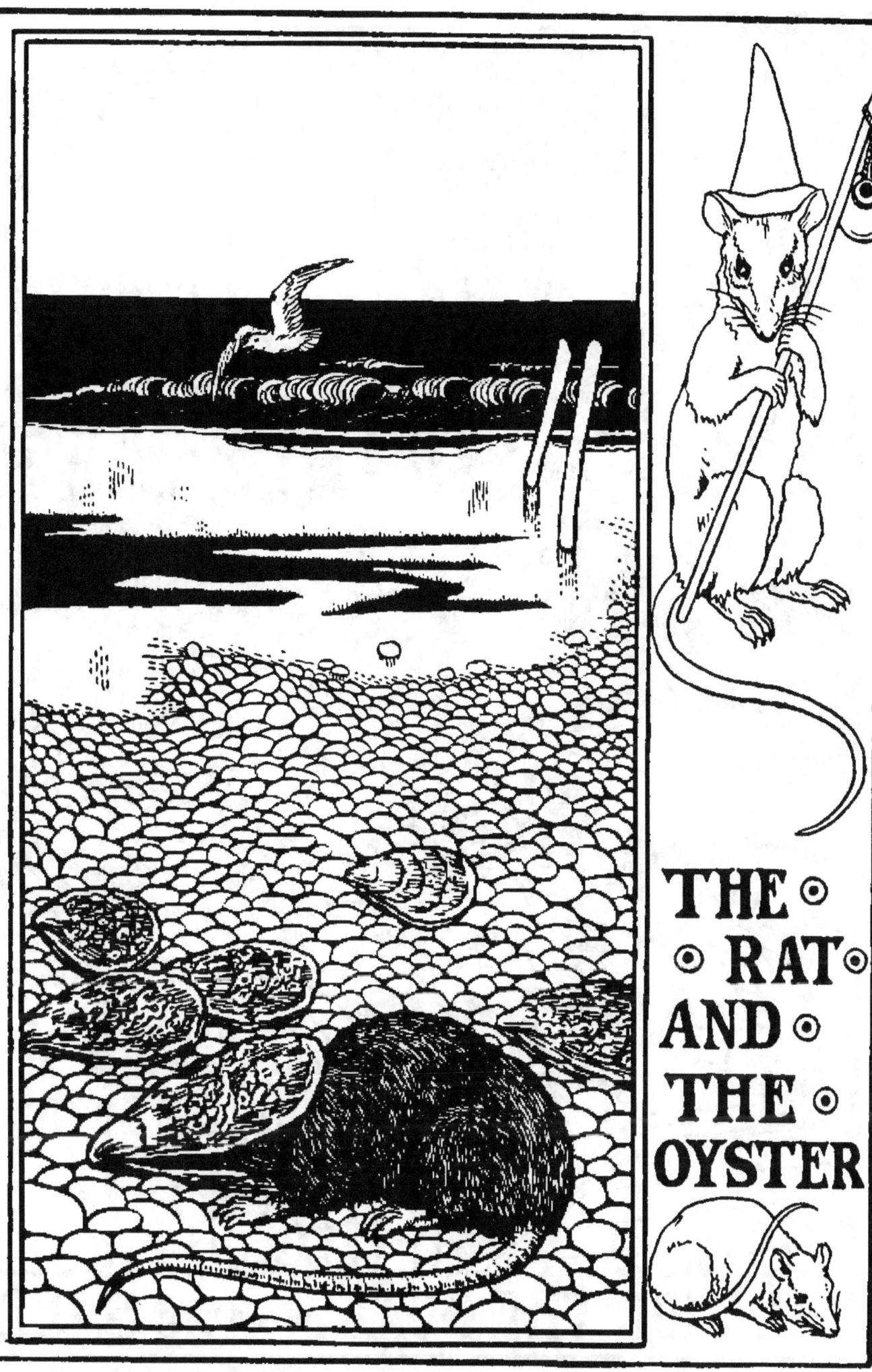

THE ⊙
⊙ RAT ⊙
AND ⊙
THE ⊙
OYSTER

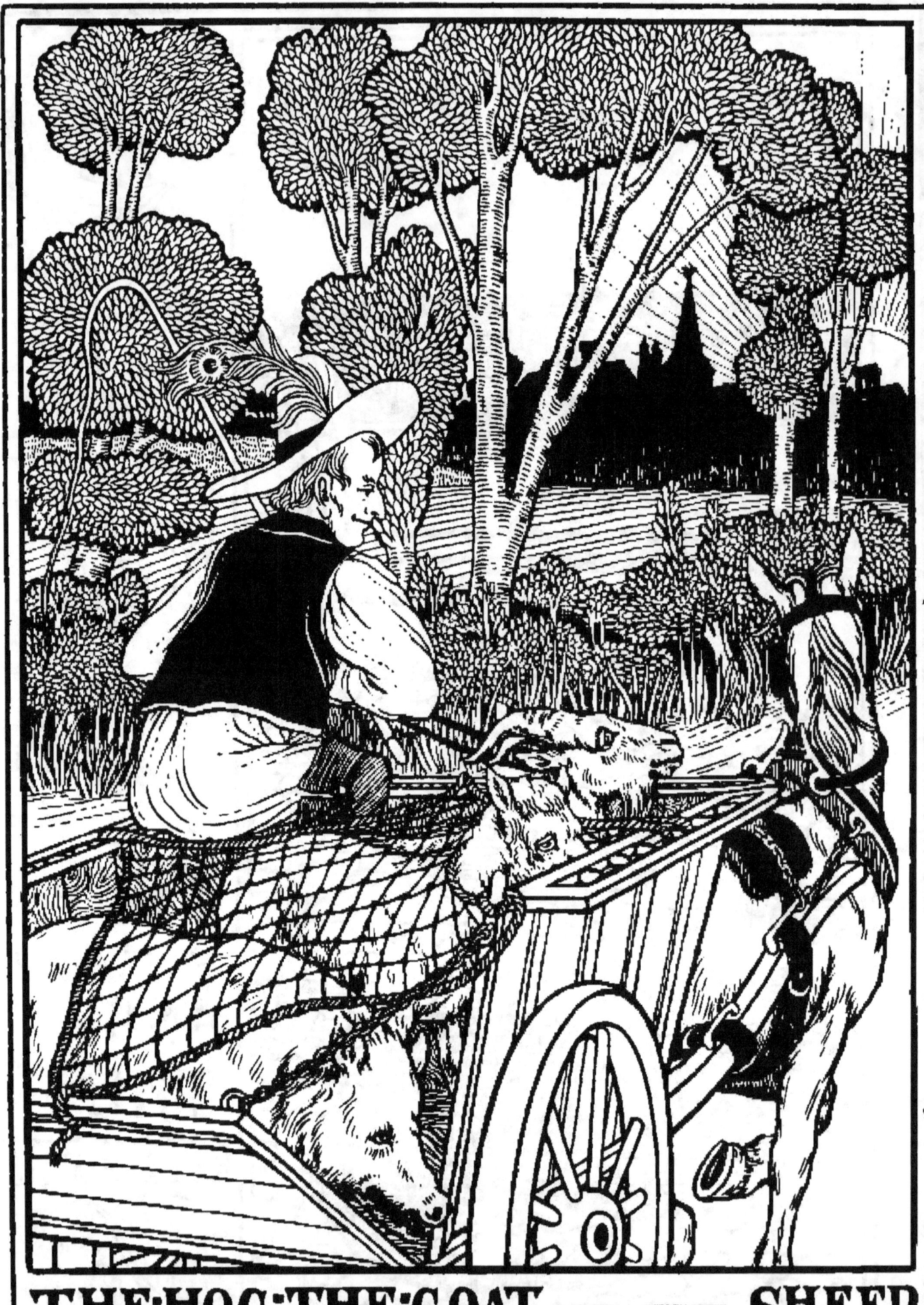

THE·HOG·THE·GOAT·AND·THE·SHEEP.

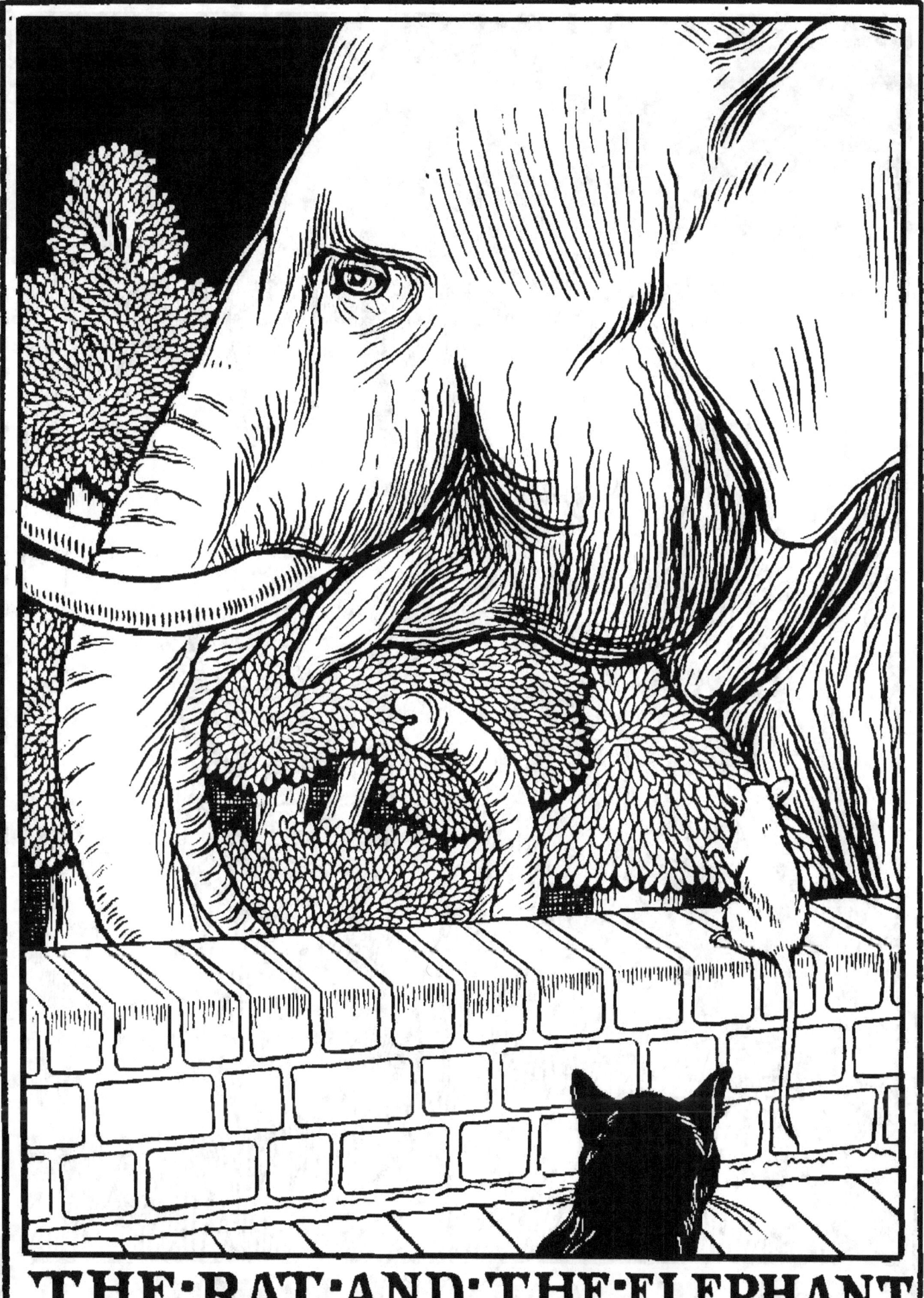

THE·RAT·AND·THE·ELEPHANT

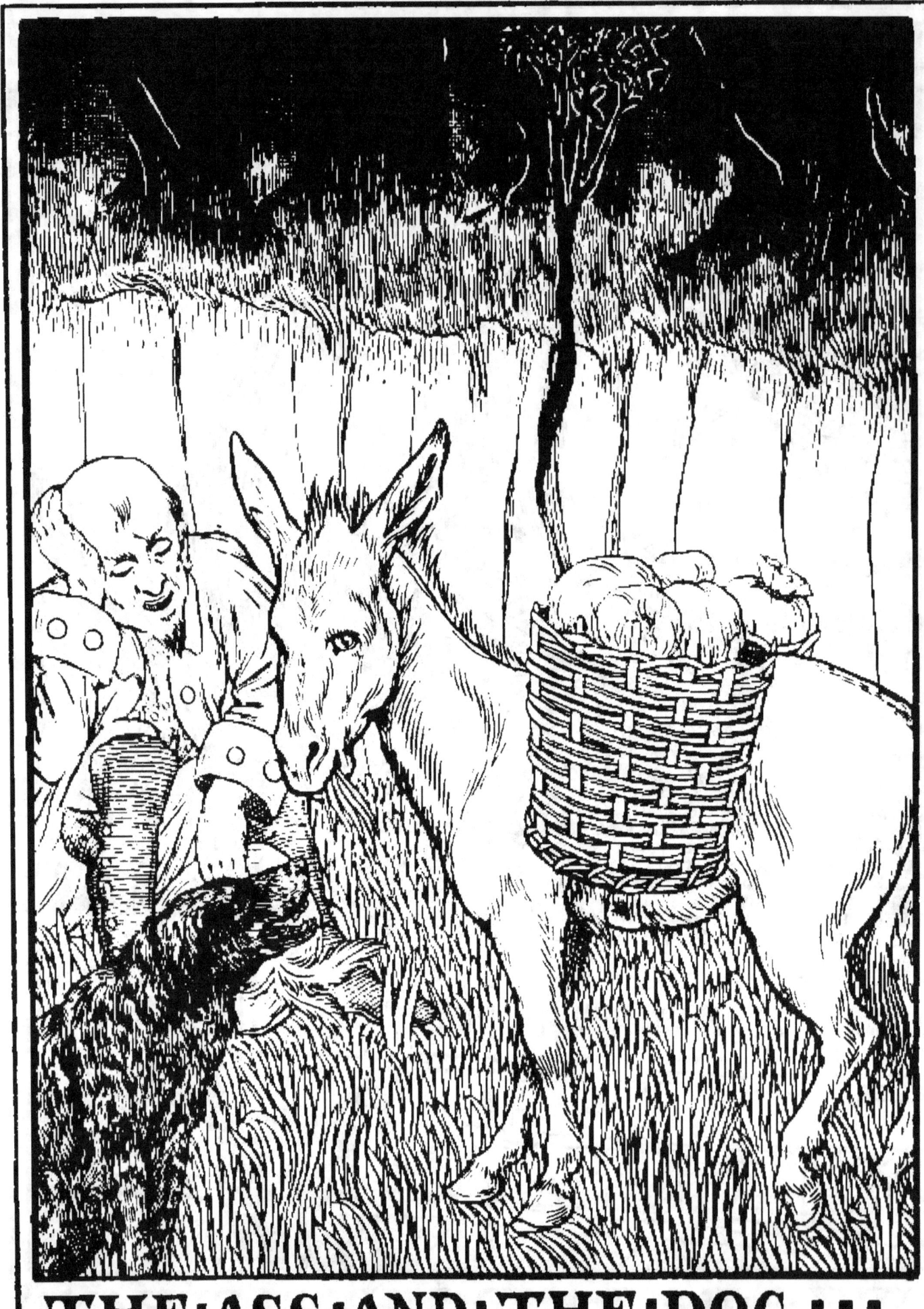

THE·ASS·AND·THE·DOG····

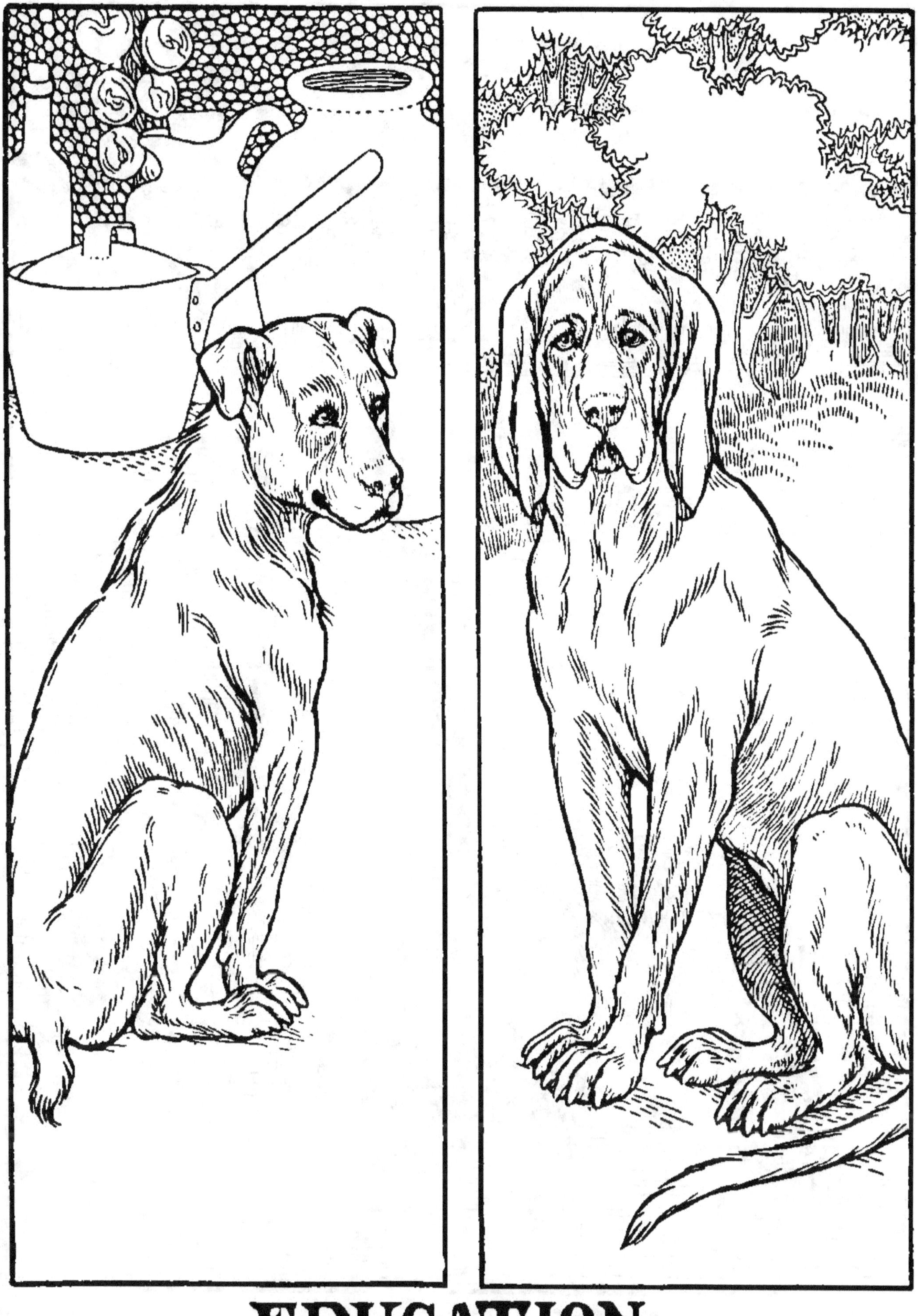

EDUCATION.

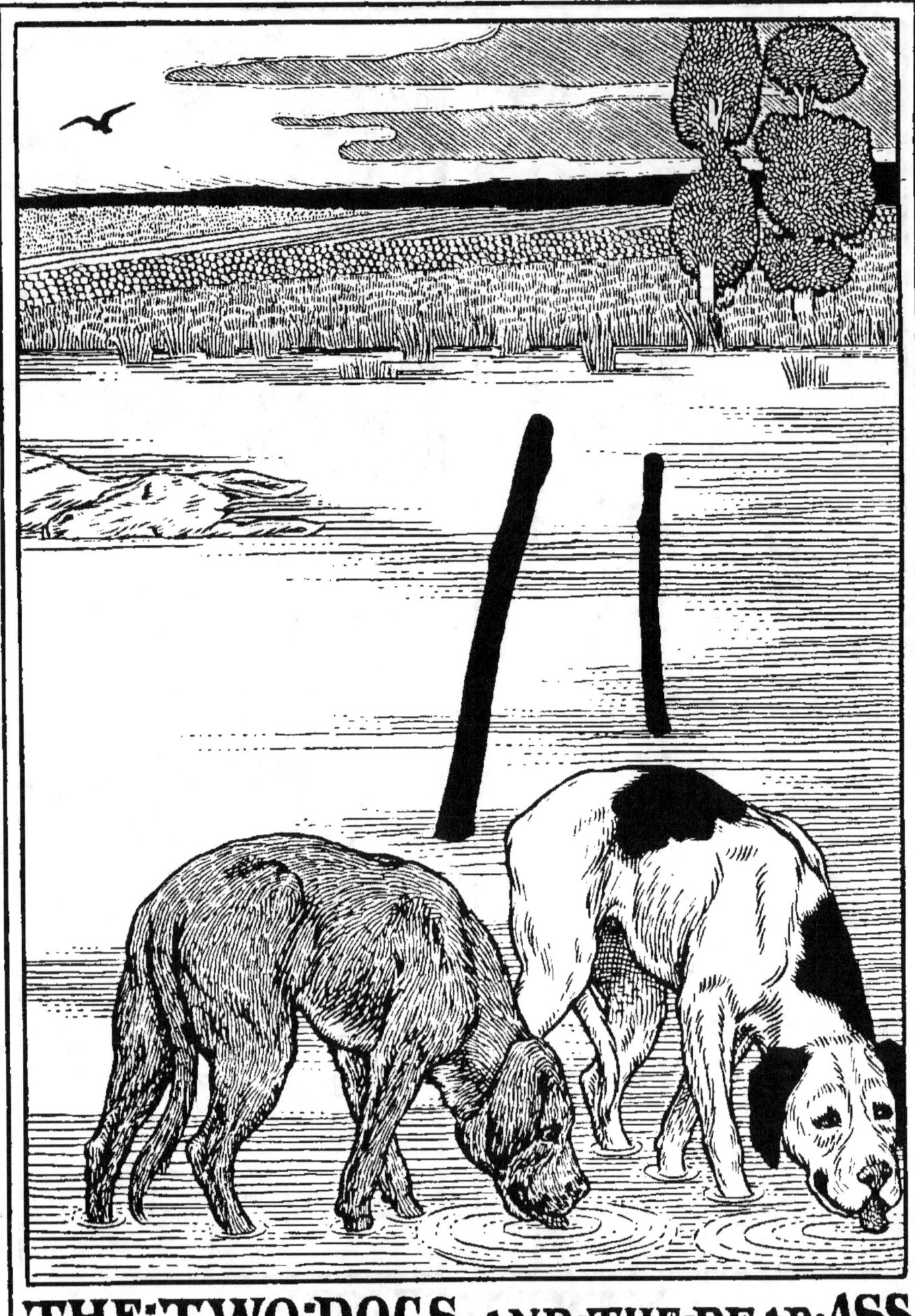

THE·TWO·DOGS·AND·THE·DEAD·ASS

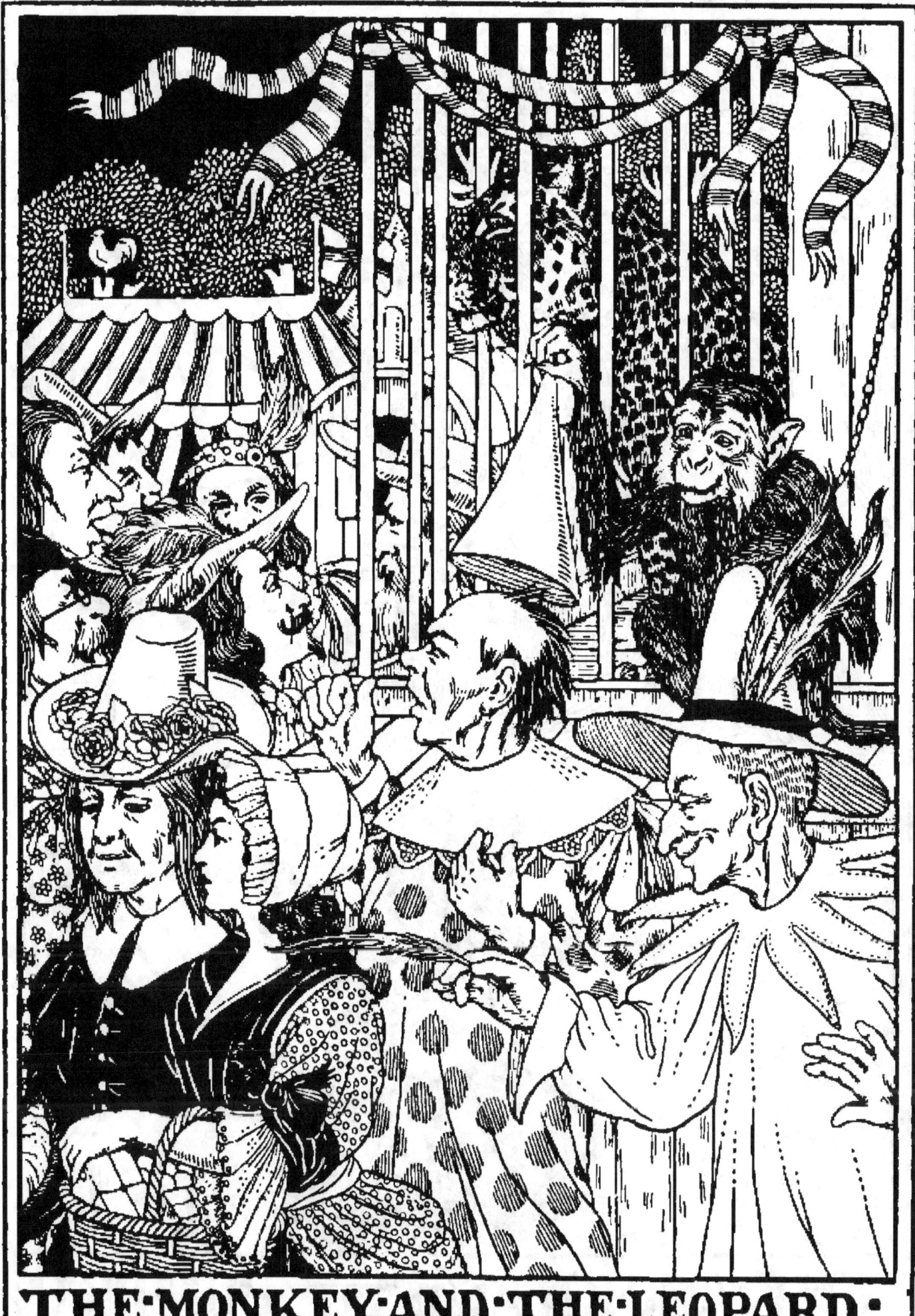

THE·MONKEY·AND·THE·LEOPARD·

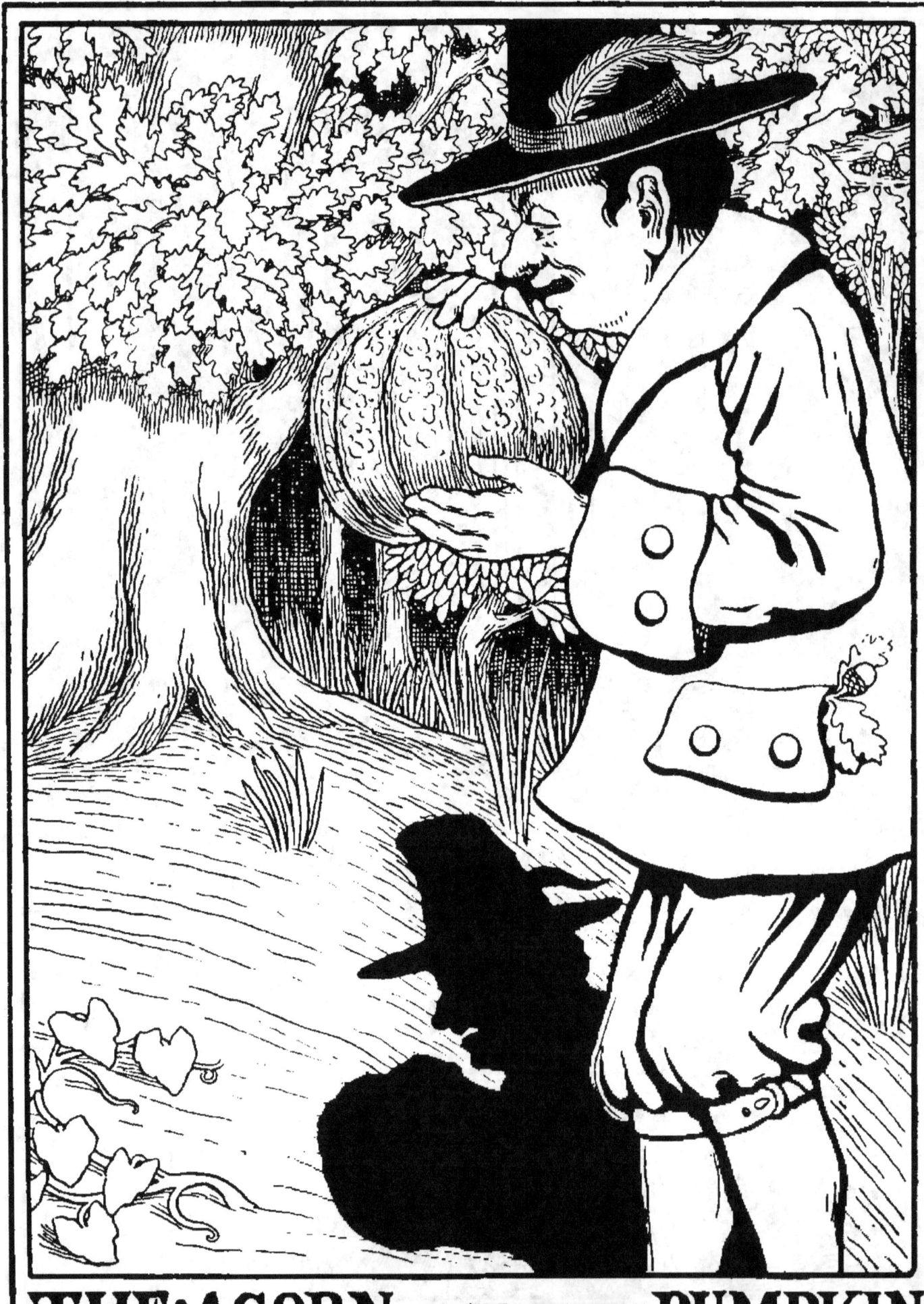

THE·ACORN·AND·THE·PUMPKIN

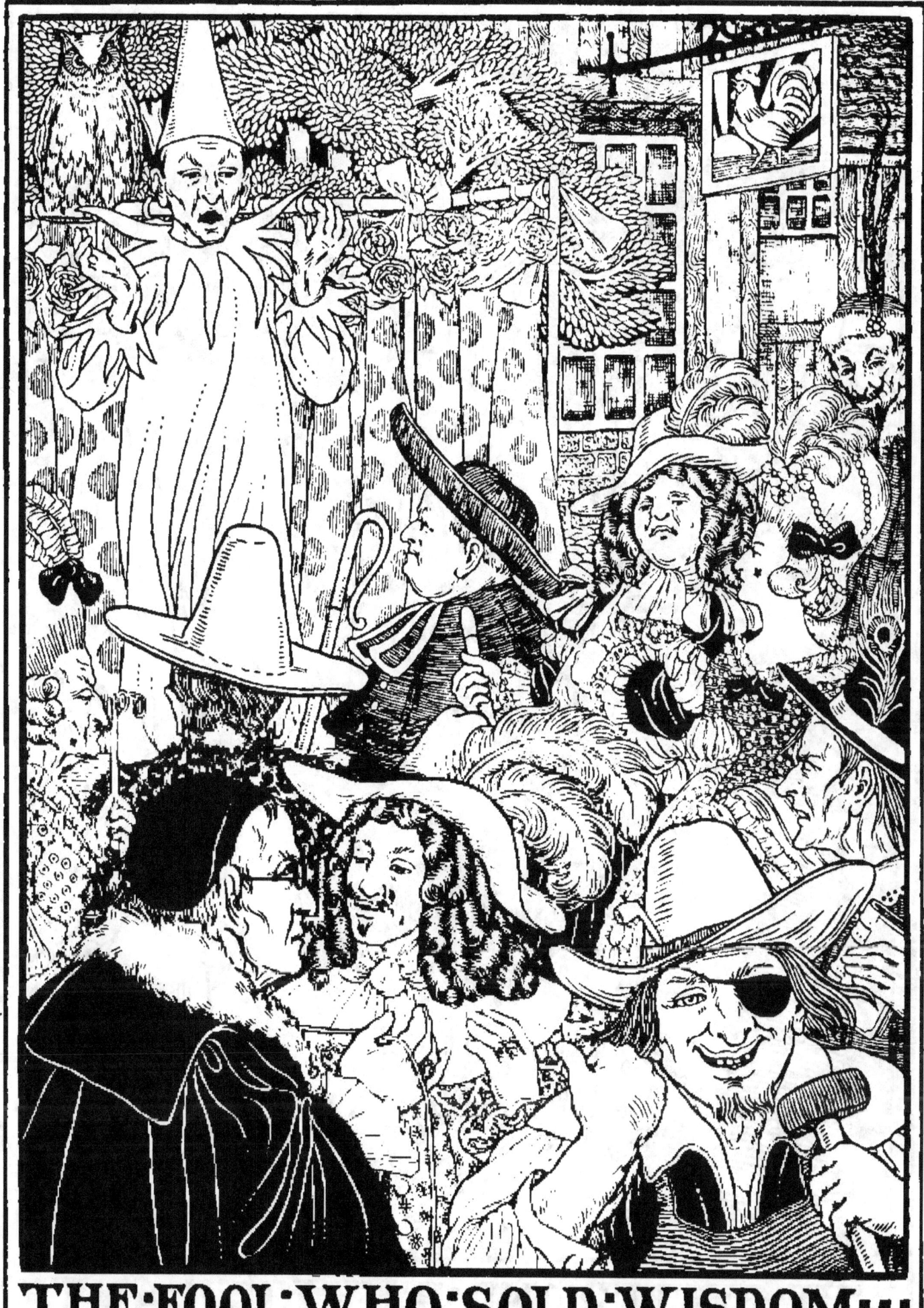

THE·FOOL·WHO·SOLD·WISDOM···

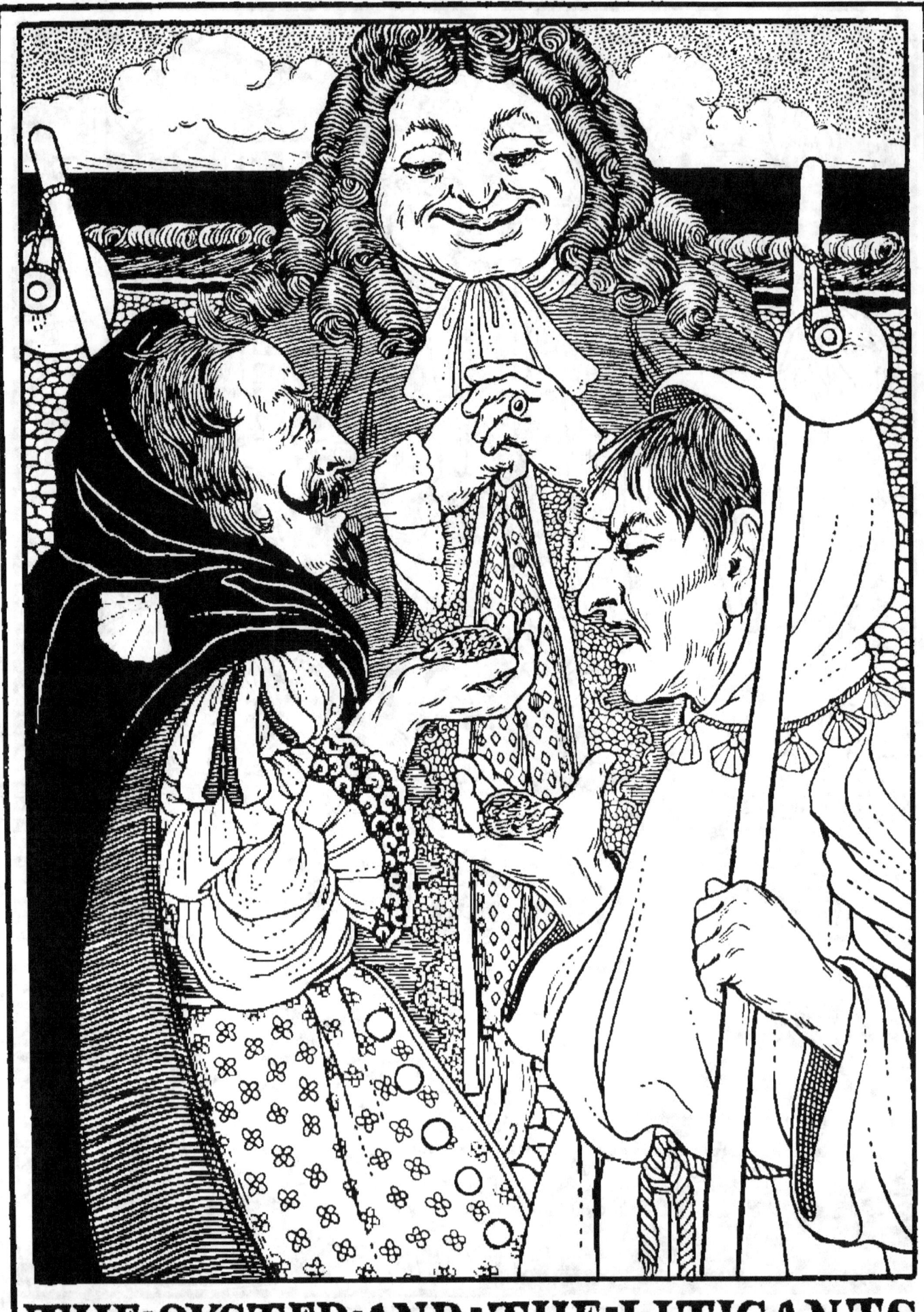

THE·OYSTER·AND·THE·LITIGANTS.

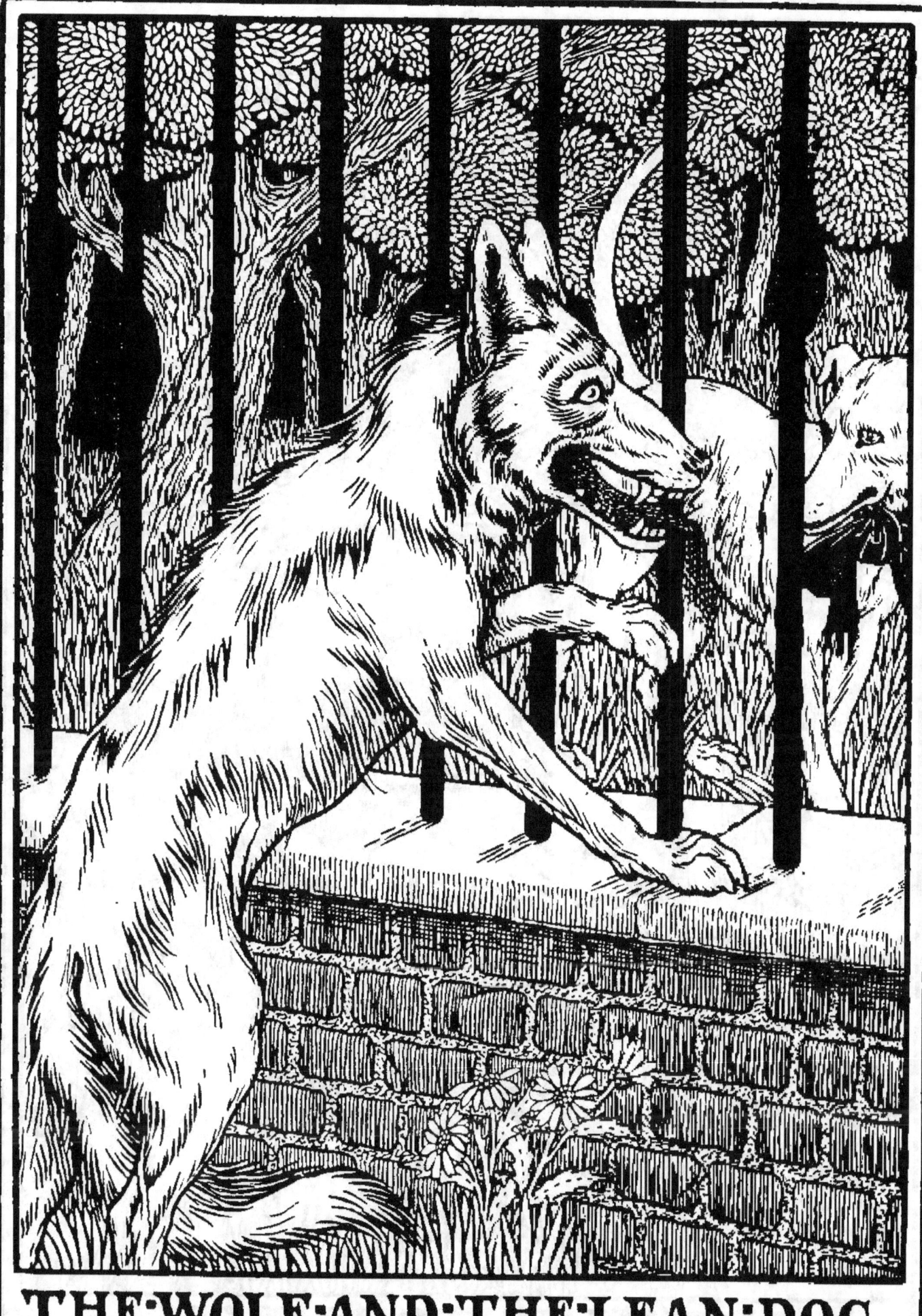

THE·WOLF·AND·THE·LEAN·DOG.

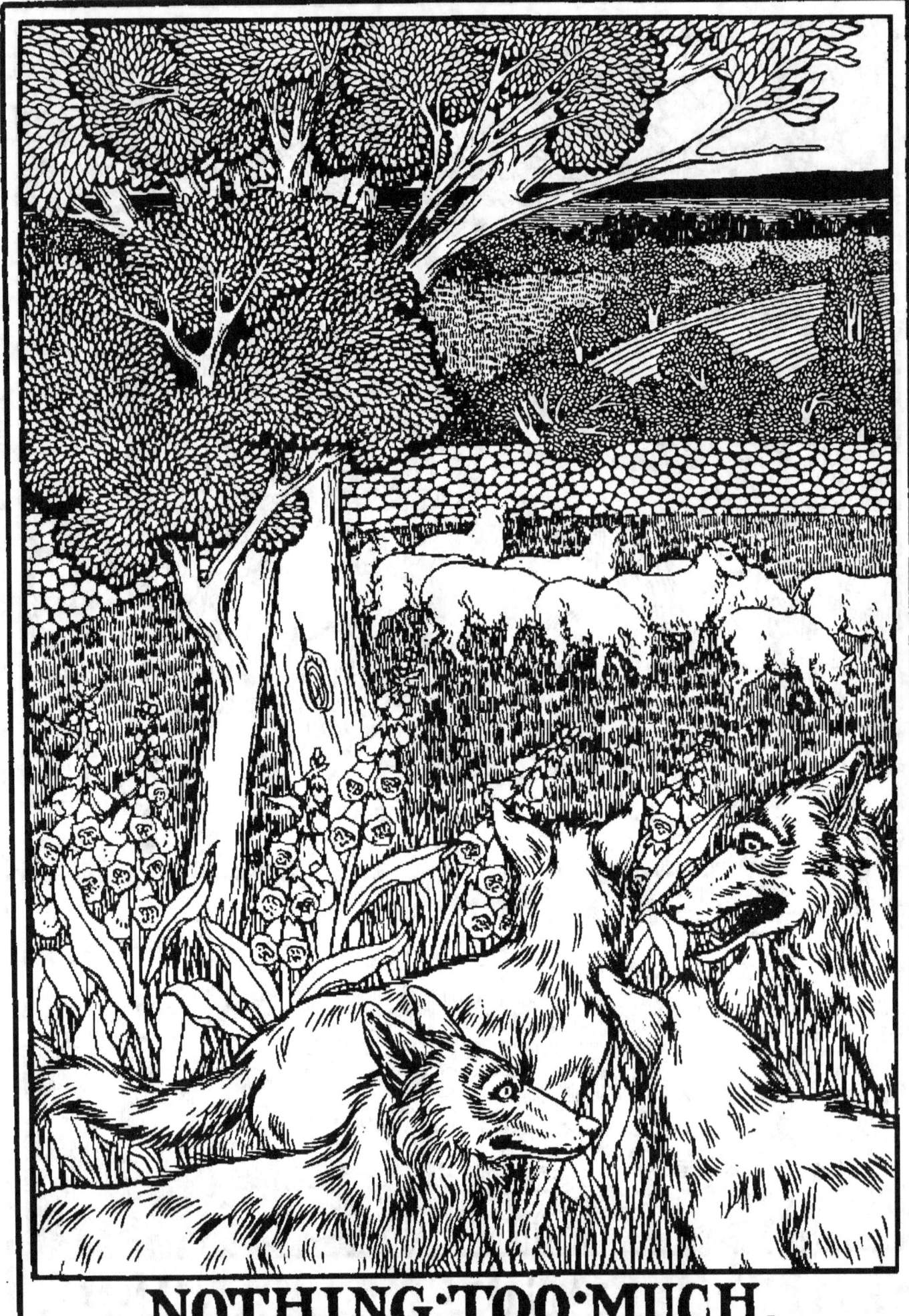

NOTHING·TOO·MUCH.

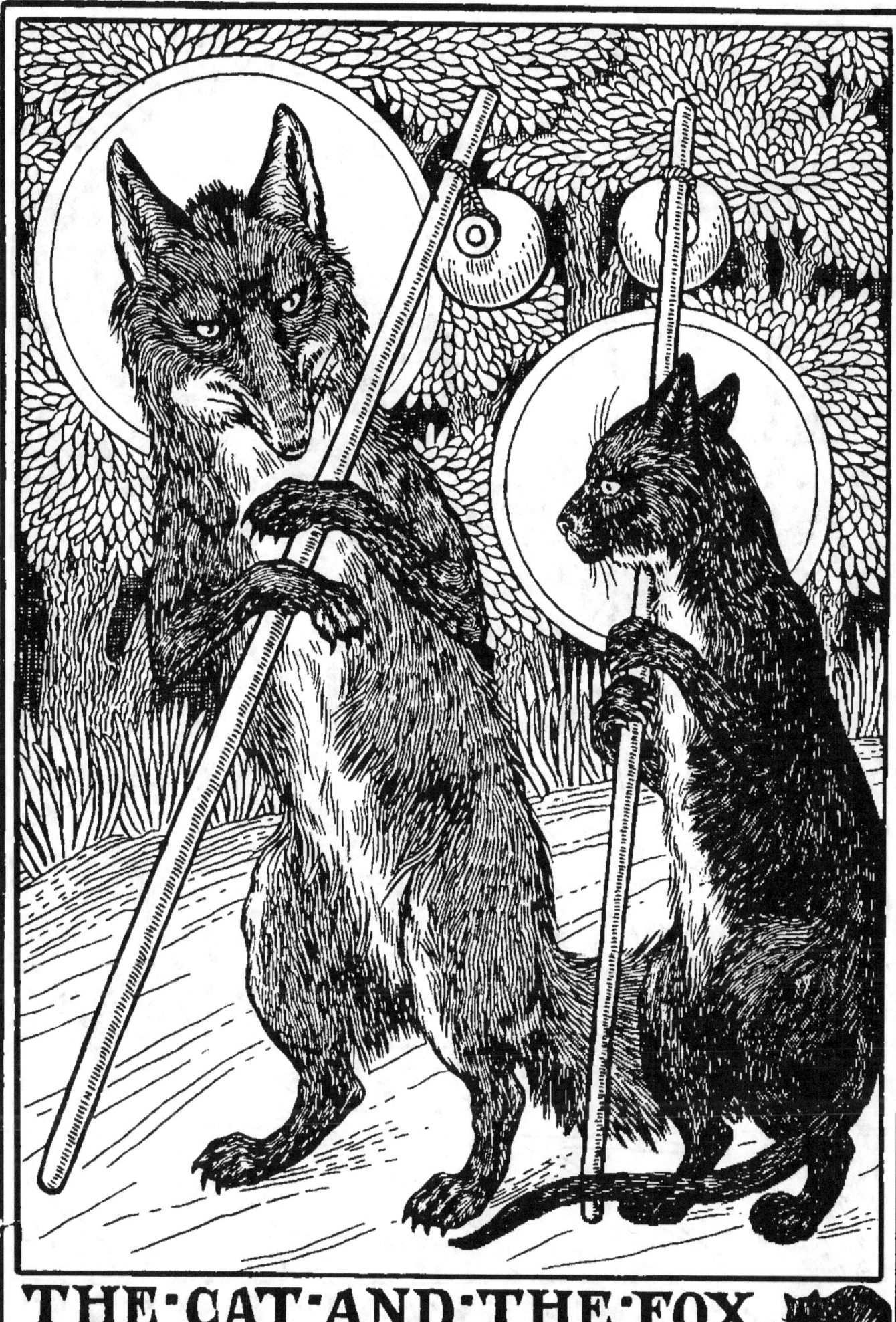

THE·CAT·AND·THE·FOX.

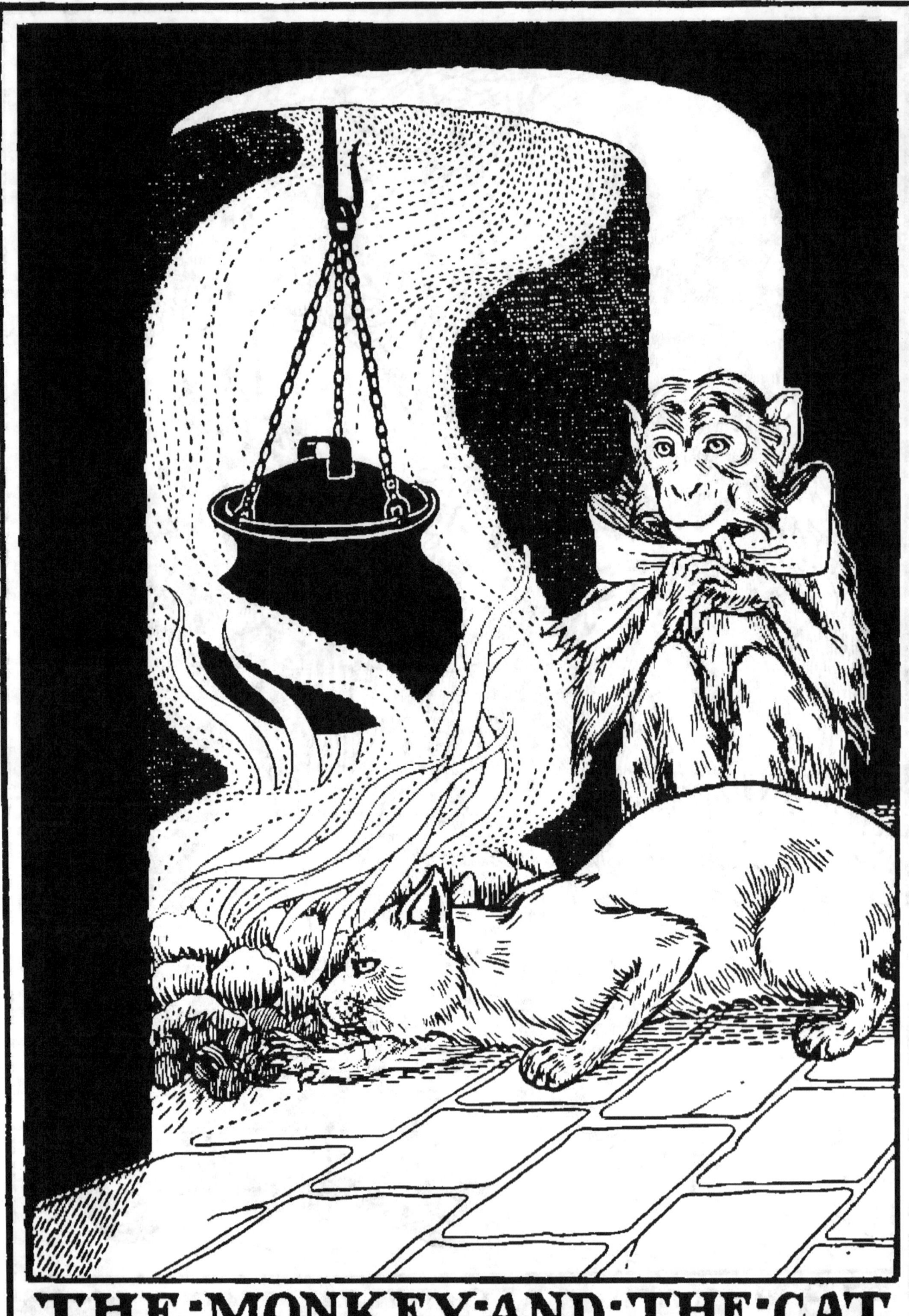

THE·MONKEY·AND·THE·CAT.

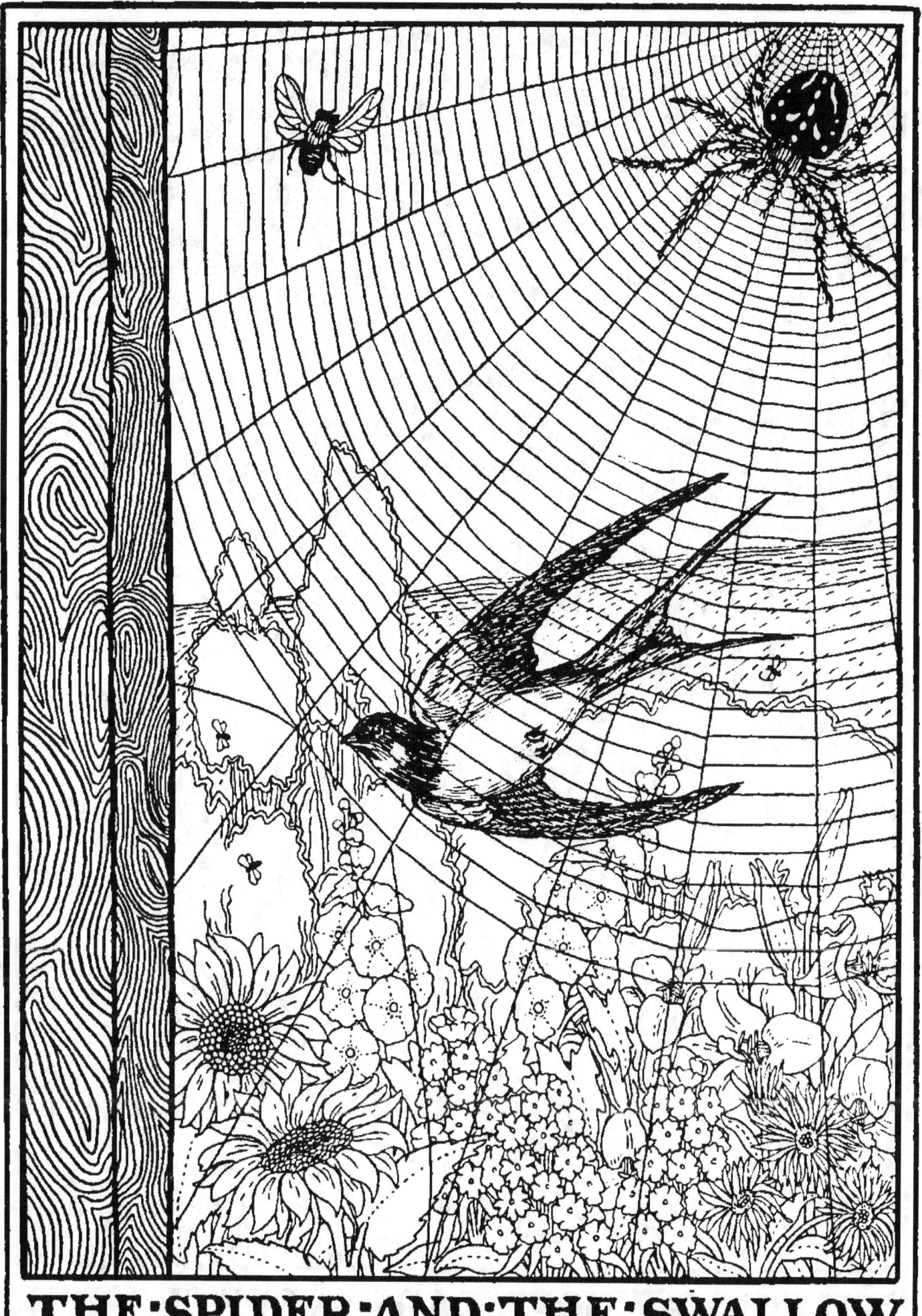

THE·SPIDER·AND·THE·SWALLOW.

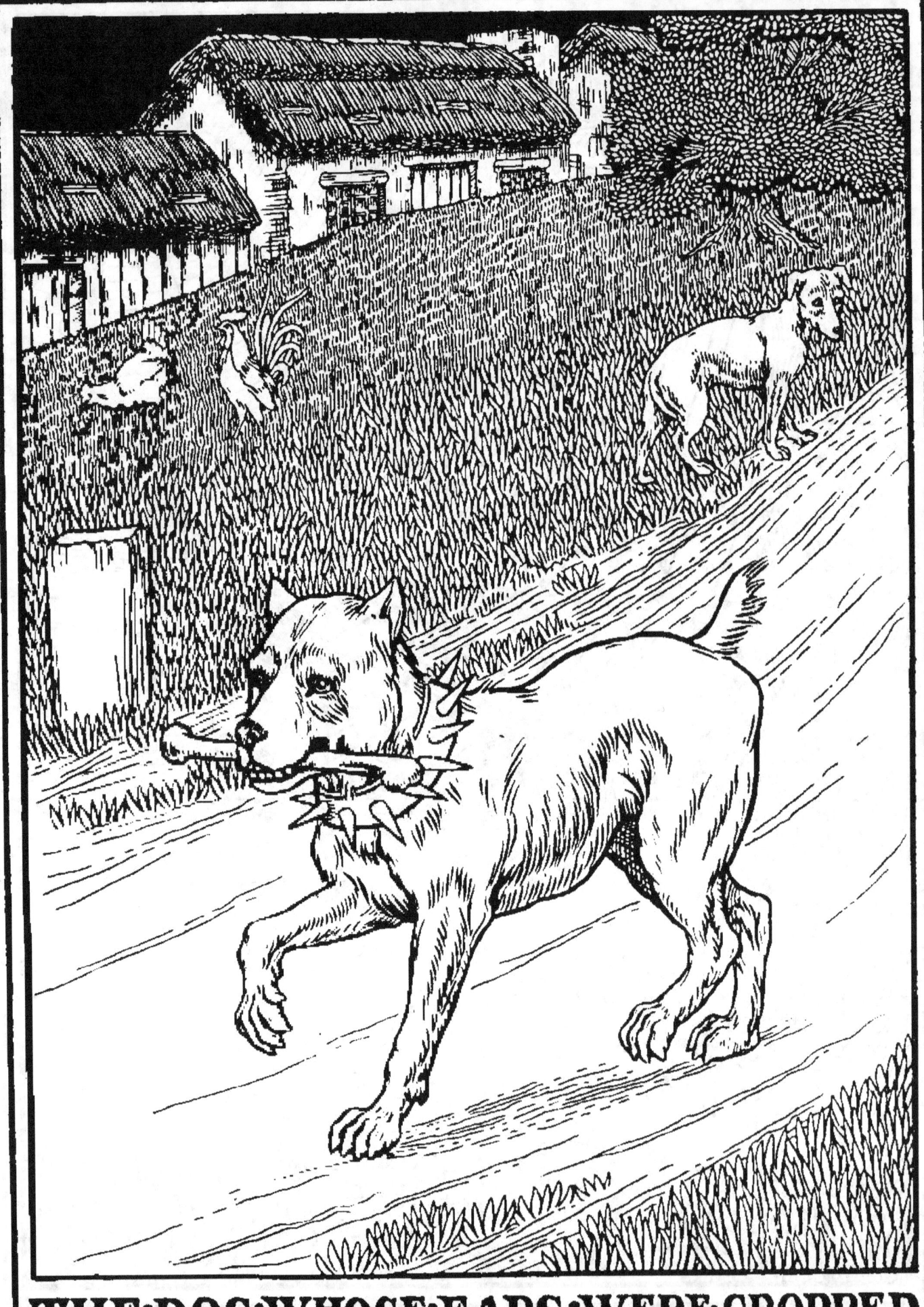

THE·DOG·WHOSE·EARS·WERE·CROPPED

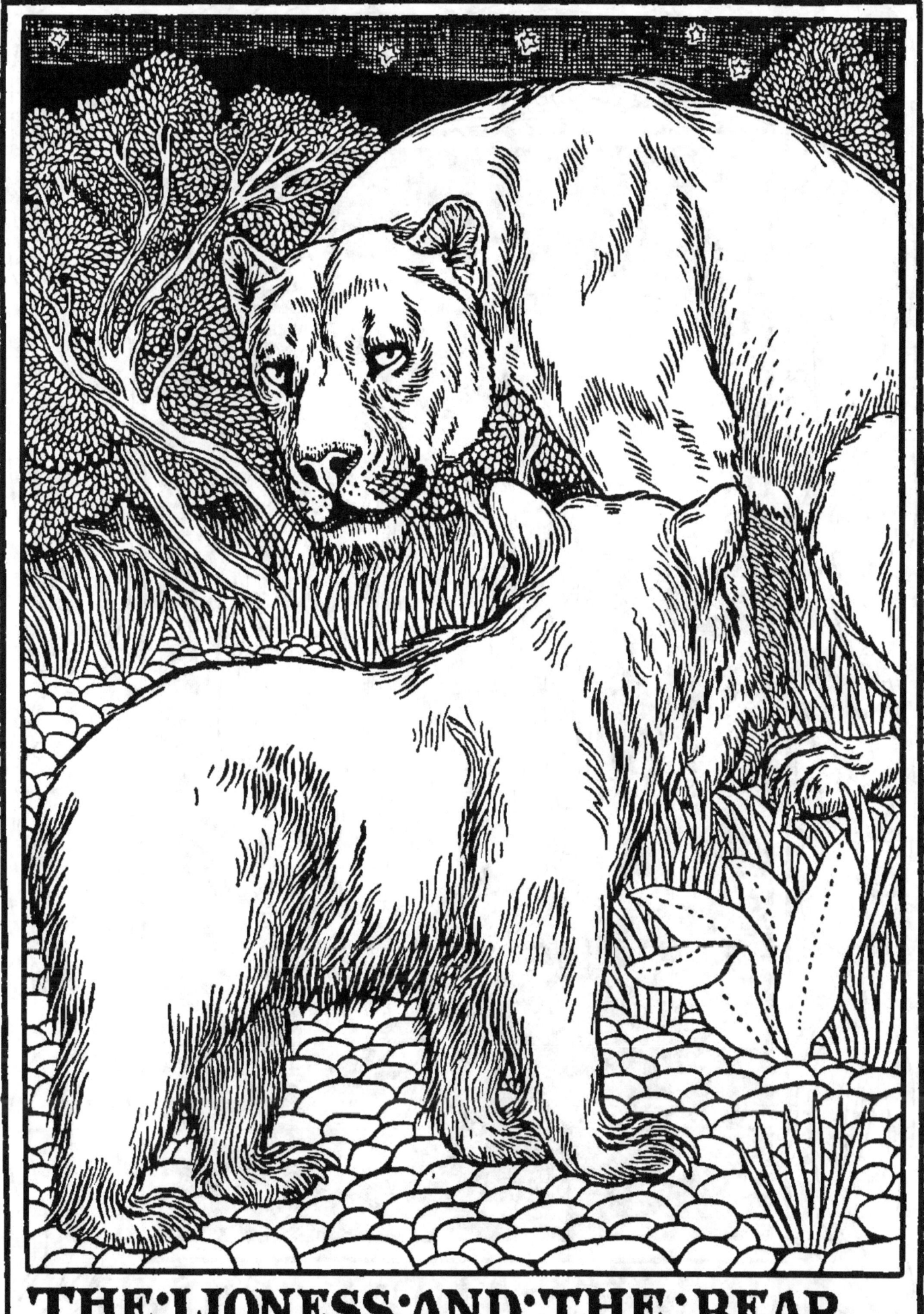

THE·LIONESS·AND·THE·BEAR.

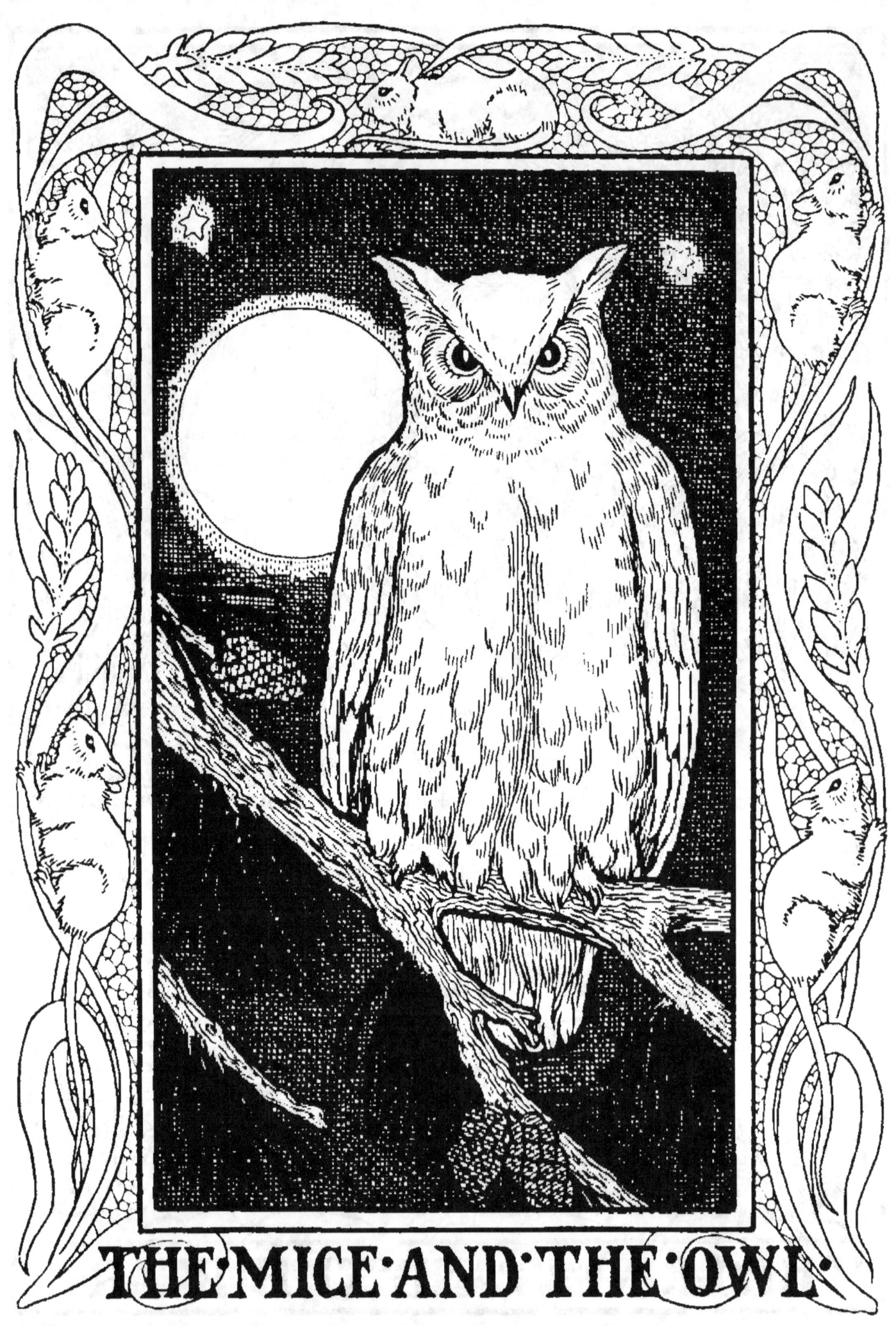

THE·MICE·AND·THE·OWL·

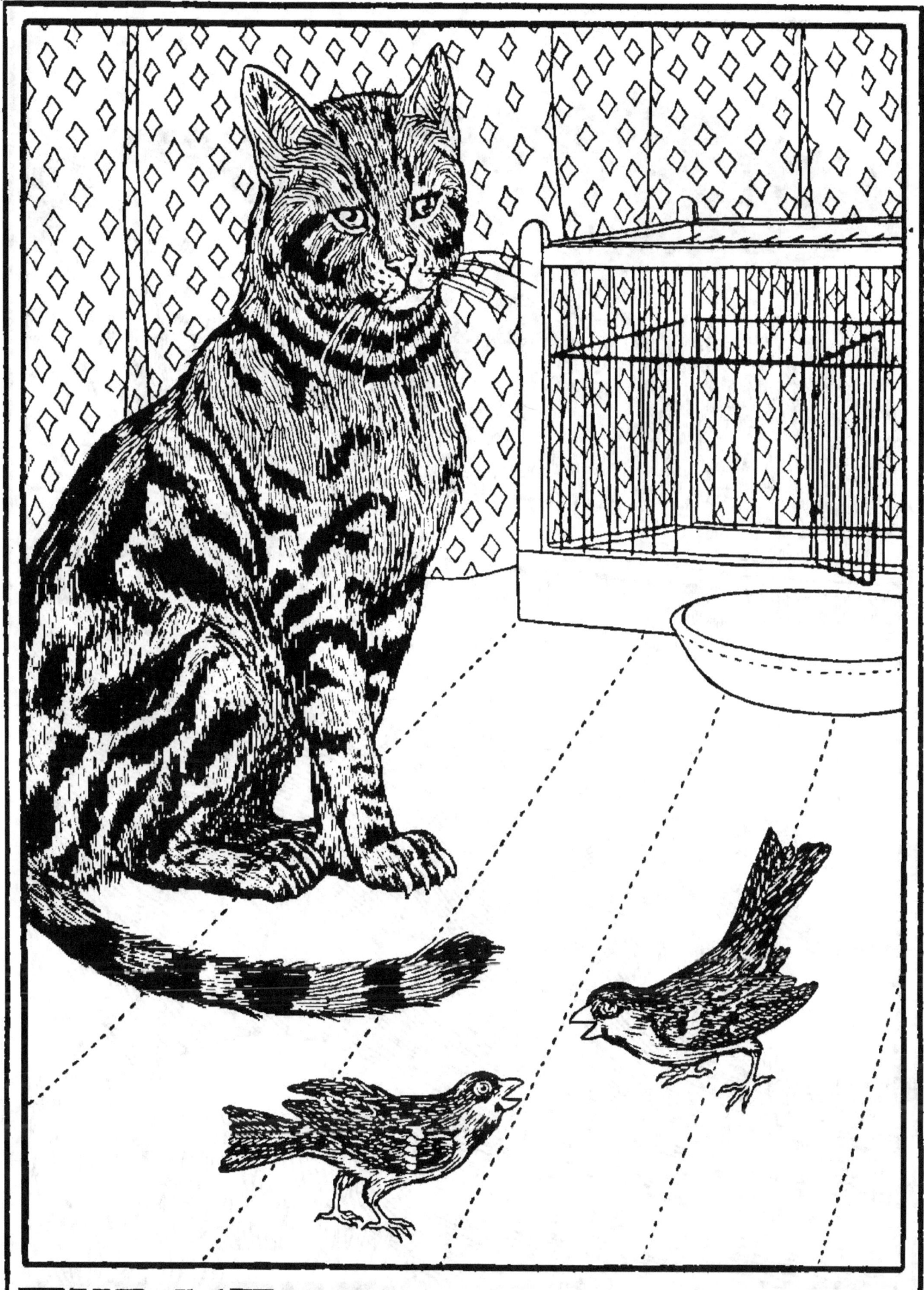

THE·CAT·AND·THE·TWO·SPARROWS

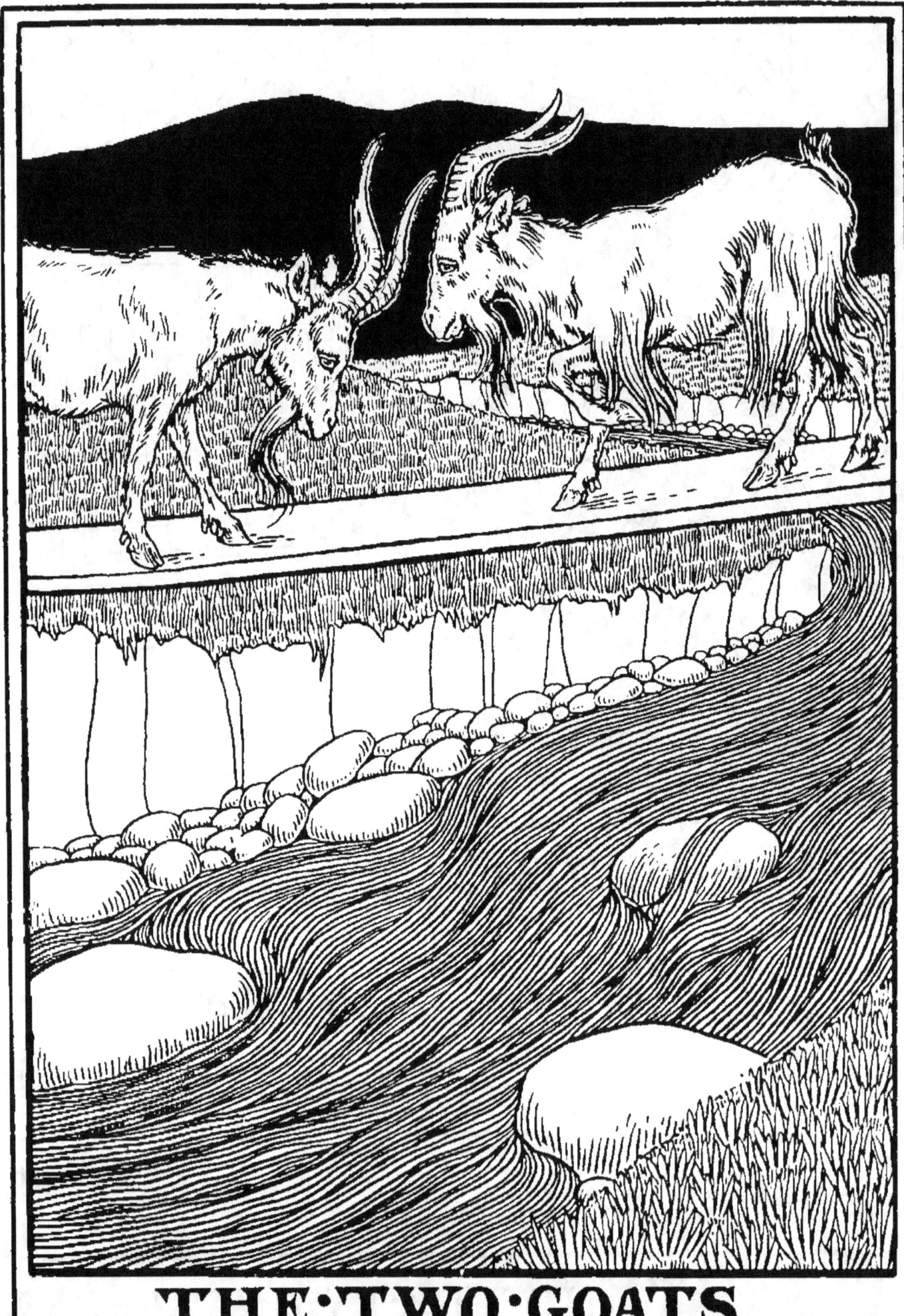

THE·TWO·GOATS

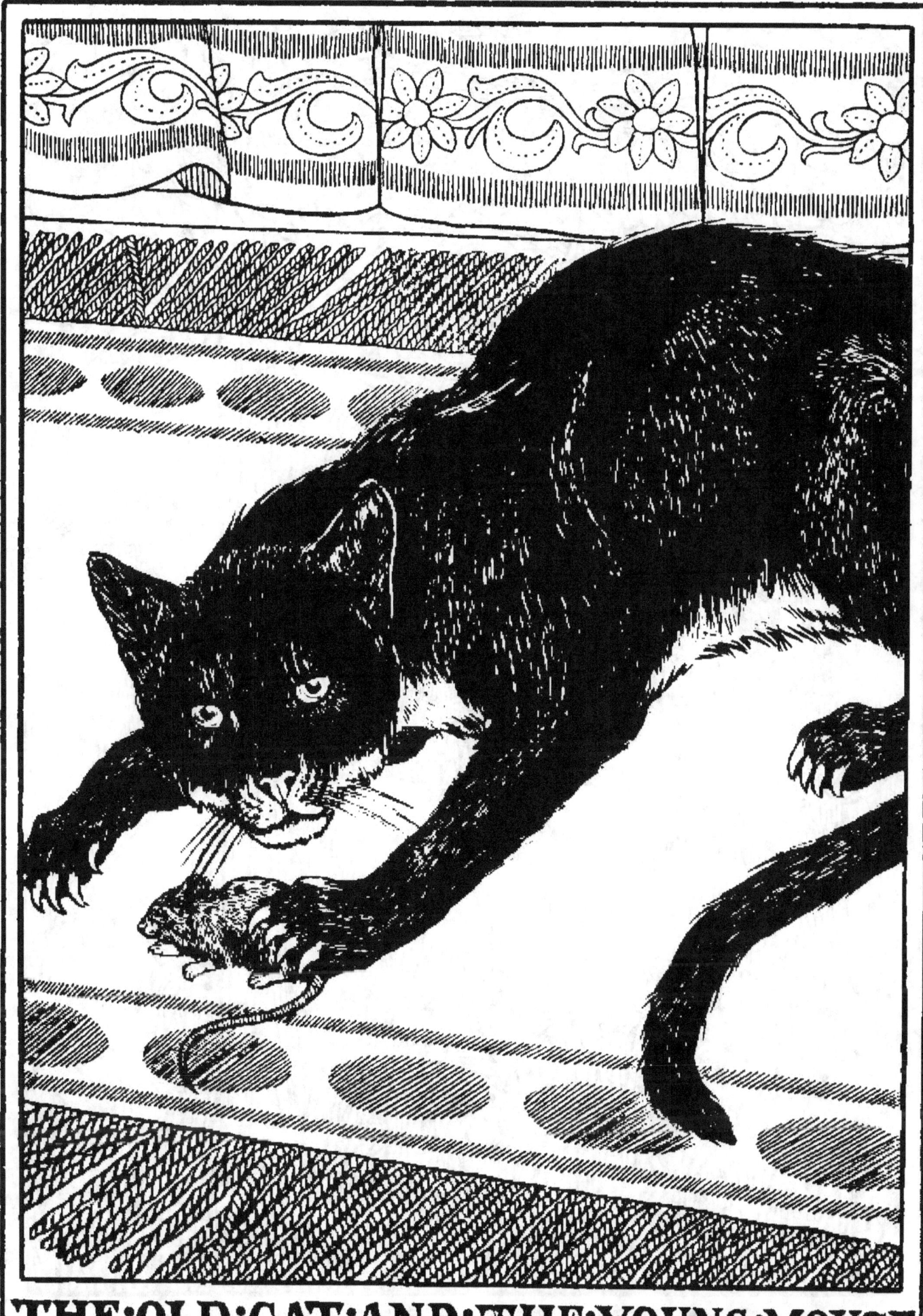

THE·OLD·CAT·AND·THE·YOUNG·MOUSE

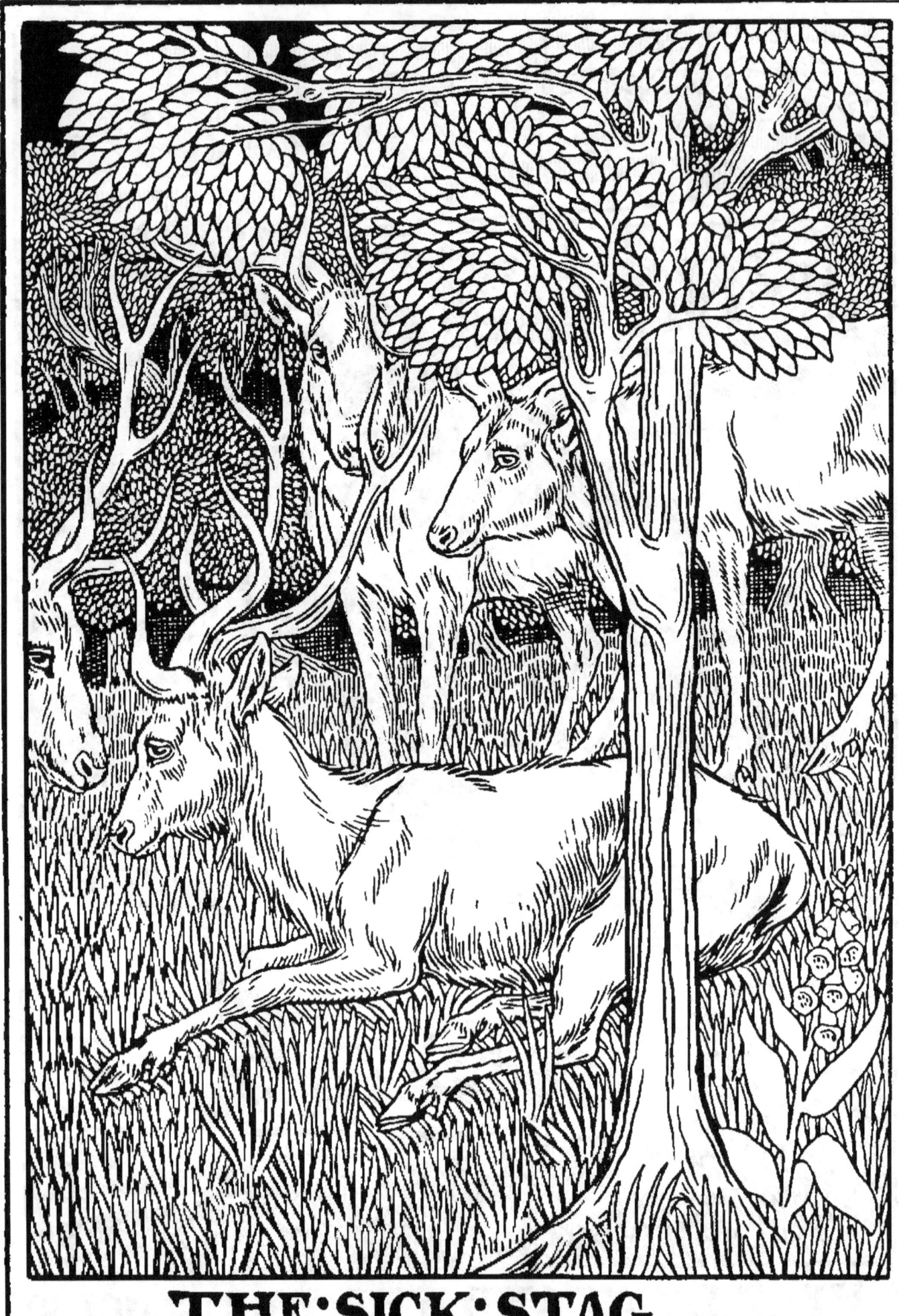

THE·SICK·STAG.

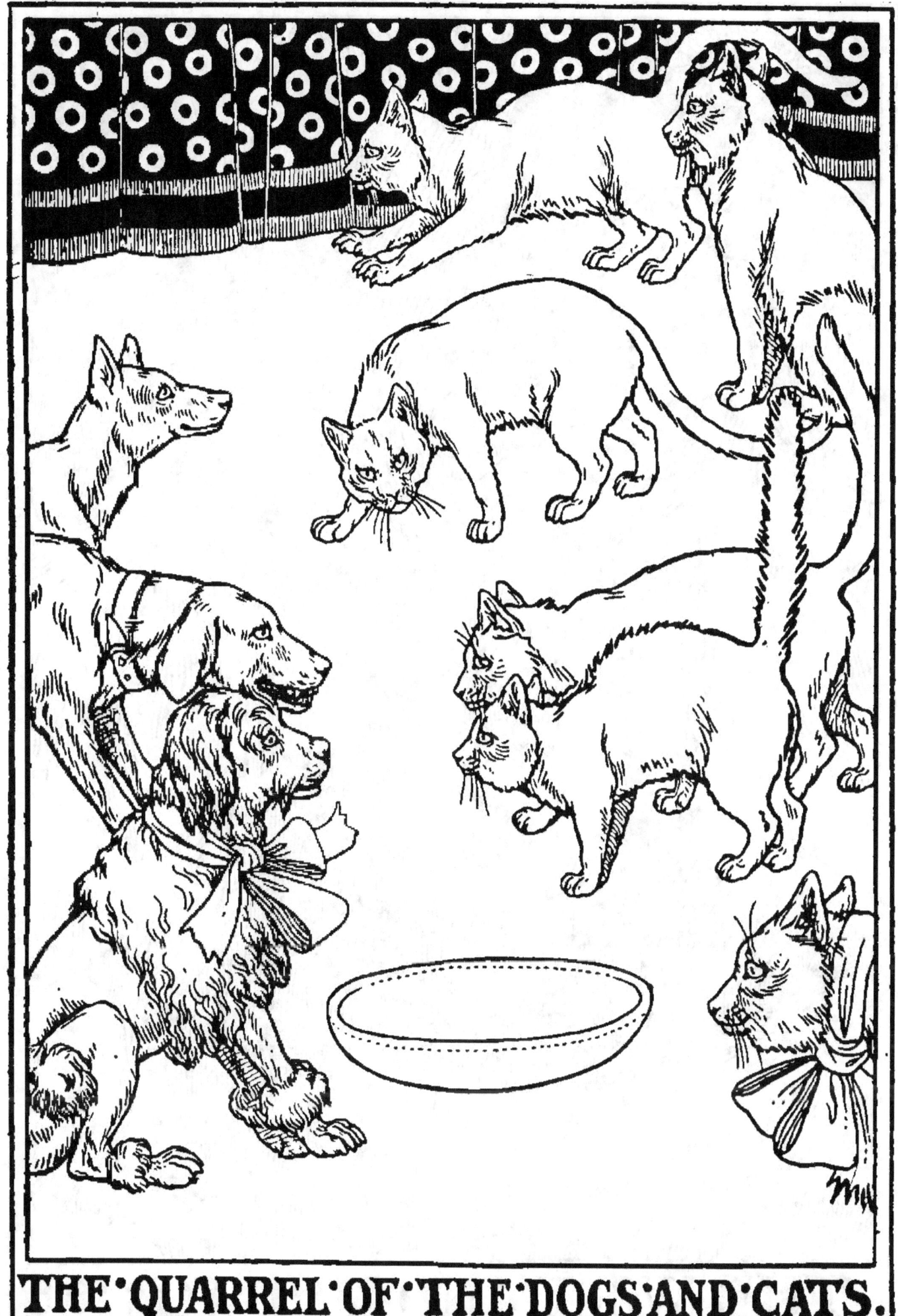

THE·QUARREL·OF·THE·DOGS·AND·CATS.

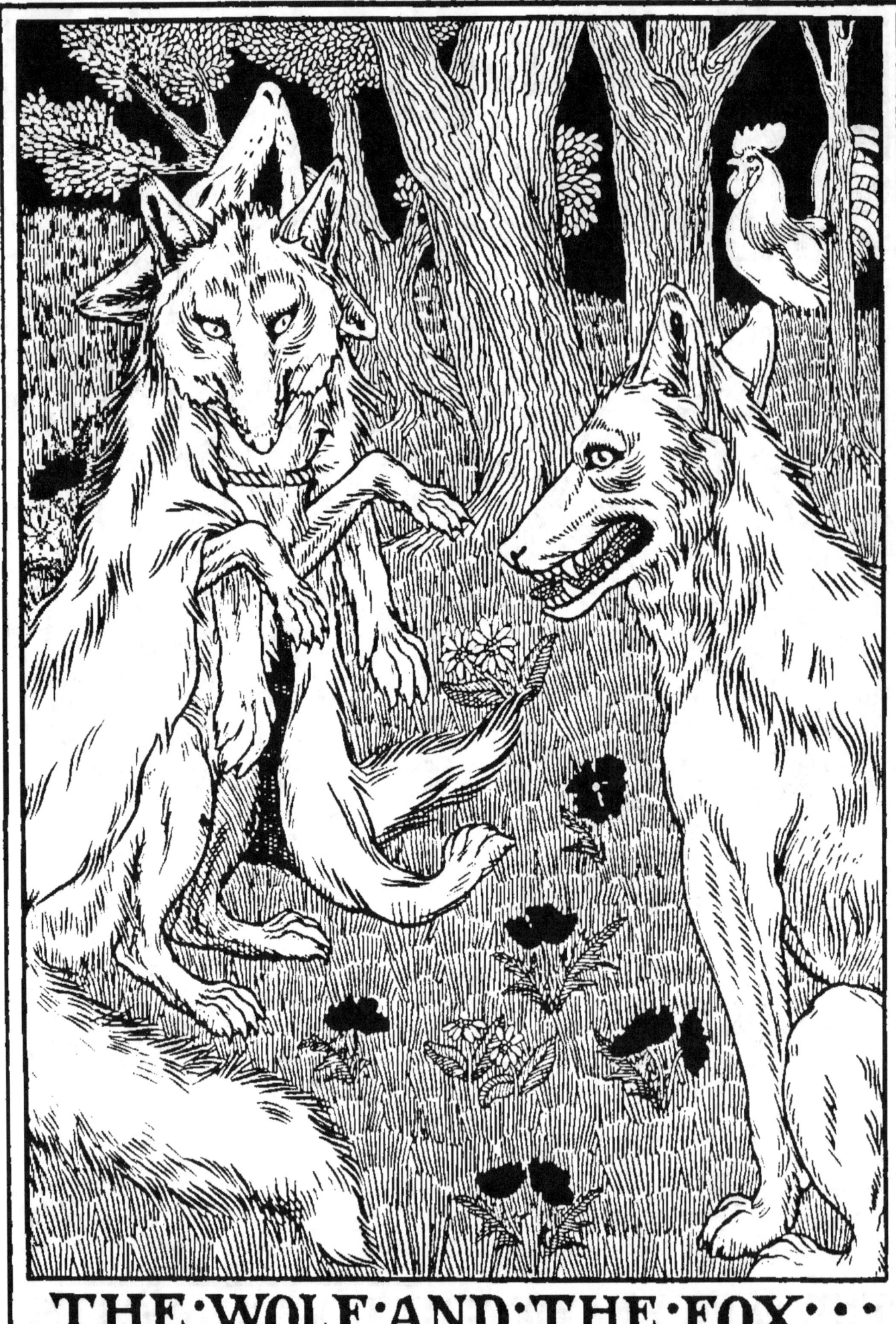

THE·WOLF·AND·THE·FOX···

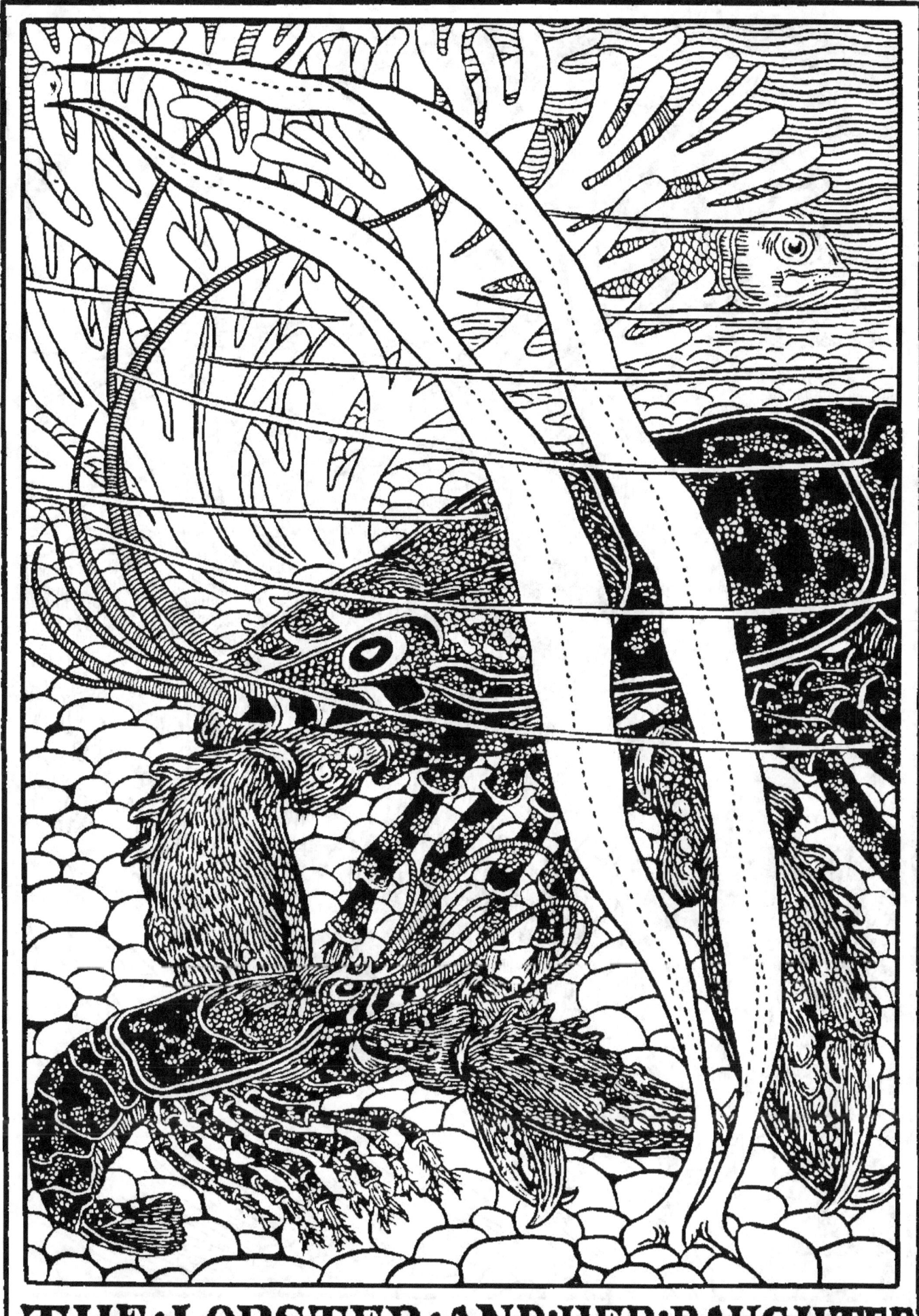

THE·LOBSTER·AND·HER·DAUGHTER

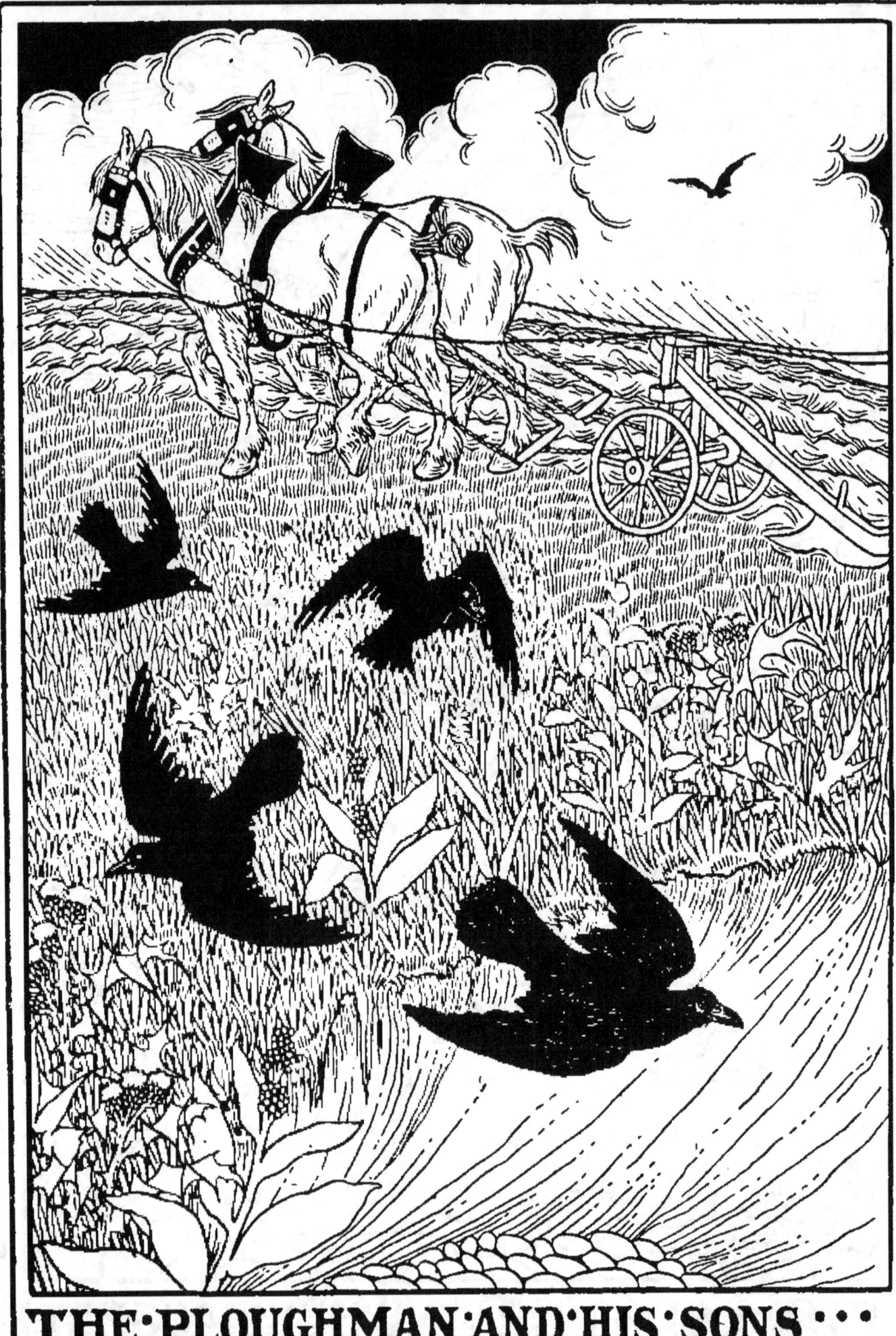

THE·PLOUGHMAN·AND·HIS·SONS···

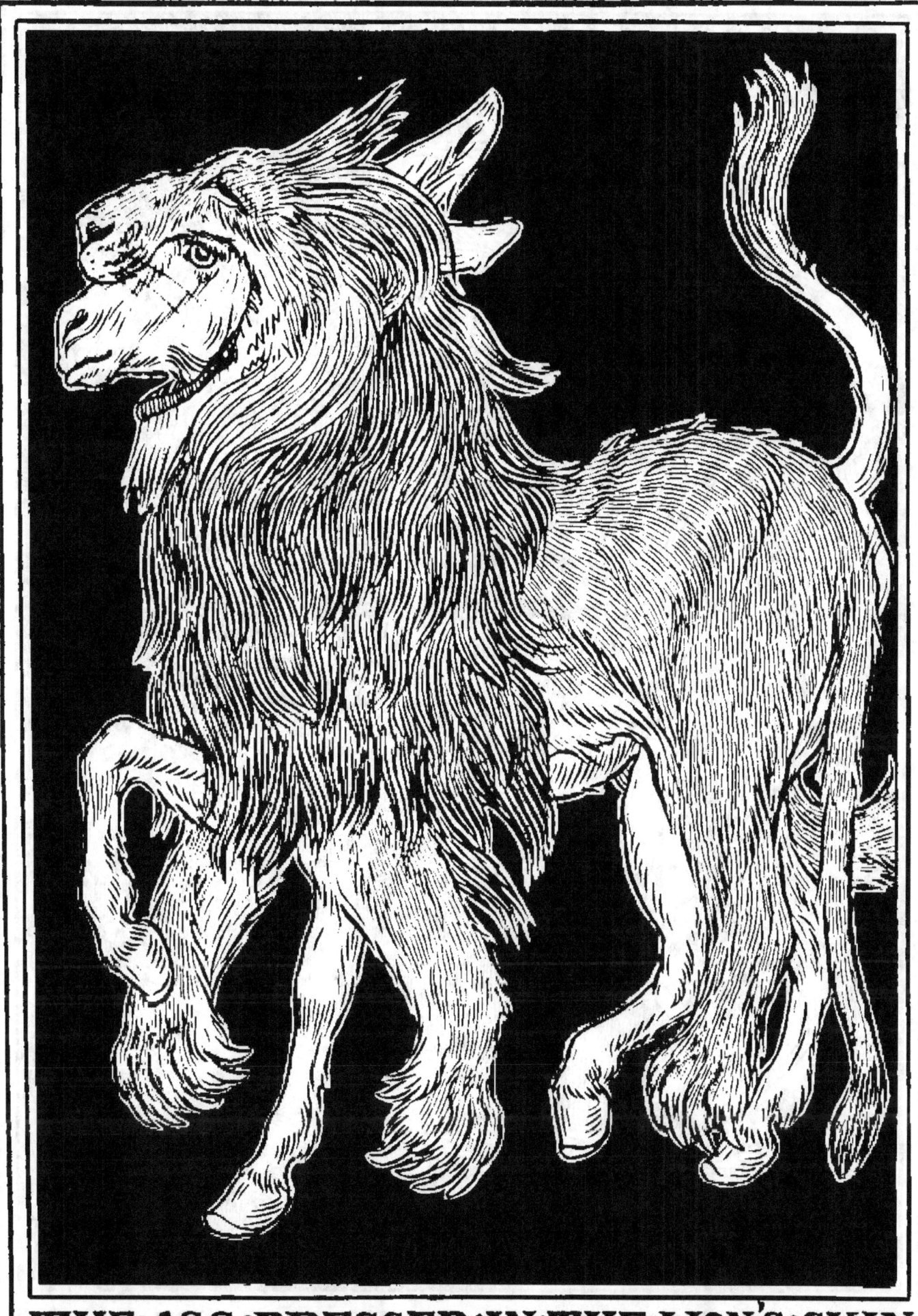

THE·ASS·DRESSED·IN·THE·LION'S·SKIN

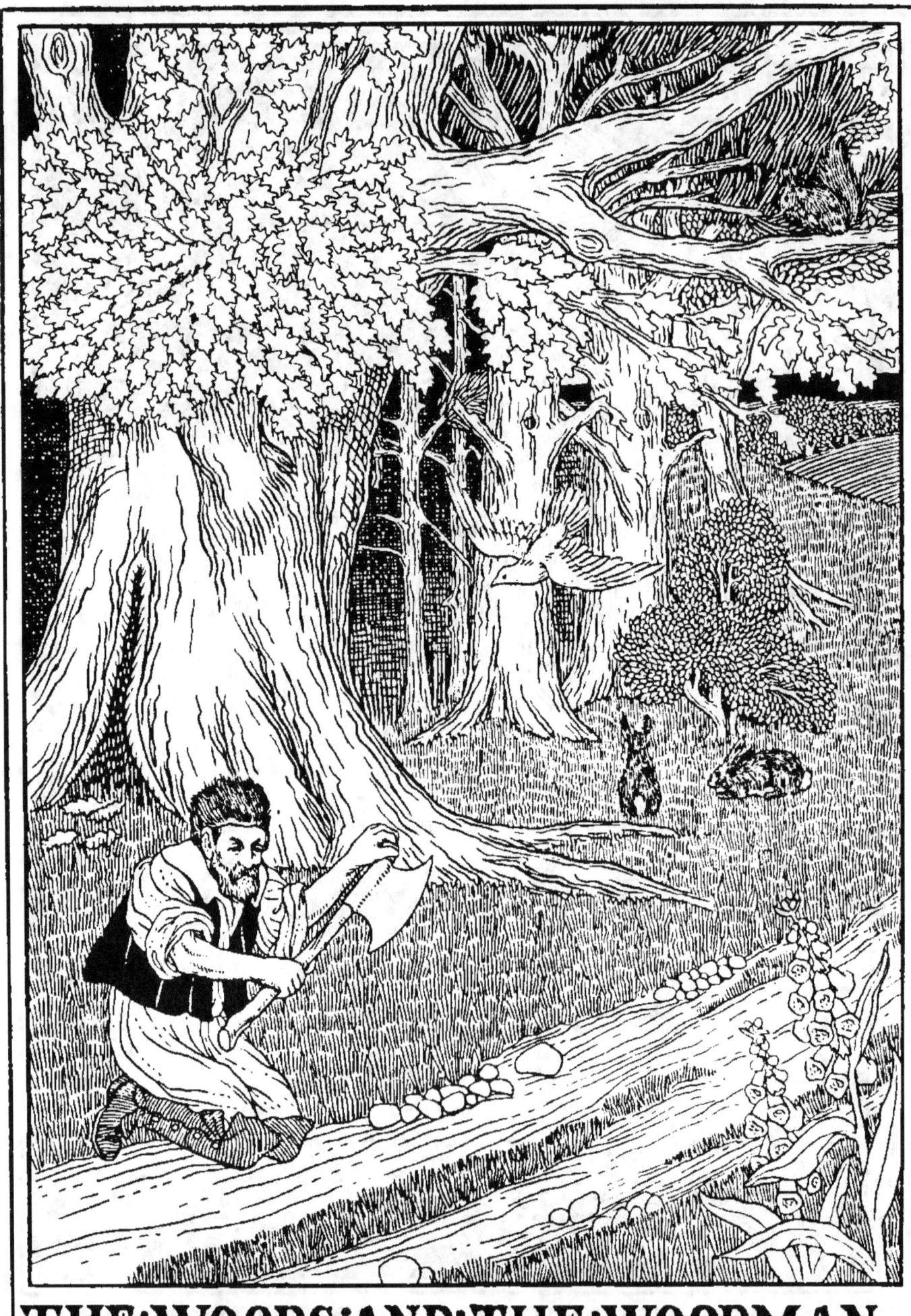

THE·WOODS·AND·THE·WOODMAN.

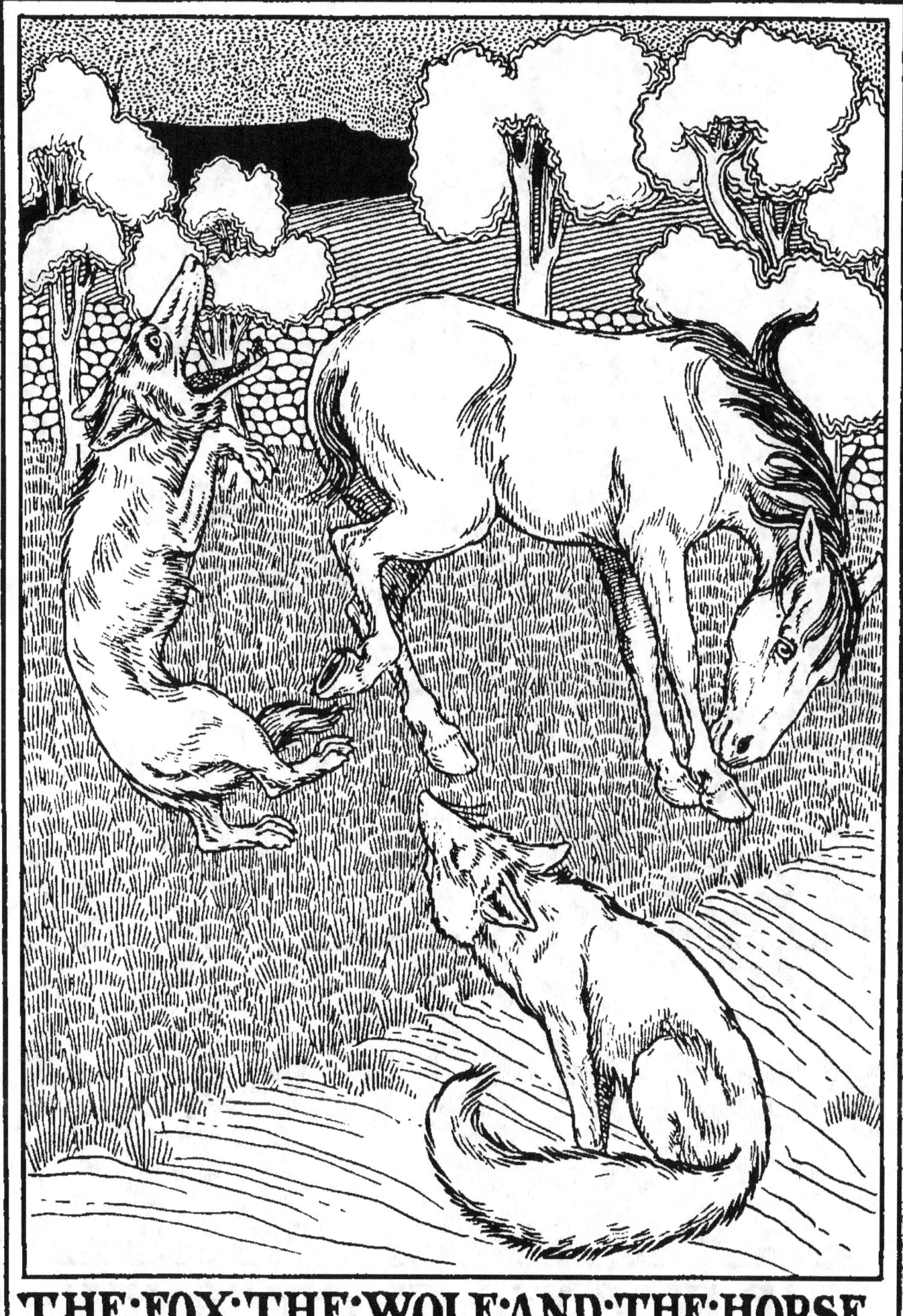

THE·FOX·THE·WOLF·AND·THE·HORSE.

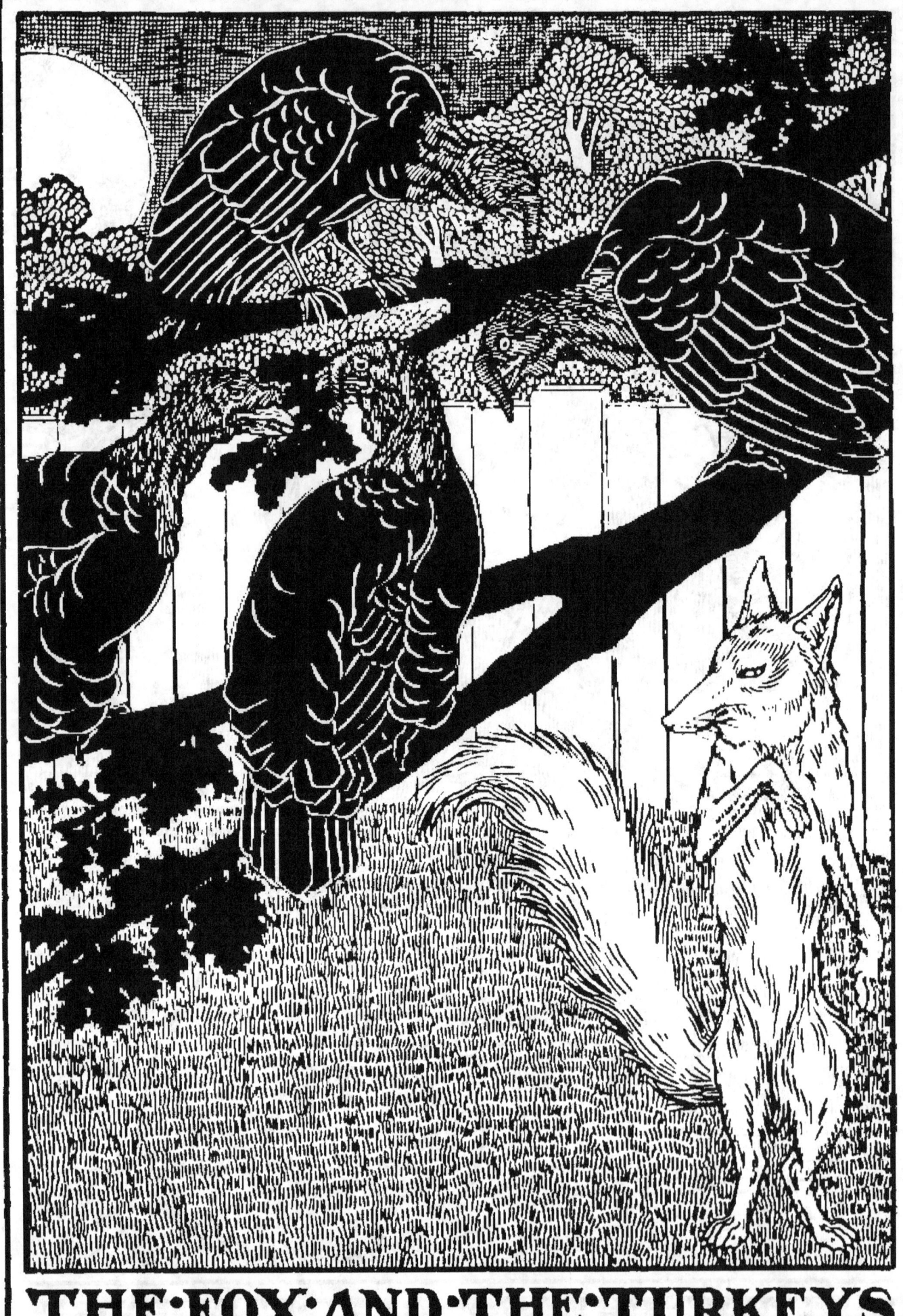

THE·FOX·AND·THE·TURKEYS.

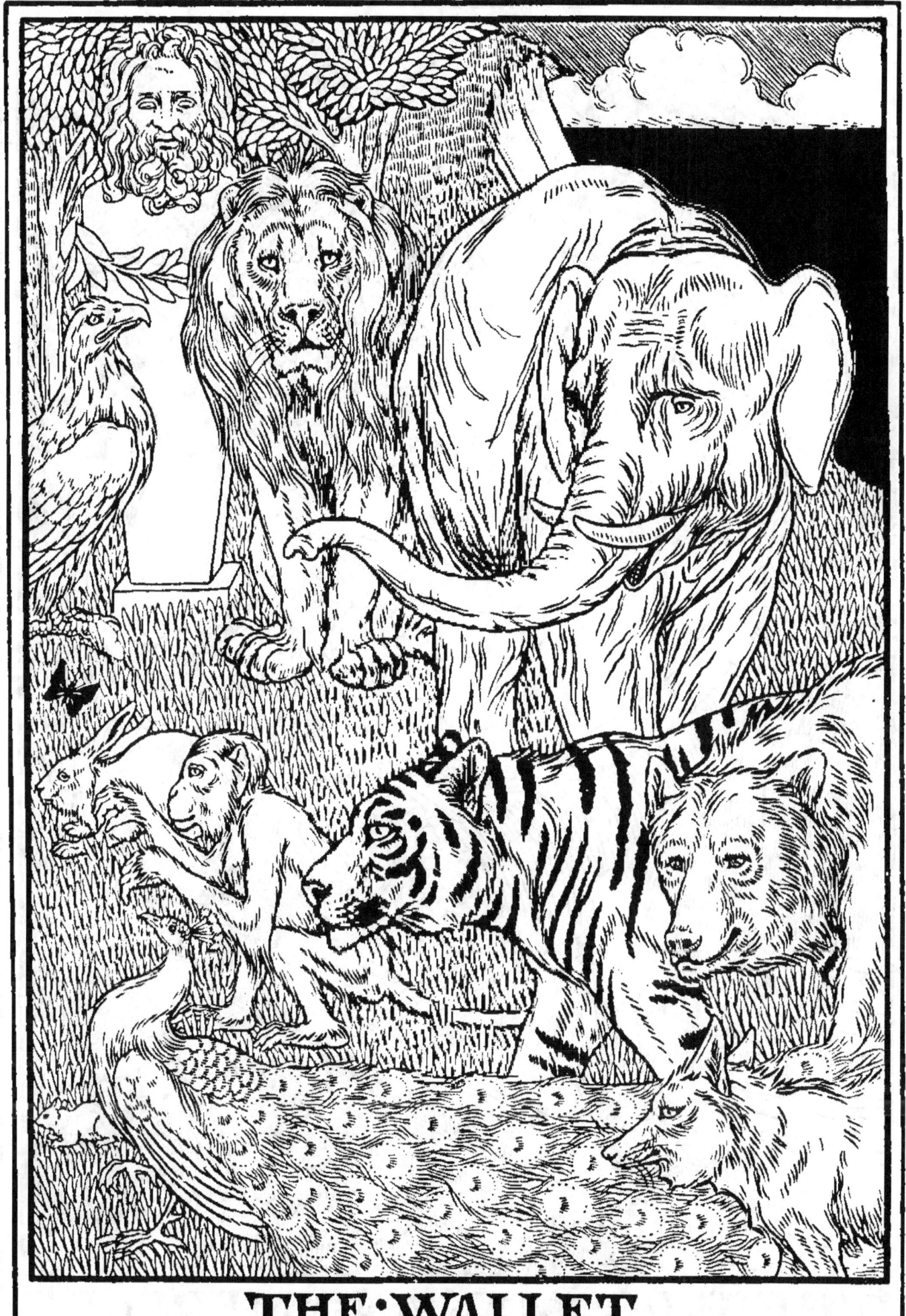

THE·WALLET.

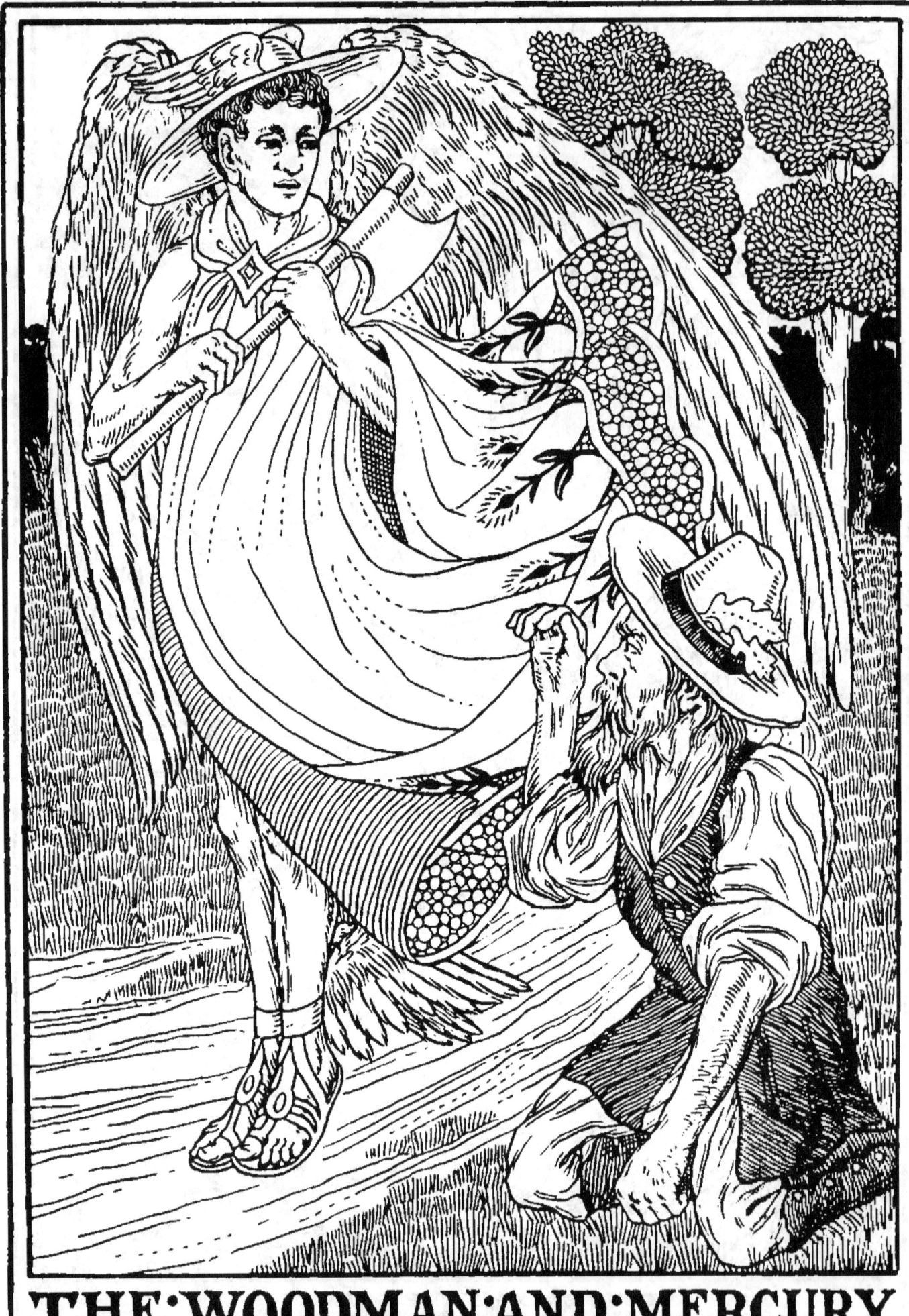

THE·WOODMAN·AND·MERCURY.

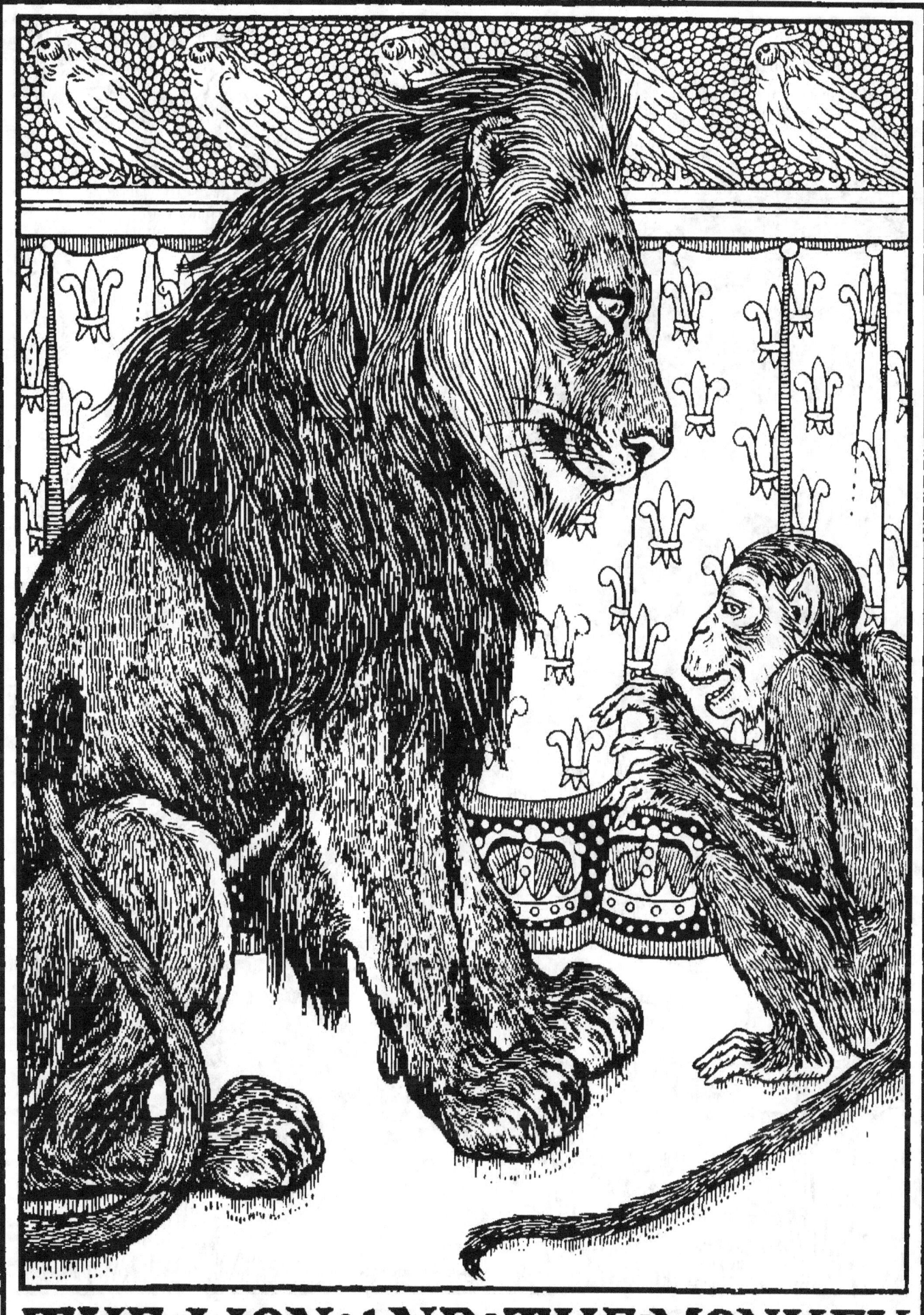

THE·LION·AND·THE·MONKEY·

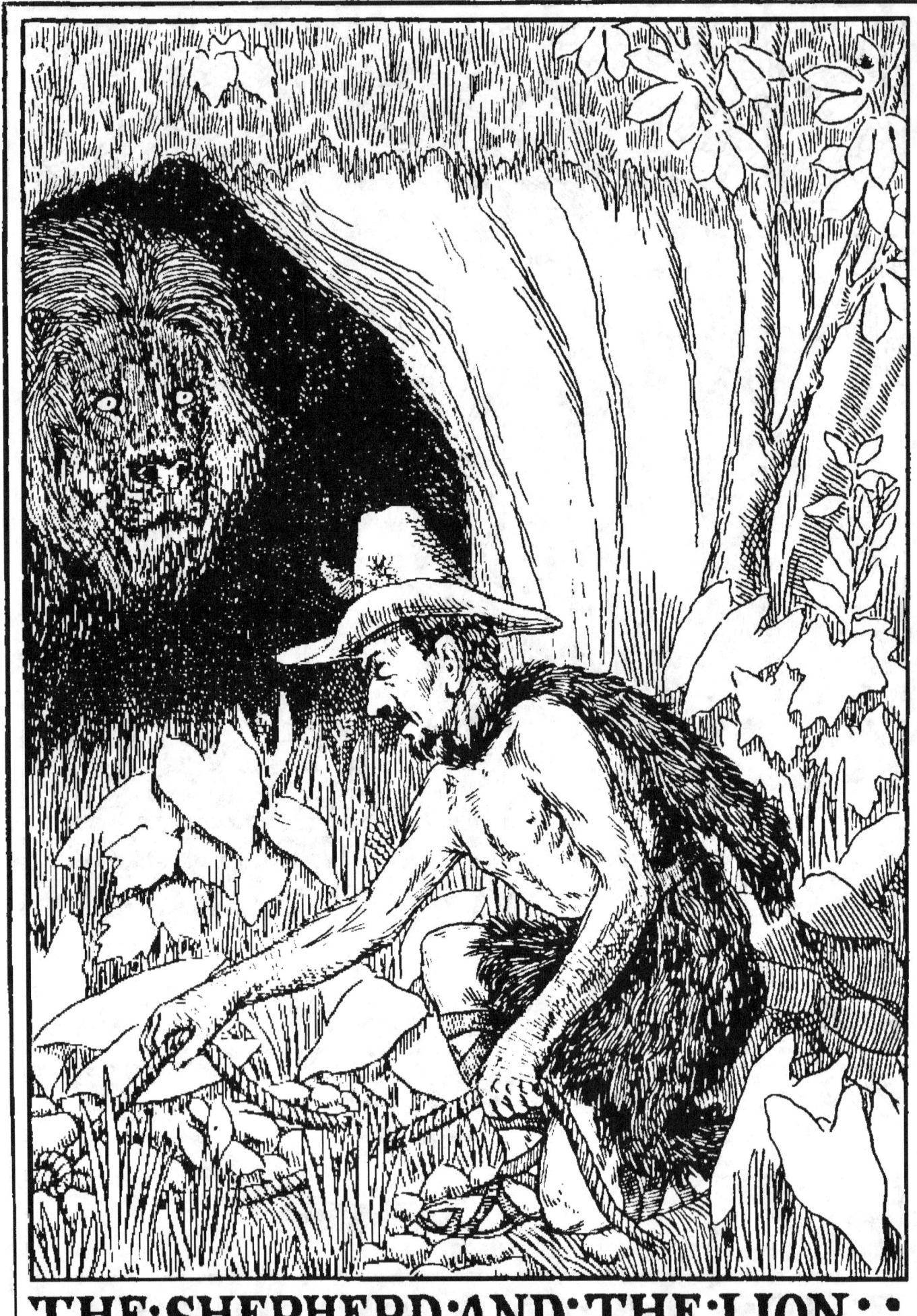

THE·SHEPHERD·AND·THE·LION··

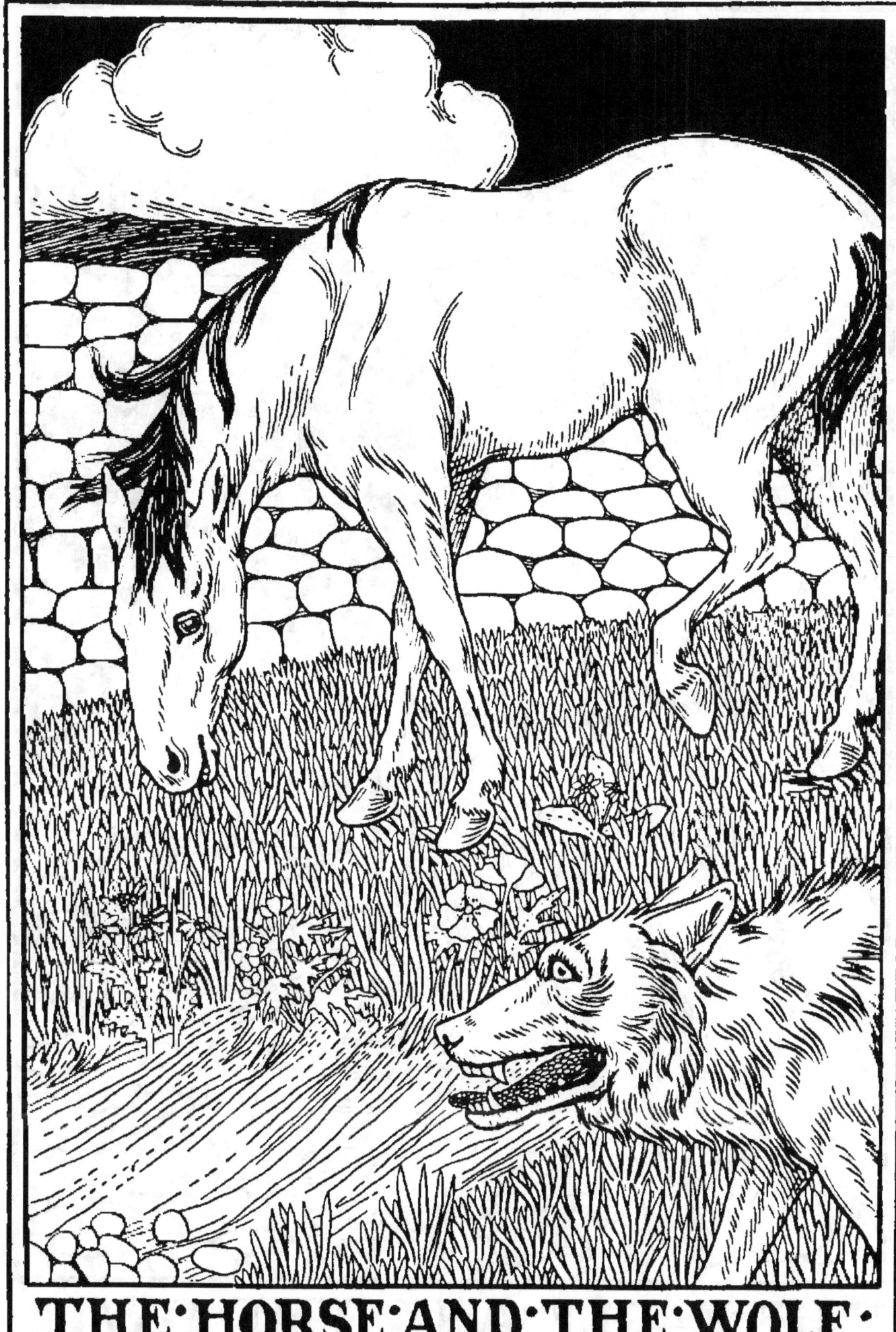

THE·HORSE·AND·THE·WOLF·

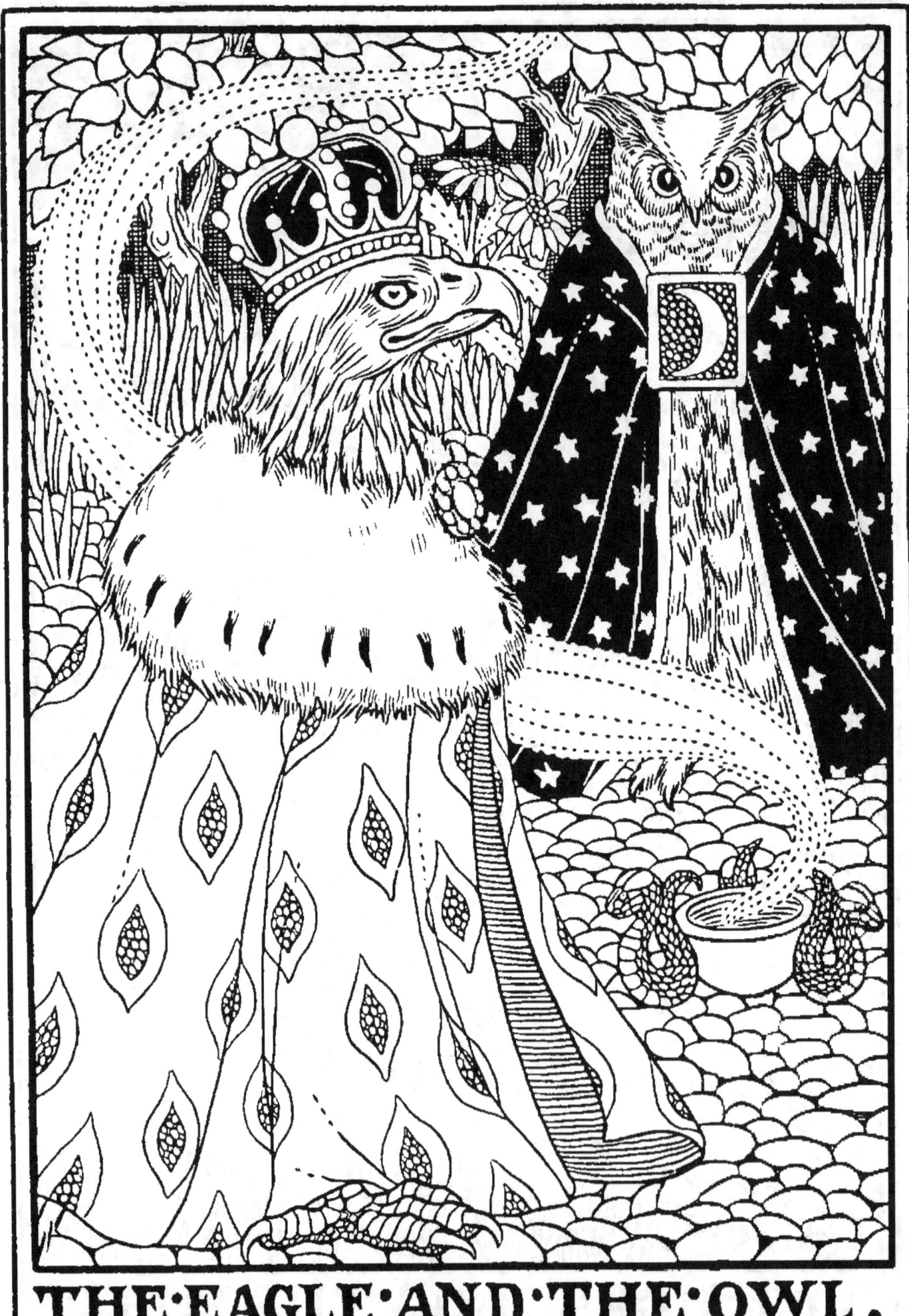

THE·EAGLE·AND·THE·OWL.

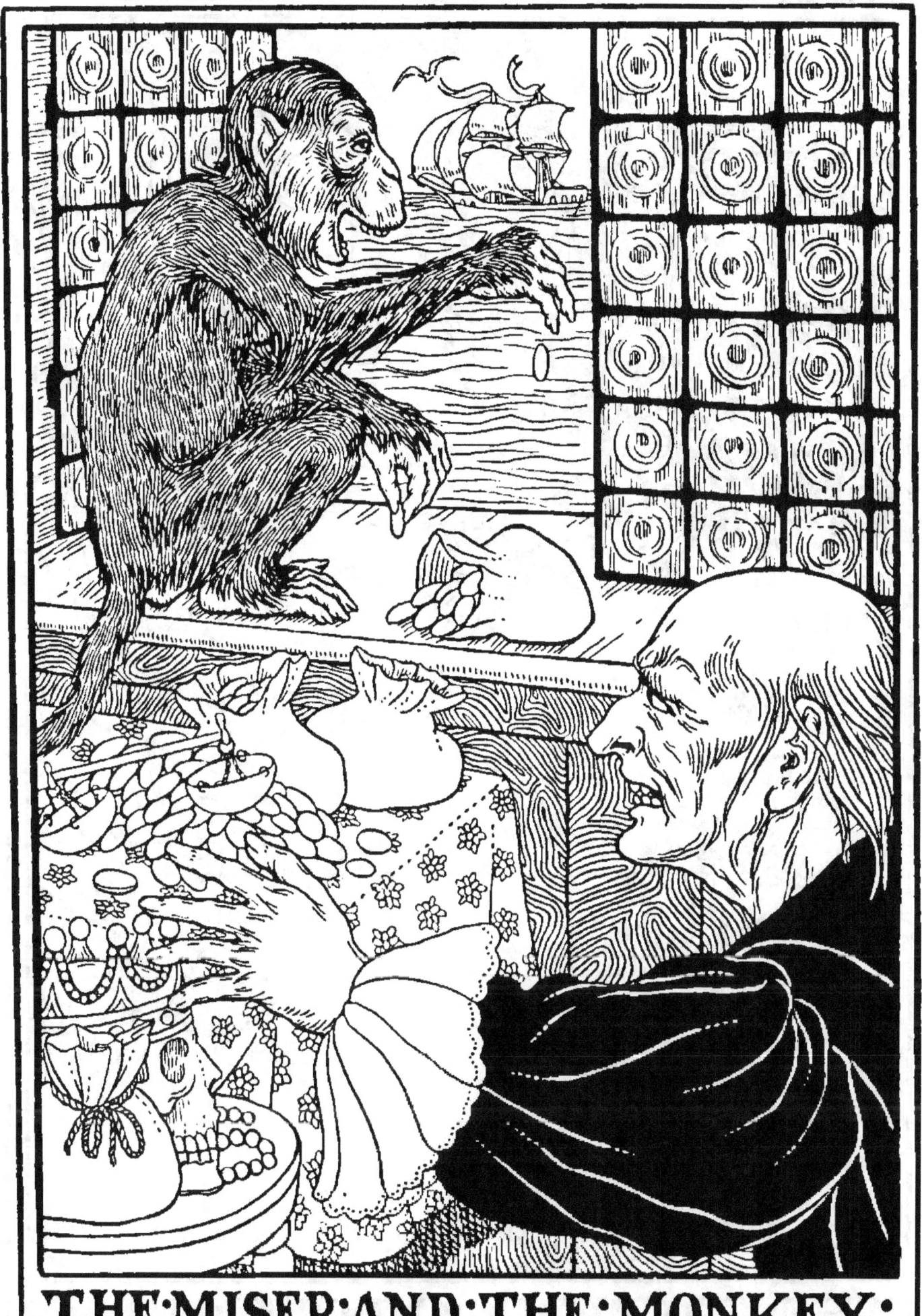

THE·MISER·AND·THE·MONKEY·

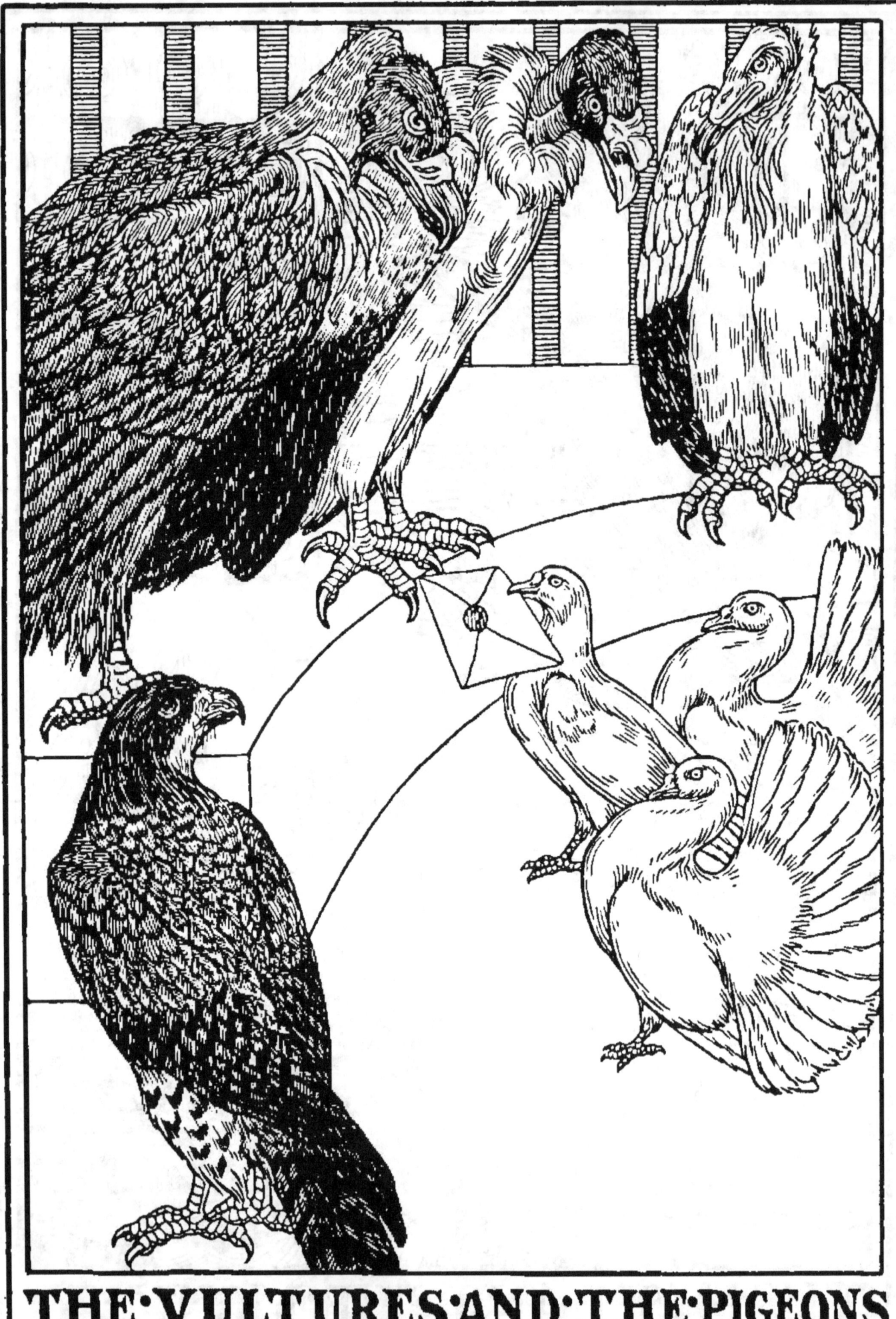

THE·VULTURES·AND·THE·PIGEONS

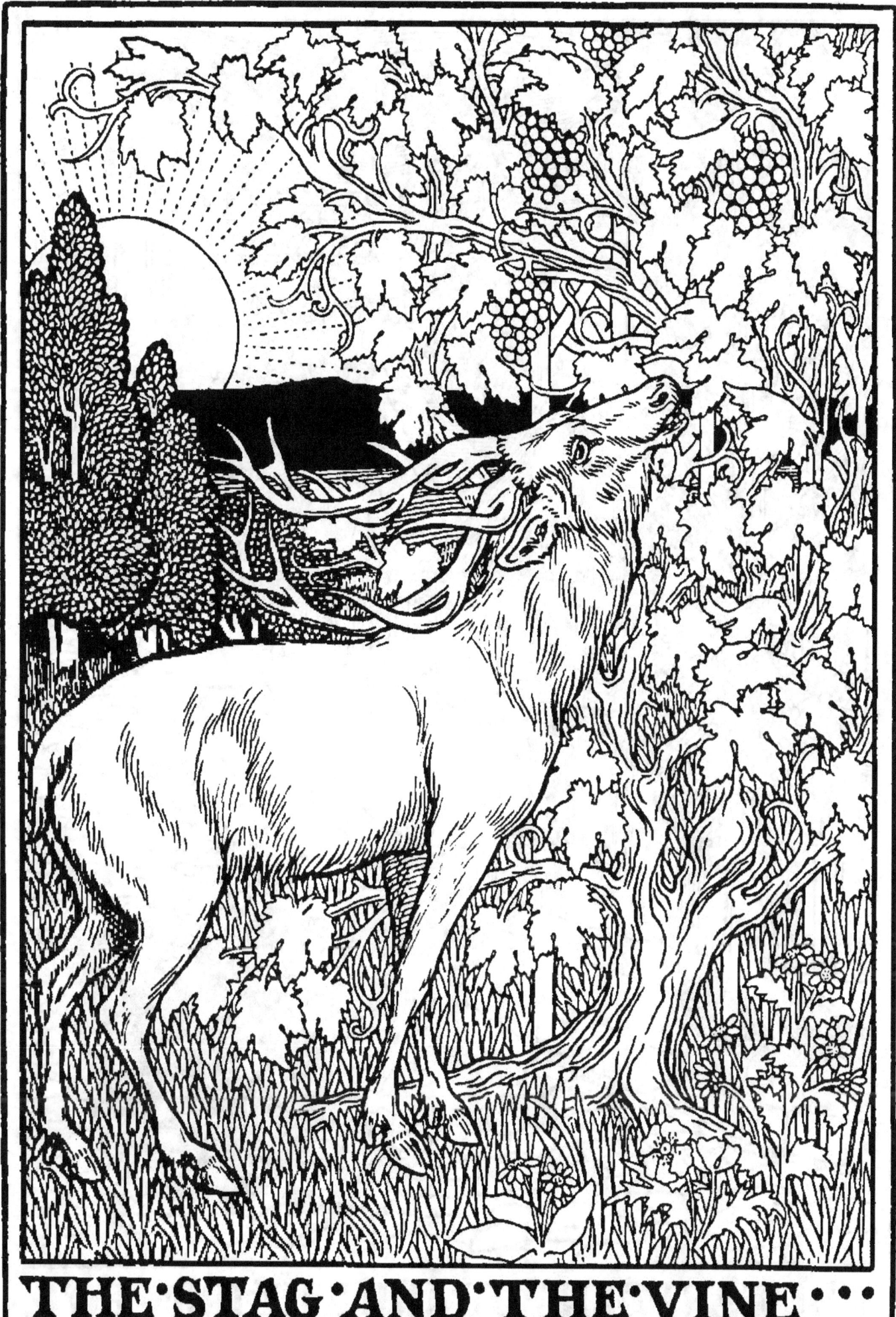

THE·STAG·AND·THE·VINE·•·•

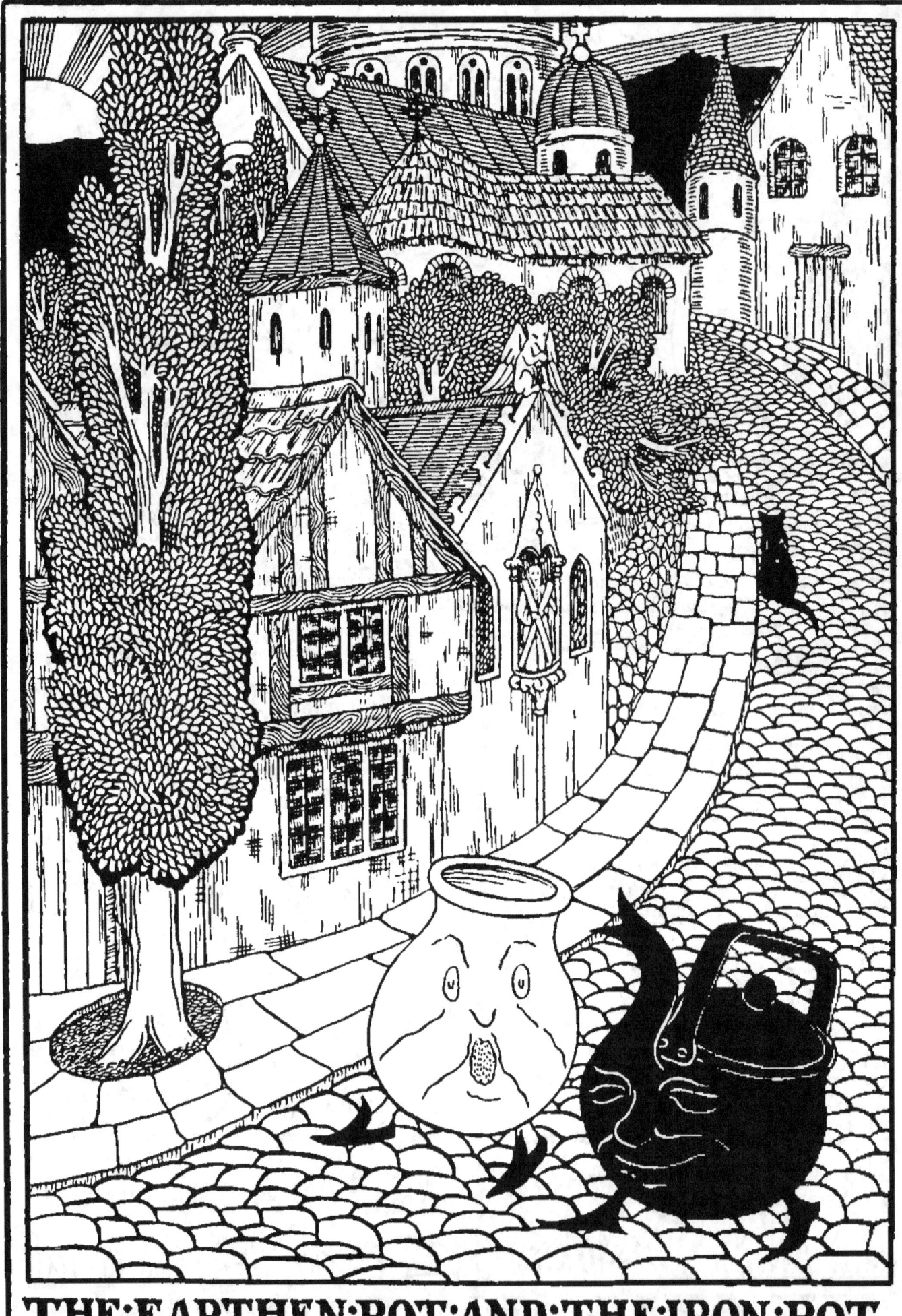

THE·EARTHEN·POT·AND·THE·IRON·POT.

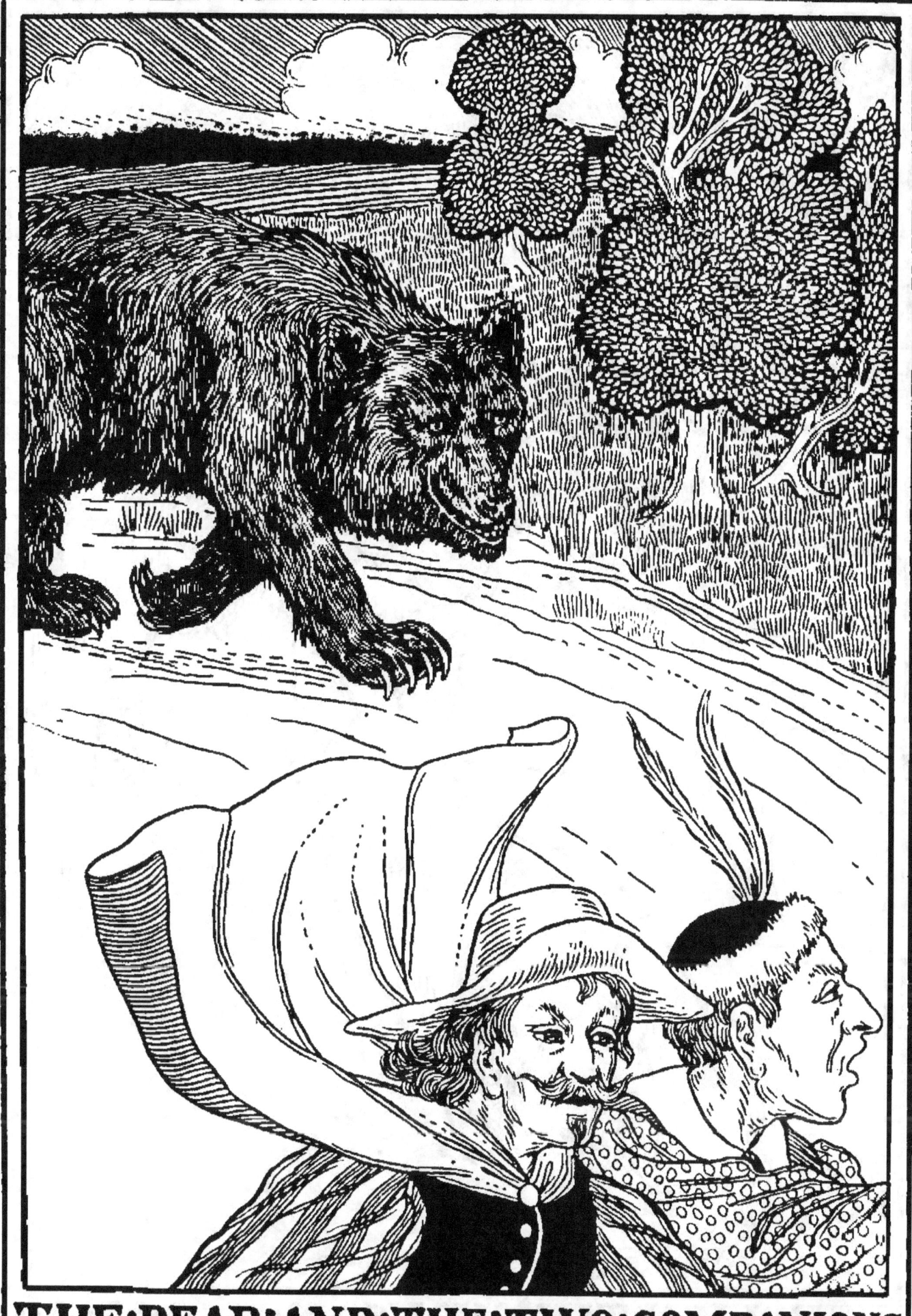

THE·BEAR·AND·THE·TWO·COMPANIONS

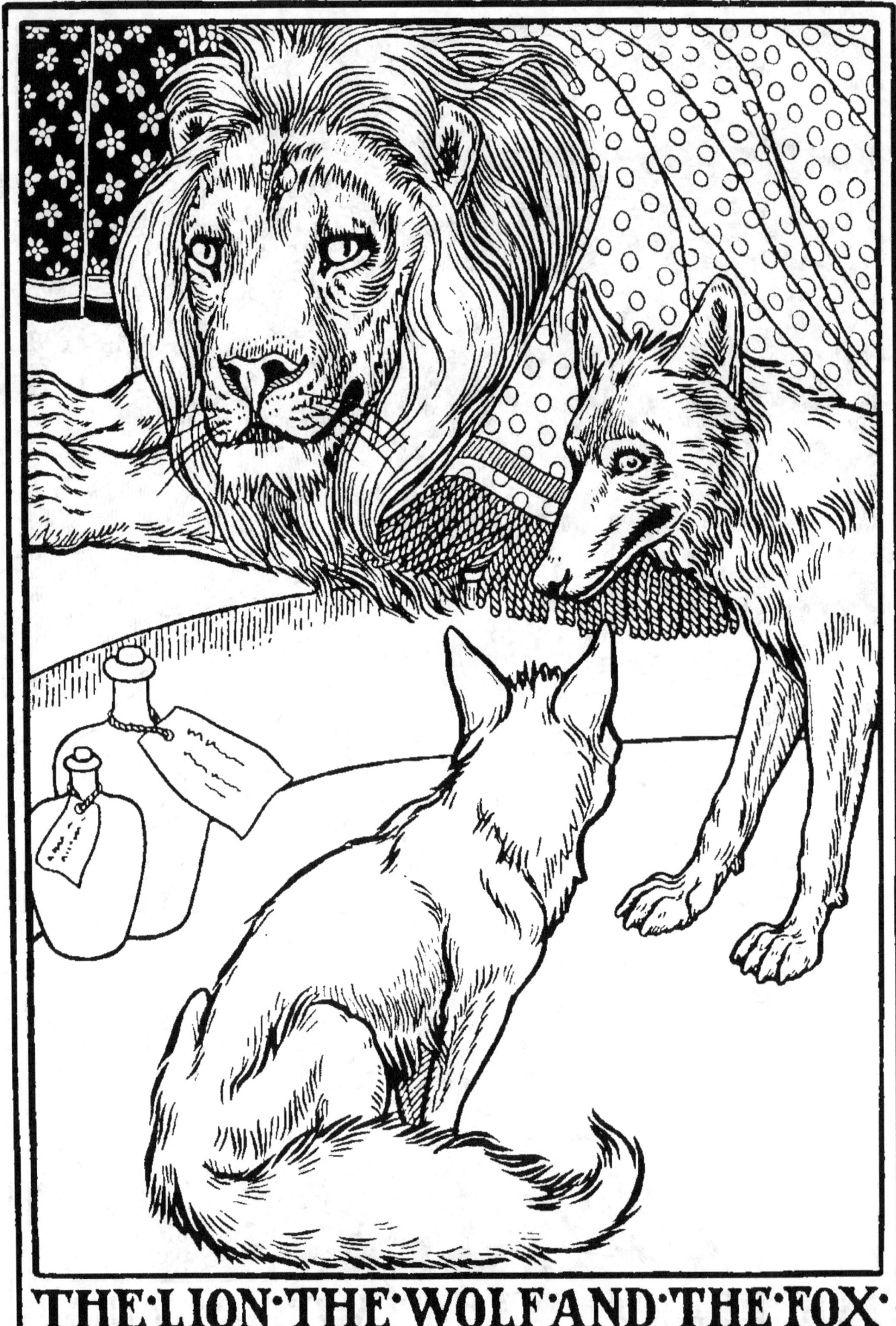

THE·LION·THE·WOLF·AND·THE·FOX·

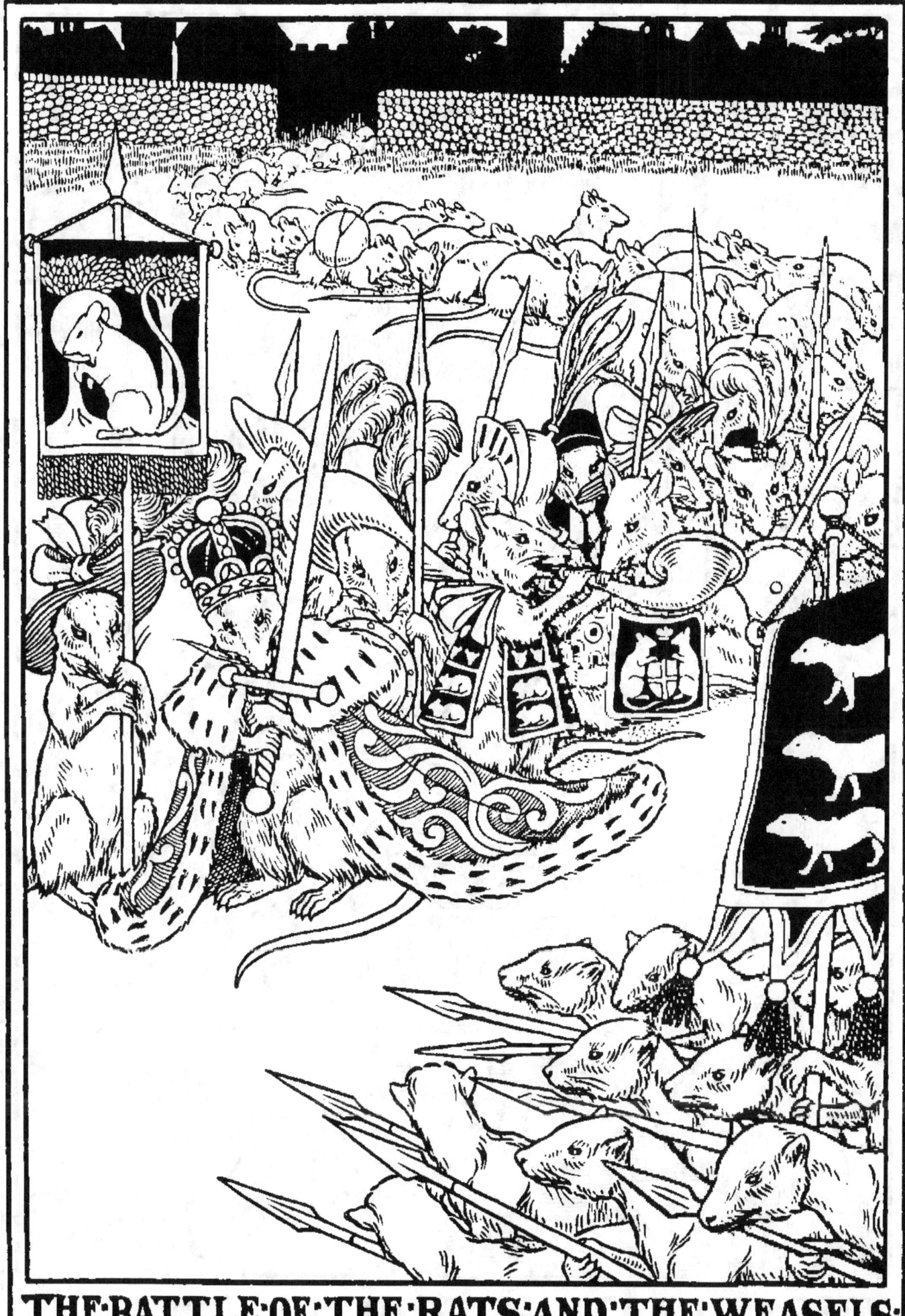

THE·BATTLE·OF·THE·RATS·AND·THE·WEASELS·

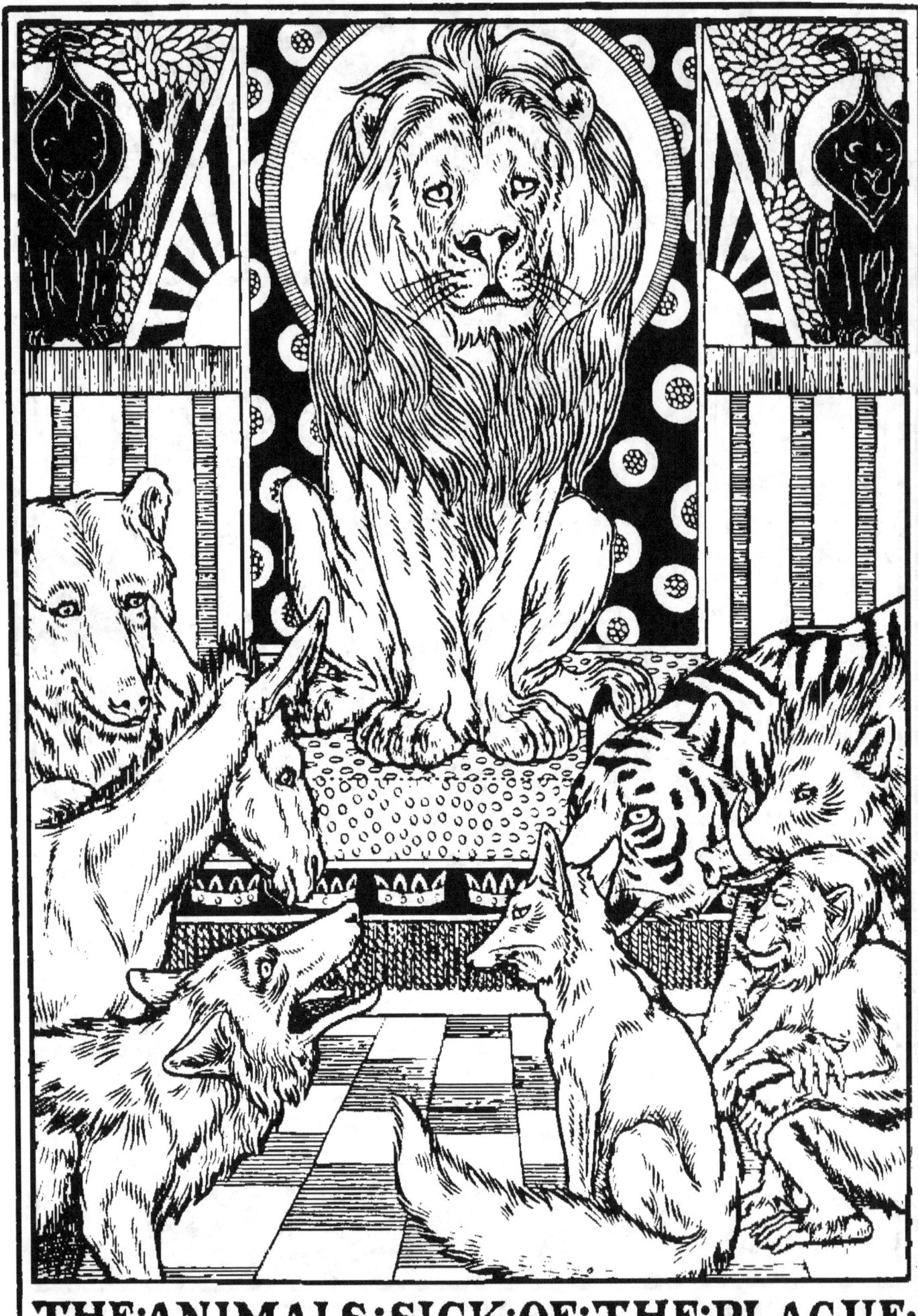

THE·ANIMALS·SICK·OF·THE·PLAGUE·

www.ingramcontent.com/pod-product-compliance
Lightning Source LLC
Chambersburg PA
CBHW081604220526
45468CB00010B/2759